ID : 11850

JCE

CU00923407

STROUD'S JUDICIAL DICTIONARY OF WORDS AND PHRASES

Third Cumulative Supplement

EIGHTH EDITION

HUGH JAMES SOLICITORS
HODGE HOUSE
114-116 ST MARY STREET
CARDIFF CF10 1DY
Tel: (029) 2022 4781
Fax: (029) 2038 8222
DX33000 CARDIFF
e-mail: cardiff@hughjames.com

STROUD'S JUDICIAL DICTIONARY OF WORDS AND PHRASES

THIRD CUMULATIVE SUPPLEMENT TO THE EIGHTH EDITION

BY DANIEL GREENBERG

Barrister, Lincoln's Inn; Legal Adviser, Office of the
Speaker's Counsel, House of Commons;
Parliamentary Counsel, Berwin Leighton Paisner LLP

SWEET & MAXWELL

THOMSON REUTERS

*Published in 2015 by Thomson Reuters (Professional) UK Limited
trading as Sweet & Maxwell, Friars House, 160 Blackfriars Road, London, SE1 8EZ
(Registered in England & Wales, Company No. 1679046.
Registered Office and address for service: 2nd floor, 1 Mark Square,
Leonard Street, London EC2A 4EG)
Typeset by Wright and Round Ltd., Gloucestershire
Printed and bound in Great Britain by
CPI Group (UK) Ltd, Croydon, CR0 4YY*

*No natural forests were destroyed to make this product; only farmed timber was
used and re-planted.*

ISBN 978–0–414–05112–6

All rights reserved.

*Crown copyright material is reproduced with the permission of the
Controller of HMSO and the Queen's Printer for Scotland.*

*All rights reserved. No part of this publication may be reproduced or transmitted in
any form or by any means, or stored in any retrieval system of any nature without
prior written permission, except for permitted fair dealing under the
Copyright, Designs and Patents Act 1988, or in accordance with the terms of a
licence issued by the Copyright Licensing Agency in respect of photocopying
and/or reprographic reproduction. Application for permission for other use of
copyright material including permission to reproduce extracts in other
published works shall be made to the publishers. Full acknowledgement of
author, publisher and source must be given.*

© Thomson Reuters (Professional) UK Limited
2015

PREFACE

As with recent editions of *Stroud*, the intention is to provide annual cumulative supplements noting new judicial and statutory definitions.

The editorial policy remains as stated in the preface to the Seventh Edition. In particular, *Stroud* is a judicial dictionary, and not a legal dictionary: it is dependent, as it always has been, on the courts and legislatures for the provision of definitions. The result is that there will be expressions of importance to lawyers or related professions that do not feature in *Stroud* because their definition has not fallen to be considered in a decided case or glossed by statute. Equally, there are many expressions that would have no place in a legal dictionary—not being terms of art forming part of the mechanism or structure of the law—that have been defined by the courts or legislature in a way likely to be helpful to lawyers and related professions and that are therefore included in *Stroud*.

In this respect *Stroud* sees itself as a companion work to *Jowitt's Dictionary of English Law*, which aims to define terms forming part of the structure of the law whether or not they have received recent judicial or statutory definition. The Third Edition of *Jowitt* was published in 2010; a Fourth Edition is due to be published later this year.

This supplement is up to date to the end of July 2015.

Stroud has benefited greatly over the years from comments and suggestions provided by readers. All communications are always most gratefully received and should be sent to the publishers in the first instance.

Daniel Greenberg
London
August 2015

ABNORMAL OCCURRENCE.

"53. A similarly realistic approach has in our view to be adopted to the determination of the essentially factual question whether the event giving rise to the particular casualty is to be characterised as an 'abnormal occurrence' or as resulting from some 'normal' characteristic of the particular port at the particular time of year. We emphasise the word 'normal' in the term 'normal characteristic'. . . .

63. In deciding whether the critical combination was itself a normal characteristic of the port or an abnormal occurrence, what the judge should have done was to evaluate the evidence relating to the past frequency of such an event occurring and the likelihood of it occurring again. He should have also, in our view, have taken into account what appears to have been the unchallenged evidence of Mr Lynagh referred to above relating to the exceptional nature of the storm that affected Kashima on 24th October 2006 in terms of its rapid development, its duration and its severity. Had he done so, then, on the basis of his own finding that 'the concurrent occurrence of those events was rare', and on the basis of the evidence which we have summarised above, there would, in our view, have been only one conclusion which he could have reached—namely that the event which occurred on 24th October 2006 was indeed an abnormal occurrence."

Gard Marine & Energy Ltd v China National Chartering Co Ltd (Rev 1) [2015] EWCA Civ 16.

ABSCOND.

"The words 'abscond' or 'absconded' are not defined in the [Children (Scotland) Act 1995]. The word 'abscond' is defined in the *Shorter Oxford Dictionary* as 'to leave hurriedly in secret, to escape from justice'. The *Collins English Dictionary* defines 'abscond' as 'to run away secretly especially from an open institution or to avoid prosecution or punishment'. It is, in our judgment, necessary, in the absence of a statutory definition of 'abscond', to construe it in the context of the other statutory language among which it finds its place. . . . In the present case the position was that the two girls had told two members of staff at the home that they intended to visit the flat in question. They were given verbal instructions not to do so but otherwise there was no restriction upon them leaving the home. In going to the flat for the purposes they said they did, there was no indication that they did so with the intention of 'running away' from the home and not returning. They, as noted, said they went there for cigarettes. In doing so they, no doubt, defied a valid express instruction of the

members of staff at the home not to do so. In that respect their liberty had been restricted by the orders of the staff which orders they disobeyed. But they cannot, in our view, be said thereby to have 'absconded' from the Home as that word falls to be construed, having regard to its context in the legislation. As seen two members of staff gave evidence to the effect that in such circumstances they would have been concerned about the girls' safety and would have called the police. That is what occurred in this case."
Welsh v Procurator Fiscal, Aberdeen [2012] Scot HC HCJAC 114.

ABUSE. Stat. Def., "physical, sexual, psychological, emotional or financial abuse (and includes abuse taking place in any setting, whether in a private dwelling, an institution or any other place)" (Social Services and Well-being (Wales) Act 2014 s.197).

ABUSE (Financial abuse of a person). Stat. Def., "includes having money or other property stolen, being defrauded, being put under pressure in relation to money or other property, and having money or other property misused" (Care Act 2013 s.42); Stat. Def., Social Services and Well-being (Wales) Act 2014 s.197.

ABUSIVE. Stat. Def. (in context of tax), Finance Act 2013 s.207.

ACCEPTABLE.
"The ordinary meaning of the phrase 'acceptable under the legislation of the State Party' does not predicate, or require, specific additional enabling legislation, expressly defining what is 'acceptable' for the purposes of the 1995 Act. It simply means that the guarantee must be regarded as 'acceptable' under any relevant United Kingdom legislation. 'Acceptable' in this context does not need to be construed as having any technical meaning. It could equally mean a guarantee which was not regarded as 'unacceptable' under any United Kingdom legislation; in other words, simply a guarantee that did not contravene any relevant statutory provision. A guarantee which satisfied the requirements of the Statute of Frauds—because the guarantee itself, or some note or memorandum of it, was in writing and signed by the guarantor or his authorised agent—would be likely to be regarded as 'acceptable' as a guarantee for the purposes of the 1995 Act (at least, under English and Welsh legislation), because it was enforceable. Conversely, an oral guarantee, which did not satisfy the requirements of the Statute, and was therefore not enforceable, clearly would not be 'acceptable' for the purposes of the 1995 Act.
33. In particular circumstances, in order to qualify as 'acceptable', a guarantee might also have to satisfy other requirements of United Kingdom legislation. For example, if the guarantee were one given by an institution in the course of carrying on insurance business, then, in order to be 'acceptable', the guarantee would also have to be provided by a person who was duly authorised by The Prudential Regulation Authority under

3

the relevant provisions of the Financial Services and Markets Act 2000 to carry on insurance business of that type in the United Kingdom (as indeed Owners' P&I Club is in the present case). But the fact that the Statute of Frauds is directed at the circumstances in which a court action can be brought to enforce a guarantee, does not in my judgment preclude the statutory provision from being used as a reference point for 'acceptability'."
Kairos Shipping Ltd v Enka & Co LLC [2014] EWCA Civ 217.

ACCIDENT.

"1. The question in this appeal is whether, in the circumstances of this case, the act of giving an air passenger an injection of a diuretic in the course of an international commercial flight, which injection (it is assumed for present purposes) thereby exacerbated the passenger's physical discomfort caused by fluid retention resulting from urethral stenosis, constituted 'an accident' for the purposes of Article 17.1 of the Montreal Convention 1999 'for the Unification of Certain Rules for International Carriage by Air' . . .

28. I have concluded that the circumstances in which the injection was administered by the doctor cannot be characterised as 'unusual' for the purposes of Article 17.1. There is no evidence that the actual administration of the injection was done in an abnormal way. The only 'unusual' aspect of the whole process was that it was carried out in the course of an international flight by a passenger doctor on another passenger (with proper consent) as a result of a request to the doctor for assistance by a crew member. But the key point is that there is no evidence that any of those characteristics had any causative effect in the chain of events that led to Mrs Ford's 'bodily injury'. The same chain of events would have taken place wherever the injection had been administered. It seems to me that the simple fact that the injection was administered in mid-flight rather than elsewhere cannot provide the circumstances with the necessary 'unusual' characteristics so that this event constitutes an 'accident' within Article 17.1. I would adopt the language quoted by Lord Phillips of Worth Matravers M.R. in his judgment in the Deep Vein Thrombosis case: [37] 'If the event on board an airplane is an ordinary, expected and usual occurrence, then it cannot be termed an accident. To constitute an accident, the occurrence on board the aircraft must be unusual, or unexpected, an unusual or unexpected happening'. The event in this case is the actual administration of the injection. That, in itself, was not unexpected, or unusual."
Ford v Malaysian Airline Systems Berhad [2013] EWCA Civ 1163.

Stat. Def., "an act of non-consensual physical violence done to a person at work" (Reporting of Injuries, Diseases and Dangerous Occurrences Regulations 2013 reg.2).

See DISEASE.

ACCOMMODATION.

"The word 'accommodation' in itself is neutral. It is not in its ordinary sense to be equated with 'unit of accommodation'. It is no abuse of language to speak of a family being 'accommodated' in two adjoining flats. The limitation, if any, must therefore be found in the words 'available for occupation . . . together with' the other members of his family. The statutory test will be satisfied by a single unit of accommodation in which a family can live together. But it may also be satisfied by two units of accommodation if they are so located that they enable the family to live 'together' in practical terms. In the end, as Mr Arden submits, this comes down to an issue of fact, or of factual judgment, for the authority. Short of irrationality it is unlikely to raise any issue of law for the court."
Sharif v The London Borough of Camden [2013] UKSC 10.

ACQUITTAL.

"10. For our part, it seems clear, as a matter of ordinary language that a person found 'not guilty by reason of insanity' has indeed been acquitted of the offence. That is what a finding of 'not guilty' is, whatever the basis upon which that verdict is returned."
AJR v R. [2013] EWCA Crim 591.

"26. For all these reasons we conclude that a finding that a person did the acts charged against him is not an 'acquittal', and it therefore does not give the court the power to make a restraining order under section 5A of the Protection from Harassment Act 1997."
Chinegwundoh v R. [2015] EWCA Crim 109.

ACT, NEGLECT OR DEFAULT.

"10. The phrase 'act, neglect or default' has appeared in statutory provisions concerned with limitation periods since the Public Authorities Protection Act 1893. It appeared, in particular, in section 6(1)(a) of the Law Reform (Limitation of Actions) Act 1954 ('the 1954 Act'), which was the predecessor of section 17(1) of the 1973 Act. The meaning of the phrase in that context was considered by the House of Lords in *Watson v Fram Reinforced Concrete Co (Scotland) Ltd* 1960 SC (HL) 92. Lord Reid construed 'default' as meaning 'breach of duty'" (p.109). Lord Keith of Avonholm was of the opinion that the phrase did not refer to a historical event, as the Inner House had considered in that case, but referred to negligence or a failure of duty (p.111). Lord Denning, echoing the Book of Common Prayer, stated at p.115: 'The words "act, neglect or default" are perhaps a little tautologous: for "act" in legal terminology often includes an omission as well as an act of commission: and "default" certainly includes "neglect". But tautologous as they may be, the words are apt to cover all breaches of legal duty, no matter whether it be by leaving undone those things which we ought to have done, or by doing those things which we ought not to have done.' "

*David T Morrison & Co Ltd (tla Gael Home Interiors) v ICL Plastics Ltd
(Scotland)* [2014] UKSC 48.

ACT OF TERRORISM. Stat. Def., Counter-Terrorism and Security Act
2015 s.14.

ADDED MATTER.
"1. This appeal raises an issue about what patent lawyers call 'added matter'. Added matter refers to the rule that a patent application or patent
may not be amended in such a way that it contains subject matter which
extends beyond the content of the application as filed. If it has been so
amended, and the added matter is not or cannot be removed, the patent
will be invalid."
AP Racing Ltd v Alcon Components Ltd [2014] EWCA Civ 40.

ADDITIONAL POLICE BODY. Stat. Def., Police Reform Act 2002 Sch.3
as inserted by Police (Complaints and Conduct) Act 2012.

ADEQUATE ACCOUNTING RECORDS. Stat. Def. (in context of local
authorities), Local Audit and Accountability Act 2014 s.3.

ADEQUATE AND APPROPRIATE INSURANCE. See INSURANCE.

ADJUDICATION.
"In my judgment it is wrong to describe the exercise of disciplinary power
by the employer as a form of adjudication. The purpose of the procedure is
not 'a determination of any issue which establishes the existence of a legal
right', as Lord Bridge put it in *Thrasyvoulou*, nor is it properly regarded as
'determining a dispute'."
Christou v London Borough of Haringey [2013] EWCA Civ 178.

ADVERTISEMENT.
"The word 'advertisement' in Class 13 has the meaning given to it by section 336(1) of the 2009 Act: . . . 'This is difficult drafting', as was observed
by Popplewell J. in *Westminster City Council v Secretary of State for the
Environment* [1990] 59 P & CR 496 (at page 500). . . . As Sullivan L.J.
observed in *Butler* (at paragraph 23), 'advertisement' was given a very
broad meaning for the purposes of the Act. We should not lose sight of the
fact that the primary purpose of Part VIII of the 1990 Act and the 2007
Regulations is to facilitate the control of advertising. It appears under the
rubric 'Special Controls'. Provisions which benefit a landowner and limit
control, such as deemed consent by way of Class 13, are in the nature of
exceptions. A control mechanism is relaxed because there has been a
lengthy period of official acquiescence or tolerance. It seems to me that the
reason for the very broad definition of 'advertisement' is that it facilitates
control by guarding against the exploitation of loopholes. It is a form of

anti-avoidance measure. Thus, within the ten year period, it enables the local authority to control not just a sign etc. but also the structure to which it is attached. But does that necessarily mean that a bare, unadorned structure remains an 'advertisement' in circumstances such as those of cessation in the present case, with the consequence that there is continual display? In my judgment, it does not."
Winfield v Secretary of State for Communities and Local Government [2012] EWCA Civ 1415.

"It ought nevertheless to be acknowledged that our purposive construction of the definition in s.336(1) has been required in order to make working sense of Class 13. This is not an ideal mode of legal reasoning. Although, as the Vice-President says, the appellant's construction of the definition is counter-intuitive, it has the primary virtue of apparent loyalty to the text. I would hope that departmental attention will be given to clarifying the legislation." (Above.)

ADVOCACY. Stat. Def., Legal Aid, Sentencing and Punishment of Offenders Act 2012 s.42.

AFTER-CARE.
"7. Although the [Mental Health Act 1983] has in s145 an interpretation section there is, some might think surprisingly, no definition of 'after-care services'. Parliament, whether by design, or by accident, left the interpretation of that compound noun to the judges. . . .
19. I therefore hold that as a matter of law s117(2) is only engaged vis-à-vis accommodation if:
 i) The need for accommodation is a direct result of the reason that the ex-patient was detained in the first place ('the original condition');
 ii) The requirement is for enhanced specialised accommodation to meet needs directly arising from the original condition; and
 iii) The ex-patient is being placed in the accommodation on an involuntary (in the sense of being incapacitated) basis arising as a result of the original condition."
Afework, R. (on the application of) v London Borough of Camden [2013] EWHC 1637 (Admin).

AGGRAVATED DAMAGES.
"38. The formulation of the preliminary issue in this case begs the question of what is meant by 'aggravated damages'. The term has sometimes been used to refer to a monetary award which is intended to serve a punitive or partly punitive purpose. It is common ground, however, that the reference to 'aggravated damages' is to be understood as denoting damages which are purely compensatory in purpose and which are awarded for a tort as compensation for mental distress caused by the manner in which the tort has been committed, or the motive with which it was committed,

or by subsequent conduct of the defendant: see *Rookes v Barnard (No1)* [1964] AC 1129, 1221, per Lord Devlin; and see the report of the Law Commission on 'Aggravated, Exemplary and Restitutionary Damages' (September 1997), pp.10–11, paras 1.1 and 1.4."
Iraqi Civilians v Ministry of Defence [2014] EWHC 3686 (QB).

AGGRIEVED.
"The authorities also demonstrate that there are circumstances in which a person who has not participated in the process may nonetheless be 'aggrieved': where for example an inadequate description of the development in the application and advertisement could have misled him so that he did not object or take part in the inquiry, as in *Cumming v Secretary of State for Scotland* and the analogous English case of *Wilson v Secretary of State for the Environment* [1973] 1 W.L.R. 1083. Ordinarily, however, it will be relevant to consider whether the applicant stated his objection at the appropriate stage of the statutory procedure, since that procedure is designed to allow objections to be made and a decision then to be reached within a reasonable time, as intended by Parliament."
Walton v The Scottish Ministers (Scotland) [2012] UKSC 44.

"While the wording of Article 143(5) is deceptively simple and while the applicant clearly feels a grievance in relation to the way in which the Official Receiver has conducted the sale of the shares case law authority is against the applicant. For a party to be entitled to claim that he is 'aggrieved' he must have some arguable legal interest or right which has been infringed by the actions or decisions of the liquidator."
Curistan v The Official Receiver for Northern Ireland [2015] NI Ch 10.

AGREEMENT FOR THE SALE OR OTHER DISPOSITION OF AN INTEREST IN LAND.
"I conclude that the compromise agreement is not an agreement 'for the sale or other disposition of an interest in land' within the meaning of section 2(1) of the [Law of Property (Miscellaneous Provisions) Act 1989], so that despite being oral it is a valid contract."
Yeates v Line [2012] EWHC 3085 (Ch).

AGRICULTURAL ACTIVITY.
"7. As explained below, the notion of 'agricultural activity' used for the purposes of the EU's SPS regime is a wide one. It covers both active use of farmland for production of crops or animals and also the maintenance of land in 'good agricultural and environmental condition' without putting it to productive use. Thus usage hectares which are declared in order to activate entitlement hectares may be land which is employed for production of food or which is simply being maintained to appropriate 'good agricultural and environmental condition' standards."
Bickford-Smith, R. (on the application of) v Secretary of State for Environment, Food and Rural Affairs [2013] EWHC 3371 (Admin).

AIR TRANSPORT SERVICES. Stat. Def., Civil Aviation Act 2012 s.69.

AIRPORT. Stat. Def., Civil Aviation Act 2012 ss.66, 67.

AIRPORT OPERATION SERVICES. Stat. Def., Civil Aviation Act 2012 s.68.

ALL REASONABLE ENDEAVOURS.
"Guidance as to the correct construction of the term 'all reasonable endeavours' is to be found in the judgment of Ackner J. in *Agroexport State Enterprise for Foreign Trade v Compagnie Européene de Cereales* (supra). That case concerned a dispute between the plaintiffs as sellers and the defenders as purchasers of Romanian maize. The dispute arose on account of difficulties the plaintiffs had encountered in obtaining the necessary licences to export the full tonnage of the maize contracted for from Romania. The licence granted covered only half of the contracted tonnage. In such circumstances, when there had been a partial prohibition of export, the sellers were not only under an obligation to apply for a licence, they were obliged to use all reasonable efforts to obtain permission to export the full tonnage. In order to take advantage of the exemption clause, implied into the contract, the sellers required to show that despite having taken all reasonable steps to obtain permission they had been unable to achieve success or alternatively that it would have been useless for them to take any further steps because they were foredoomed to failure (page 506). [28] In our opinion it is clear that the obligation to pursue a project or seek a planning consent with all reasonable endeavours is one that requires the court to consider whether there were reasonable steps which the obligant could have taken but did not. For that reason it is a higher or more onerous obligation than one restricted to using 'reasonable endeavours'. However, whether the phrase used is 'all reasonable endeavours', as in Clauses 6 and 13, or 'reasonable endeavours' we agree with the view expressed by Lord Hodge in *MacTaggart & Mickel Homes Ltd v Hunter*, at para.[63], that an obligation in either terms does not require the obligant to disregard its own commercial interests. Where the balance between the obligation to use reasonable endeavours and countervailing commercial considerations falls to be struck depends on the wording of the obligation in question. In considering what steps would be reasonable, the court also has to consider whether any further steps would have been successful. We agree with Lord Hodge (at para.[64]) that if an obligant can show that it would have been useless for it to have taken a particular step (or steps), because it would not have been sufficient to achieve success, that would provide an answer to any claim that the obligant had acted in breach of contract (see also *Agroexport State Enterprise for Foreign Trade v Compagnie Européene de Cereales*, Ackner J. at page 506). Equally if there was an insuperable obstacle, it is irrelevant that there may have been other obstacles which could have been overcome, or at any rate in respect

of which the obligant had not yet done all that could reasonably be expected of it to try to overcome (see *Yewbelle Ltd v London Green Developments Ltd* [2008] 1 P. & C. R. 17, Lloyd L.J. at para.103, cf Waller L.J. at para.126)."
EDI Central Ltd v National Car Parks [2012] ScotCS CSIH 6.

ALTERNATIVE DISPUTE RESOLUTION.
"9. The term 'alternative dispute resolution' ('ADR') is defined in the glossary to the CPR as a 'collective description of methods of resolving disputes otherwise than through the normal trial process'. One such process is, of course, mediation."
Laporte v The Commissioner of Police of the Metropolis [2015] EWHC 371 (QB).

ALWAYS.
"Whilst slavish application of the literal meaning of 'always' might appear to place a claimant in the WRAG unless he can bring himself within the description to which I refer at the end of paragraph 36 above, I consider that that would not make sense in the overall statutory context and would tend to undermine its underlying purpose."
The Secretary of State for Works and Pensions v Brade [2014] ScotCS CSIH 39.

AMEND. Stat. Def., "Any power of the Secretary of State or Lord Chancellor under this Act to amend legislation by subordinate legislation includes power to repeal or revoke legislation (and any reference to the amendment of legislation by such an order or regulations is to be read accordingly)." (Marriage (Same Sex Couples) Act 2013 s.16); note that this provision (Marriage (Same Sex Couples) Act 2013 s.18) is unnecessary, and for it to become a standard inclusion would be an unwise innovation, in that it creates or exacerbates doubt in places where it has not been incorporated in the past (or where it is inadvertently omitted in the future); it is preferable to leave this to be inferred, as it undoubtedly would be (since repeal of a provision is merely one form of amendment of the enactment of which it forms part, and the difference between repealing individual provisions and a whole enactment is one only of quantity and not of quality).

AMOUNT TO BE PAID.
"44. The phrase the 'amount to be paid' which appears in the latter half of section 10(4) of the 1980 Act must be construed consistently with the opening words of that subsection. In my view it means the amount to be paid in respect of the actual damage caused to C. It does not refer to or include the amount of costs which D must pay to C, even though those costs can be the subject of a contribution claim."
Hampshire Constabulary v Southampton City Council [2014] EWCA Civ 1541.

AND/OR.

"26. That this document is not the product of skilful drafting is also evidenced by the presence of the expression 'and/or.' Its use in this clause is unnecessary and confusing. In this case 'and/or' in clause 4.2 can only mean 'or'. If the vendors agree with the purchaser not to remain as directors, then the occasion for a request by the purchaser to that effect would not arise. It would only arise as an alternative to a failure to agree on whether the vendors stay or go. I would add that the use of the expression 'and/or' in any legal document is in any case open to numerous more fundamental objections of inaccuracy, obscurity, uncertainty or even as being just plain meaningless, as explained by Sir Robert Megarry in his erudite philological discussion of 'and/or' in 'Andorandororand' to 'Law at the Centre' (1999) at pp 71 to 78)."
Situ Ventures Ltd v Bonham-Carter [2013] EWCA Civ 47.

ANGIOGRAPHY.

"Angiography is a medical imaging technique used to visualise the inside of blood vessels done by injecting a radio-opaque contrast agent into the blood vessel via a catheter introduced into a patient's arterial system with the assistance of guide wires and imaging the vessels so injected using X-ray techniques. The film or image of the blood vessels is called an angiogram and that term is commonly used to encompass the whole procedure."
Connolly v Croydon Health Services NHS Trust [2015] EWHC 1339 (QB).

ANGIOPLASTY.

"Angioplasty is a procedure in which initially the same techniques are used as for the production of an angiogram but after insertion of a catheter into a patient's arterial system various other items may also be introduced into the arterial system via the catheter, namely guide balloons and stents. A balloon may be used to open a narrowed or blocked artery. Most modern angioplasty procedures also involve inserting a stent, i.e. a short wire-mesh tube, into the artery during the procedure. The stent is left in place permanently to allow blood to flow more freely."
Connolly v Croydon Health Services NHS Trust [2015] EWHC 1339 (QB).

ANNOUNCE.

"77. As a matter of first impression, the GMC's interpretation of the word 'announce' seems highly improbable. The definition of 'announce' in the *Oxford Dictionary* is 'make a formal public statement about a fact, occurrence, or intention', which suggests strongly that the approach of the GMC requires a distortion of the natural meaning of the word. But one must not only consider the natural meaning of the word, but also consider it in the context of the relevant Rules and the role of the Panel.

78. The starting point must be to consider the role of the Panel. Its task under the Rules is to determine allegations of misconduct against profes-

sional men and women, and hearing evidence to that end. Those allegations can, if proved, lead to a conclusion that the doctor's fitness to prac-
tise was impaired, and in some cases to erasure from the register or
suspension. In carrying out that function, it must sit in public (Rule 41)
unless it decides to sit in private for good reasons. The public interest, and
in particular the interests of open justice, requires that such proceedings
are held in public. That applies with no less force to the parts of its proceedings where its decisions are given.

79. It would be illogical if a Tribunal which is required to conduct its
proceedings in public is then able to issue factual determinations otherwise than in public, unless some good reason under Rule 41 required it.

80. The use of the word 'announce' is therefore apt in that context. A
finding under Rule 17(2)(i) is 'announced', so that all interested in the outcome of the hearing (including but not limited to the doctor concerned)
know what has been concluded and why. If what was permitted was, as Mr
Hare contended, simple notification to the parties, the word 'announce'
could not have been chosen. Still less could it be achieved by the issue to
the parties of an embargoed draft, as the Panel seem to have thought."
TZ v General Medical Council [2015] EWHC 1001 (Admin).

ANTARCTIC TREATY. Stat. Def., Antarctic Act 2013 s.13.

ANTI-SOCIAL BEHAVIOUR. Stat. Def., Anti-social Behaviour, Crime
and Policing Act 2014 s.2.

ANY APPROPRIATE RELIEF.
"105. The non-exhaustive words 'any appropriate relief' are capable of
being given a wide literal meaning. However, the very width of their literal
meaning, which is illustrated in paragraph 79 above, makes me somewhat
cautious about construing the words literally. Those considerations suggest to me that it was not intended that the words should be given such a
wide literal meaning."
Fibria Celulose S/A v Pan Ocean Co Ltd [2014] EWHC 2124 (Ch).

APPEAL. See REFERENCE.
Stat. Def., (including reference to retrial) Serious Crime Act 2015 s.65.

APPEARANCE. See ENTERS AN APPEARANCE.

APPLIED.
"Agreeing that a law is 'to be applied' to disputes between parties is a com-
mon means of expressing a choice of substantive law, a choice that is fre-
quently made express."
Shagang South-Asia (Hong Kong) Trading Co Ltd v Daewoo Logistics [2015]
EWHC 194 (Comm).

APPROPRIATE. See ANY APPROPRIATE RELIEF.

APPURTENANT.

"Appurtenant property, as defined by section 112(1), includes appurtenances belonging to or usually enjoyed with the building, part of a building or flat. Appurtenances such as gardens and yards are frequently enjoyed by a building, or a part of a building or a flat, in common with other buildings, parts of buildings or flats. In ordinary language, the car parking ports/spaces included in the leases of the flats 'belong to' the flats which comprise the self contained block, whereas the bin area, access road and gardens are 'enjoyed with' the flats which comprise the two blocks. The fact that the occupiers of other property, in this case the two coach houses, also enjoy those appurtenances does not mean that they fall outside the definition in section 112(1). The fact that the definition is not limited to appurtenances which belong to the building in question is a powerful indication that Parliament did not intend that appurtenant property for the purpose of section 72(1)(a) should be limited to property that is exclusively appurtenant to the self contained building in question. In effect, Mr. McGurk's approach is an attempt to substitute in section 72(1)(a) the words 'self contained premises' for premises which consist of a self contained building together with appurtenant property. In my judgment, the wording of section 72(1)(a) is clear: there is no requirement that the appurtenant property should appertain exclusively to the self contained building which is the subject of the claim to acquire the right to manage. The prospect of dual responsibility for the management of some of the appurtenant property in this and other similar cases is not a happy one. As Mr. McGurk submitted, there is the potential for duplication of management effort and for conflict between the 'old' management company and the new RTM company in respect of such appurtenant property, but I am not persuaded that these consequences are so grave, or that the end result is so manifestly absurd, that we would be justified in adding a gloss to words—appurtenant property—which are already defined in the Act. It is always open to the parties, if they wish to avoid duplication and/or conflict, to reach an agreement which would make economic sense for all parties (see paragraph 18 of the President's decision); if they are unable to do so, paragraph 17 of the President's decision suggests a means of resolving disputes arising from dual responsibility for maintenance."
Gala Unity Ltd v Ariadne Road RTM Company Ltd [2012] EWCA Civ 1372.

AREA.

"32. A 'conservation area' has no further definition than in s.91 where it is . . . 'an area for the time being designated under section 69'. There is no very useful authority on what constitutes an 'area'. I note the contrast for these purposes with s.1 of the 1990 Act, which deals with listed buildings, and applies only to buildings. A building can be listed having regard to the interest of any man-made object fixed to the building or forming part of the land within the curtilage of the building. English Heritage has listed some sports pavilions and stands, and a lido, both pool and changing rooms, but has not listed a whole stadium with curtilage as a building. . . .

36. In my judgment, the designation is of an 'area' for the purposes of s.69. The question is not one of rationality in the first place. The question of what the lawful requisites are for an area to be an 'area' for the purposes of s.69 must be established; the Council must then approach the application of those requisites to the facts rationally. It is plain that the word 'area' has a very wide scope. It connotes some size unspecific but going beyond a mere mathematical square footage. There is sound practical sense of general application behind Mr Hill's contention that a single building with curtilage is not intended to be designated as a conservation area. The provisions governing conservation areas are to be contrasted with those governing listed buildings, to avoid undermining the clear distinction between the protections given to each. A conservation area is not a form of inferior protection to be bestowed on a single building with a curtilage, which simply fails to make the listing grade. However, if as a general proposition, the single building and its curtilage signpost the distinction between the two regimes, there is no exclusive or exhaustive statutory rule to that effect, good for all single buildings and their curtilages, whatever their nature, scale or relationship to each other. The fact that the proposed area is enclosed as a single entity, albeit now in disparate uses or abandoned, does not prevent in law the enclosure, and the land and buildings within being an 'area' for s.69 purposes. The absence of public access or visibility goes only to the desirability of preserving or enhancing the area. Single ownership is irrelevant other than perhaps to that issue. The Council did not err in its understanding of the concept of an 'area' for the purposes of s.69. . . .

38. That is why I emphasise that Parliament has not defined 'area' as distinct from 'a building and its curtilage'. Had it done so, then whatever the circumstances, and for all the variety of forms and purpose of spaces and buildings which are to be found, the question of whether a site was an 'area' for the purposes of s.69 would have had to be answered by pigeon-holing the site into one or other category, however artificial that would have been. But it has not done so, and such artificiality should not be imposed on the statutory provisions. This case illustrates how difficult such an exercise would have been and how it would have distracted from the main purpose of s.69 and its test."

GRA Acquisition Ltd, R. (on the application of) v Oxford City Council [2015] EWHC 76 (Admin).

ARISING FROM.

"145. Mr Chamberlain submits that in the present context the expression 'arising from' clearly has a narrow meaning. A right 'arises from' an instrument referred to in para.30 if and only if it is contained in that instrument, not by reason of some looser connection. The expression 'arising from' (rather than, for example, 'under') has been used simply because each of the instruments in question has to be implemented in domestic law—the Refugee Convention by means of the Immigration Rules, the Human Rights Convention by means of the Human Rights Act 1998, and the Temporary Protection Directive and the Qualification Directive by means of regulations and other measures. The use of 'arising from' makes sense in that context. The fact that LASPO lays down a set of carefully defined and restrictive conditions as to the matters in scope for legal aid also tells in favour of a narrow interpretation.

146. On that basis it is submitted that a refugee's right of family reunion is not a right 'arising from' the Refugee Convention. The right is not contained in the Refugee Convention. The Refugee Convention makes no reference whatsoever to it. It is not enough that the right is recognised in international law and is referred to in the Final Act of the Conference which adopted the Refugee Convention.

147. In our judgment, the interpretation of 'arising from' for which the appellants contend is the correct one. The expression is evidently capable of having a narrower or a wider meaning but in the present context, for the reasons given by Mr Chamberlain, we think that Parliament must have intended the narrower meaning, with the consequence that the right of family reunion is excluded from the matters in scope. On this issue, therefore, we reach the opposite conclusion from that reached by Collins J."

Gudanaviciene, R. (on the application of) v Director of Legal Aid Casework [2014] EWCA Civ 1622.

ARMED FORCES. Stat. Def., Public Service Pensions Act 2013 s.37.

ARRANGEMENTS.
"164. While it is common ground that 'arrangements' are not of necessarily legally binding agreements (although agreements are a species of arrangements and contracts are a sub-species of agreement), Mr Coppel submitted that Asset Land and its investors cannot have entered into arrangements that were contradicted by their contracts or inconsistent with them. I cannot accept this argument: it is, in my judgment, wrong to regard arrangements (either in the context of section 235 or more generally) as inchoate or imperfect contracts that are displaced if the parties enter into a different (perhaps superior) form of understanding, a contract. People do not live their lives only by reference to their legal rights, and often manage their affairs, and make arrangements, on the basis that the legal framework in which they operate will not be invoked, or is unlikely to be invoked."

The Financial Services Authority v Asset L I Inc (t/a Asset Land Investment Inc) [2013] EWHC 178 (Ch).

"68. The word 'arrangements' ordinarily has a wider ambit than agreement or contract: the focus of the section being on the intended operation

of the scheme in practice, the arrangements may qualify as such even if not stated or intended to be legally binding."
Secretary of State for Business Innovation and Skills v Chohan [2013] EWHC 680 (Ch).

"I agree with the judge's analysis. The authorities demonstrate that, when interpreted together, sections 235(1), (2) and (3) [of the Financial Services and Markets Act 2000] are drafted in such a way as to justify the giving of a very wide meaning to term 'arrangements' in section 235(1), which includes understandings and agreements that are not legally binding."
Asset Land Investment Plc v The Financial Conduct Authority (FCA) [2014] EWCA Civ 435.

ASSET.

"The principal one is whether a contractual right to draw down under an unsecured loan facility qualifies, either generally or in particular circumstances, as an 'asset' for the purpose of the order? . . .

72. I agree with the judge (judgment, [75]) that a man who is entitled to borrow and does so 'is not ordinarily to be described as disposing of or dealing with an asset'. As Sir Roy Goode has stated, albeit in the context of section 127 of the Insolvency Act 1986, '[i]f there is one thing that is still clear in the increasingly complex financial scene . . . it is that a liability is not an asset and that an increase in a liability is not by itself a disposition of an asset': *Principles of Corporate Law*, 4th ed., (2011) at 13-133. I also agree with the judge that, while in construing a legal document such as the order the court needs to have regard to the legal meaning where technical legal terminology is used to describe particular concepts, here the terms used; 'assets', 'dispose of', 'deal with', and 'diminish the value of' are not specifically legal terminology. . . . I have concluded that, in determining the meaning of the term 'assets' in a freezing order, account should be taken, as part of the background and context of such orders, of their purpose, in the way that anyone construing any document should take account of the background of it. Where the words used clearly and unequivocally lead to the conclusion that the term 'asset' includes that which cannot be the subject of execution, effect must be given to the words. Where they do not, the purpose of such orders will be a significant factor in determining the meaning of the term 'asset' in this context, and a pointer against including the particular right under consideration. . . .

Notwithstanding that, in the light of the background understanding of the purpose of such orders, the authorities on the point, and the guidance on which practitioners have relied, I have also reached the conclusion that, if the order is to treat rights of this sort as 'assets' despite their unamenability to enforcement and the inability to place a value on them, additional words are needed.

91. Accordingly, for these reasons, I would dismiss the appeal on the main question, whether the contractual right to draw down under the loan

facility agreements qualifies as an 'asset' and whether the exercise of that loan facility constitutes 'disposing of' or 'dealing with' an asset."
JSC BTA Bank v Ablyazov [2013] EWCA Civ 928.

ASSOCIATE.
"34. The dictionary meaning of 'associate' is to join, to link together or to unite with others, but includes to accompany, escort or attend. Ms Dobbin cited *Lord Dormer v Knight* [1809] 1 Taunt 417: 127 ER 895, which seems to be the only case in the legal dictionaries where the term "associate" appears. There it was held that the receiving of visits involved an association between the visitor and the person being visited. However, that was in the context of a deed where an annuity would cease if a woman should associate with a particular man, and the court held that his visiting her, albeit innocently, constituted association. That decision tells us nothing about the meaning of the term 'associate' in the context of section 31 of the [Children and Young Persons Act 1933]."
T, R. (on the application of) v Secretary of State for Justice [2013] EWHC 1119 (Admin).

AVATAR.
"42. The term 'avatar' is used to refer to the version of the real person which exists in the virtual environment. The images can be presented to the user as they would be seen through the eyes of the avatar. This is called a first person viewpoint. With a third person viewpoint, the images depict the user's avatar."
Koninklijke Philips Electronics NV v Nintendo of Europe GmbH [2014] EWHC 1959 (Pat).

AWARD.
"First, the starting point for any interpretation of Clause 2 is that those in the construction industry commonly refer to the awarding of a contract. It is the process whereby the employer accepts the offer put forward by the contractor, or where the main contractor accepts the offer put forward by his sub-contractor. It denotes a binding agreement. It is the granting of the contract by one party, with its binding rights and obligations, to the other. 13. That interpretation of the word 'award' is, I think, entirely consistent with the definitions in the dictionaries. The *Oxford English Dictionary* has, as one of its meanings of 'award', 'to grant or assign'; another definition is 'to grant or assign (a contract or commission)'. The example that is given is telling: 'the company was awarded a contract to refurbish the timber mill'. In my judgment, that is using the word 'award' in a contractual context in precisely the way that I would expect.
14. By contrast, of course, an 'offer' is something very different. In contract law, it is something which has happened much earlier in the process. You cannot have a contract award unless you have had an offer which has

been accepted. The acceptance of the offer is then formalised by the award of the contract."

Jacobs UK Ltd v Skidmore Owings & Merrill LLP Queen's Bench Division (Technology & Construction Court), November 15, 2012.

BAKER'S HONEY. Stat. Def., "honey that is suitable for industrial use or as an ingredient in another foodstuff which is then processed" (Honey (England) Regulations 2015 (SI 2015/1348) reg.2).

BARELY COLORABLE.
"40. Again, there is discussion in the case law as to what is meant by 'barely colorable' in this context, but it is clear that an error of law by arbitrators is not enough. A 'party must show that the arbitrators intentionally flouted a legal principle'. It is not disputed that there is a high threshold before a US court will invalidate an arbitration award based on arbitrators' manifest disregard of the law."
Travis Coal Restructured Holdings Llc v Essar Global Fund Ltd [2014] EWHC 2510 (Comm).

BENCHMARK. Stat. Def., Financial Services and Markets Act 2000 s.22 as inserted by Financial Services Act 2012 s.7.

BENEFICIARY.
"22. I think one has to be careful of the use of the word 'beneficiary' in this context. A charitable trust, as such, does not have beneficiaries in the same sense as beneficiaries under a private trust. No individual has any proprietary interest in the charity's assets and funds as such, but a person may become a beneficiary in a loose sense as an object of the charitable trust. The advancing of the Ethiopian Orthodox faith would, in one sense, embrace all those of that faith. That would not, I think, be sufficient to make all members of the Ethiopian Orthodox Church, anywhere in the world, who are very considerable in number, persons interested in this charity, but I do think that regular worshippers, who have contributed as such to the acquisition of the assets of the charity, as well as worshipping at the church in its various forms over many years, are undoubtedly interested persons for this purpose. Hoffman J, in considering who is an interested person noted that no definition has been attempted in any previous case. He then set out the passage from the Vice-Chancellor's judgment that I have referred to and decided (for reasons which seem tolerably obvious) that the executors could not regard themselves on the charity side of the fence simply on the grounds that the deceased settlor would have wished to see the trusts of the charity enforced. Even if the deceased had been a person interested on those grounds, that was not an interest which could have been transmitted to the executors. As Hoffman J put it, executors succeed to the property of the deceased not to the deceased's spirit and disembodied wishes."

Bisrat v Kebede [2015] EWHC 840 (Ch).

BENEFIT.
"As already stated, section 76(4) of the Proceeds of Crime Act provides that: 'A person benefits from conduct if he obtains property as a result of or in connection with the conduct.' 14. 'Obtains' is not defined in the Act, but in *R v May* [2008] 2 Cr App R 28, Lord Bingham giving the opinion of the House stated at [48]: '(4) In addressing the questions the court should focus very closely on the language of the statutory provision in question in the context of the statute and in the light of any statutory definition. The language used is not arcane or obscure and any judicial gloss of exegesis should be viewed with caution. Guidance should ordinarily be sought in the statutory language rather than in the proliferating case law. . . . (6) D ordinarily obtains property if in law he owns it, whether alone or jointly, which will ordinarily connote a power of disposition or control, as where a person directs a payment or conveyance of property to someone else. . . . Mere couriers or custodians or other very minor contributors to an offence, rewarded by a specific fee and having no interest in the property or the proceeds of sale, are unlikely to be found to have obtained that property. It may be otherwise with money launderers.'"
Hursthouse, R. v [2013] EWCA Crim 517.

BEST INTERESTS. For discussion of the "best interests" of a child in an immigration context see *Asefa R. (on the application of) v Secretary of State for the Home Department* [2012] EWHC 56 (Admin).

BETTING EXCHANGE.
"Betting exchanges are creatures of the Internet. They are properly called exchanges, because they do not themselves normally take any position in a bet. They are described as follows in the Claimant's skeleton argument: 'An internet betting exchange is an online marketplace. Users of the exchange indicate the bets they wish to make and identify the odds they are willing to offer or accept and the sums they are willing to bet. The exchange then matches up one or more "backers" (i.e. those who want to bet at particular odds that a particular event will occur: "I bet that Camelot will win the Derby") with one or more "layers" making an opposing bet (i.e. those who are prepared to bet at the same odds that the particular event will not occur: "I bet that Camelot will not win the Derby"). The exchange charges commission on the winnings of the successful party. The exchange itself takes no risk.' A betting exchange was described as follows in Betfair's prospectus for the initial public offer of its shares: 'The Betting Exchange is an order-driven system which allows customers to bet at odds sought by themselves or offered by other customers. A bet is only confirmed on the Betting Exchange once its risk is exactly matched by Betfair with another customer or group of customers with an equal and opposite view. When betting on the Betting Exchange, customers can either place a

"back" bet or a "lay" bet. A "back" bet is a bet on something to happen (for example, a football team to win a match) and a "lay" bet is a bet on something not to happen (for example, a football match not to end in a draw). Betting on the Betting Exchange allows a customer not only to "back" or "lay" a selection, but also to choose the price at which that customer wishes to "back" or "lay" and how much he or she is prepared to risk. If the price at which the customer wishes to bet improves while a customer is in the process of placing his bet, that customer will be automatically matched by at the best available price—higher for "backing", lower for "laying"—in other words, in accordance with the "best execution principle"."

William Hill Organization Ltd, R. (on the application of) v The Horserace Betting Levy Board [2012] EWHC 2039 (Admin).

BIOMETRIC INFORMATION. Stat. Def., Protection of Freedoms Act 2012 s.28.

BISHOP. See ELIGIBLE BISHOP.

BLOSSOM HONEY. Stat. Def., honey "obtained from the nectar of plants" (Honey (England) Regulations 2015 (SI 2015/1348) reg.2).

BOARDING HOUSE.
"9. It is the claimants' case that the defendant offers accommodation in a boarding house or establishment similar to a hotel or boarding house. The Recorder applied an Oxford dictionary definition of 'boarding house' as being 'a private house which people pay to stay in for a short time'. She said that it seemed to her that a bed and breakfast establishment was 'capable of falling within the meaning of the term "boarding house" in the regulation' (para 66). She also held in the alternative that the defendant's bed and breakfast establishment was similar to the category of establishments to which hotels and boarding houses belong. She said that this conclusion was not undermined by the fact that the bed and breakfast establishment was small and that the defendant provided a personal service to her guests: hotels and boarding houses may be large or small and personal services may or may not be provided in them.
10. Ms Crowther challenges these conclusions. She cites various dictionary definitions in support of the submission that a boarding house is a private home that provides a room and meals to paying guests. She says that bed and breakfast accommodation is not a boarding house. A feature of a boarding house is the provision of more than one meal a day, and bed and breakfast accommodation contemplates only the provision of breakfast and no other meals. As for the Recorder's alternative conclusion, Ms Crowther submits that the overall character of the services provided by the defendant cannot properly be said to be of the nature of a 'similar establishment'.

11. I cannot accept these submissions. I see no reason to hold that "board" must include more than one meal per day. The normal meaning of the word is the provision of accommodation and some food which is prepared, served and cleared away by the provider. In *Otter v Norman* [1989] AC 129 (an authority to which Arden LJ drew our attention), the court had to decide whether a tenancy was protected under section 7(1) of the Rent Act 1977. That question turned on whether the dwelling-house had been let 'at a rent which includes payments in respect of board, attendance . . . ' It was held by the House of Lords that the provision of breakfast by itself, with the implicit inclusion of the ancillary services involved in preparing it and the provision of crockery and cutlery with which to eat it, amounted to 'board' within the meaning of section 7(1). Their Lordships expressly rejected the submission that 'board' requires at least the provision of one main meal in addition to breakfast. I accept that the word 'board' is capable of different meanings and that the context in which it is used is important. But I can see no reason not to apply the same approach as that adopted in *Otter* in the present context.

12. Even if the defendant does not provide accommodation in a boarding-house, I would uphold the Recorder's alternative conclusion that the accommodation is in a 'similar establishment' within the meaning of regulation 4(2)(b). A bed and breakfast establishment is similar to a hotel and boarding house in that in each of them (i) accommodation is provided for varying periods of time and (ii) the guests receive at least one meal per day (some hotels and boarding houses provide full or half board, but many only provide bed and breakfast).

13. I can think of no policy reason why Parliament would have intended to protect individuals from discrimination on grounds of sexual orientation in relation to the provision of half board (ie bed, breakfast and one other meal) but not in relation to the provision of bed and breakfast accommodation. Regulation 4(2)(b) is concerned with protecting the rights of guests staying in commercial accommodation, not just the rights of those who have breakfast plus one other meal."
Black v Wilkinson [2013] EWCA Civ 820.

BODY. Stat. Def., Public Service Pensions Act 2013 s.37.

BOOKMAKER.
"In ordinary parlance, a bookmaker is a person who carries on the business of accepting bets from members of the public, commonly referred to as punters. He is so called because he normally will seek to make a book, that is to say, to accept bets at odds that ensure that whatever the result of the race or other event that is the subject of the bets, he will make a profit. If necessary he will lay off some bets with other bookmakers, particularly if he would otherwise be exposed to a loss in a particular event. The assemblage of his positions is his book."

William Hill Organization Ltd, R. (on the application of) v The Horserace Betting Levy Board [2012] EWHC 2039 (Admin).

"44. The answer to the question of construction lies in the persistence with which the legislation has maintained the difference between those who make bets and those who receive them, between the customer and the bookmaker. In light of that distinction, those who use a betting exchange do not receive or negotiate bets within the meaning of section 55 of the Betting, Gaming and Lotteries Act 1963."

William Hill Organisation Ltd, R. (on the application of) v The Horserace Betting Levy Board [2013] EWCA Civ 487.

BROUGHT.

"When an action is 'brought' for the purpose of the Limitation Act 1980 is, in my judgment, a question of construction of the Act. It is not a question of construction of the CPR, let alone a question of construction of a Practice Direction. The CPR (and perhaps the Practice Direction) may inform the construction, but the question remains: what does the Act mean? . . . Taken literally, the ratio of *Barnes v St Helens Metropolitan Borough Council* is that once the claimant has delivered his request for the issue of a claim form to the court office, he has 'brought' his action. If Mr Last's evidence is correct, Messrs Page did that in the present case. However, literalism is not fashionable, so it is also necessary to consider the policy that underpins the decision. Tuckey L.J. dealt with this too. He pointed out that this meant that a claimant had the full period of limitation within which to 'bring' his claim; and that it would be unjust if he had to take the risk that the court would fail to process it in time. It does not seem to me that the reason why the court fails to process the request in time alters the justice of the case. If it is unjust for the claimant to take the risk that the court staff are on strike, it seems to me to be equally unjust for him to have to take the risk that a member of the court staff might erroneously put his request in the shredder or the confidential waste, or that his request is destroyed by flood or fire in the court office, or is taken in a burglary. Each of these might be reasons why the court failed to process the request in time. Essentially the construction of the Act that this court favoured in *Barnes v St Helens Metropolitan Borough Council* is based on risk allocation. The claimant's risk stops once he has delivered his request (accompanied by the claim form and fee) to the court office. PD 7 cannot, in my judgment, alter the correct construction of the Act."

Page v Hewetts Solicitors [2012] EWCA Civ 805.

BUILDING.

"The issue here is whether NG's proposal for an overhead line involved the construction of a 'building' or was an 'engineering operation' for the purposes of PPG2 (the relevant provisions of which are at Annex A). SSOBT's

case was that the construction of these large pylons constituted the erection of a building, as that term is used in PPG2. The Inspectors agreed.
... In my judgment, it does not matter whether the inappropriateness of the development arises from the fact that it involves the construction of a building or the carrying out of an engineering operation. If an engineering operation does not maintain openness and conflicts with the purposes of including land in a Green Belt, then it will be inappropriate and the presumption against it will arise."
Samuel Smith Old Brewery (Tadcaster) (An unlimited company), R. (on the application of) v Secretary of State for Energy & Climate Change [2012] EWHC 46 (Admin).

"The word 'building' in section 11(1A)(a) [of the Landlord and Tenant Act 1985] is not defined, and should be given its ordinary dictionary meaning of 'structure with a roof and walls'."
Edwards v Kumarasamy [2015] EWCA Civ 20.

BUSINESS. Stat. Def., Consumer Rights Act 2015 s.2.

BUSINESS DAY. Stat. Def., "'business day' means any day except Saturday, Sunday, Christmas Day, Boxing Day, Good Friday, Easter Monday or a bank holiday" (Criminal Procedure Rules 2013 r.2.2).

C

CAPACITY.
"'Capacity' itself is an unclear concept dependent upon what work the business decides it wants to take on, and with many variables, from the nature of the steel to be cut, through the size of the starting piece to be worked on and the complexity of the cuts that have to be made, to the quality of the work done (and whether any of it has to be redone), to the number of repeat pieces to be cut and the availability of automated processes: and, critically, the type of saw required. So the question of 'capacity' within a business is one for judgment not precise computation; and the decision whether to take on or to refuse particular work is one that needs to be taken by reference to a business plan."
Breitenfeld UK Ltd v Harrison [2015] EWHC 399 (Ch).

CARAVAN.
"It was common ground that the chalet, though lacking wheels, was capable of being moved and accordingly fell within the statutory definition of 'caravan' in section 29(1) of the 1960 Act. The planning authority contended the word 'caravan' in the planning consent should be given its ordinary and natural meaning and not the extended meaning in section 29(1) of the 1960 Act. It was common ground that, if the word had its ordinary and natural meaning, the chalet was not within the planning permission. The House of Lords held that the statutory definition applied."
Royal Borough of Windsor & Maidenhead v Smith [2012] EWCA Civ 997.

CARBON CAPTURE AND STORAGE TECHNOLOGY. Stat. Def., Energy Act 2013 s.61.

CARE (MENTAL HEALTH). Stat. Def., "'mental health care' means psychiatric services, or other services provided for the purpose of preventing, diagnosing or treating illness, the arrangements for which are the primary responsibility of a consultant psychiatrist." (Care Act 2014 Sch.3 para.7.)

CARGO. Stat. Def. "includes mail" (Civil Aviation Act 2012 s.72).

CARRIER BAG. Stat. Def., "a bag of any material supplied or designed for the purpose of enabling goods to be taken away or delivered", Single Use Carrier Bags Charge Regulations (Northern Ireland) 2013 reg.3 amended by Carrier Bags Act (Northern Ireland) 2014 s.9.

CARRIES ON.

"The two expressions 'carries on or manages' in section 11(1) are used in the alternative. The expression 'carries on', as in 'carries on or manages an establishment', seems to me to be capable of encompassing a broad range of personal involvement and control, extending beyond that involved in the phrase 'manages an establishment', so that they cannot be said to be interchangeable terms. The *Oxford English Dictionary* defines the expression 'carry on' as including 'to conduct, manage, work at, prosecute' and its scope is plainly broader than the term 'manages'. Given that it encompasses a range of involvement or control, the correct interpretation of this expression, in my view, is one which has regard to the context, and the purpose for which it has been used. The primary purpose of the Act is the proper regulation of independent hospitals, in order to ensure the safety and welfare of all those who seek medical advice and treatment there, many of whom will be vulnerable individuals. It seems to me that the restrictive definition of 'carrying on an establishment', contended for by the Appellant in this case, runs contrary to the fundamental purpose of the legislation in requiring compulsory registration. I do not consider that it was Parliament's intention to permit an unregistered surgeon, working entirely on his own, to perform an invasive, surgical procedure on a patient on an ad hoc basis, in a one room hospital owned and managed by another or other persons unknown, and yet escape the reach of section 11(1) of the Act. In my judgment the only sensible conclusion on the facts of this case is that, on 27 March 2010, the Appellant was carrying on the hospital, as that word is defined by the Act."

Waghorn v Care Quality Commission [2012] EWHC 1816 (Admin).

CASH BENEFIT. Stat. Def., Pension Schemes Act 2015 s.75.

CASH LOAN.

"There is no definition of what is meant in this context by 'a cash loan', although section 189 of the Consumer Credit Act 1974 provides that cash includes money in any form, while section 9 of the Act provides that: 'In this Act "credit" includes a cash loan, and any other form of financial accommodation.'

26. Evidently, therefore, the provision of credit includes the making of a cash loan, but is not limited to this. The statute recognises a distinction between a cash loan and other forms of financial accommodation, although the word 'other' suggests that a cash loan is itself one form of financial accommodation. This is in accordance with the ordinary meaning of these terms. One form of financial accommodation is the giving of further time for payment of an existing debt. As a matter of everyday language, that would not normally be regarded as the provision of a cash loan, although there may be some circumstances in which it could be so described. . . .

29. It seems to me to be clear that paragraph 4(1) draws a distinction between credit which takes the form of a cash loan and credit which does not. I would accept that 'cash', and therefore 'cash loan', are terms which are capable of being given and in some contexts should be given a wide meaning, but the question is what they are intended to mean in the context of these transitional provisions. Clearly, it was not intended that any variation of an existing unregulated credit agreement, or even any variation of an existing unregulated agreement which provided further credit to the borrower, should be brought within the statutory regime for regulation of consumer credit agreements. The touchstone chosen for bringing an existing unregulated agreement within the scope of regulation under the Act was that it should constitute the provision of a cash loan. That must have been intended to operate as a limiting factor.

30. In my judgment the mere restructuring of an existing agreement by allowing the debtor further time to pay without making any new funds available does not constitute the provision of a 'cash loan' for the purpose of paragraph 4(1). It constitutes the giving of a form of financial accommodation, but not the making of a cash loan. I reach that conclusion for two reasons.

31. First, it accords with the natural meaning of the words and gives effect to the distinction between the provision of credit which takes the form of a cash loan and the provision of credit which does not. The borrowers' submissions could give no real content to that distinction. In the end their case was that although the giving of further time to pay might be a form of financial accommodation which did not amount to the provision of a cash loan, if the arrears outstanding were added to the capital amount outstanding, that would necessarily constitute the making of a cash loan. I do not accept this. Unless unpaid arrears are written off altogether, allowing further time to pay inevitably means that such arrears must be added to the amount which the borrower will eventually have to pay. However, although the timing of the borrower's repayment obligations is altered, the overall effect of such an agreement is neutral. The increase in the capital outstanding is matched by the elimination of an immediate liability to pay the outstanding arrears.

32. Second, in this context the consequences of interpreting 'cash loan' as the borrowers propose would be startling, as their case in this action demonstrates. They contend in effect that a routine deferral of an instalment due under an unregulated credit agreement, even if perfectly valid and enforceable when it was concluded, could cause the whole agreement to become unenforceable, for example if it had not been concluded in the form which would have been necessary if the agreement had been regulated from the outset. That would represent a trap to any lender under an existing unregulated agreement who agreed to assist a borrower experiencing cash flow difficulties and can hardly have been intended. I consider that it was not the purpose of the legislation to apply the provisions applicable to regulation under the Consumer Credit Act 1974 to existing unreg-

ulated agreements unless new money was being advanced, in which case it would be reasonable to expect the lender to comply with the statutory provisions applicable to agreements concluded after the removal of the £25,000 financial limit."

Santander UK Plc v Harrison [2013] EWHC 199 (QB).

CAUSE.

"23. As for the first point, the word 'cause' is a word of wide ambit. It is defined in rule 1(3) of the Rules of the Court of Session 1994 as meaning 'any proceedings'. And it does not make sense of section 40(1) of the 1998 Act to regard the cause in question as the arbitration proceedings out of which the application for the stated case arose. The cause in question must be taken to be the cause or matter that was before the Inner House. Section 40 is concerned only with the proceedings in the Inner House in which the interlocutor was pronounced. There is no indication anywhere in the section that it is concerned in any way with proceedings in any lower court or tribunal. The proceedings in the Inner House must be regarded for this purpose, both in form and in substance, as a separate process from the proceedings before the arbiter. The dismissal of the stated case was final, in just the same way as if the interlocutor had encompassed the court's opinion on the questions that were before it: see *Davidson v Scottish Ministers (No 3)* 2005 SC (HL) 1, paras 12-14. In either case the court had, or would have had, no further functions to perform under the procedure that brought the matter before it."

Apollo Engineering Ltd v James Scott Ltd (Scotland) [2013] UKSC 37.

CAUSE OF ACTION.

"4. To understand merger, it is necessary to understand the meaning of 'a cause of action'. It is not a legal construct. The term 'cause of action' is used to 'describe the various categories of factual situations which entitle[d] one person to obtain from the court a remedy against another' (per Diplock LJ in *Letang v Cooper* [1965] 1 QB 232 at 242). A complaint to the ombudsman need not be a cause of action but (as further discussed below) it may involve consideration of an underlying cause of action and the facts on which a complaint is based may be or include facts constituting a cause of action."

Clark v In Focus Asset Management & Tax Solutions Ltd [2014] EWCA Civ 118.

CEASE TO EXIST.

"Section 132(2) draws a distinction between person A ceasing to exist and another person succeeding to the business of A. The words 'ceased to exist' must be given their ordinary meaning. In relation to a natural person it means when that person has died. That interpretation also accords with a purposive of construction of the statute."

Kerman & Co LLP, R. (on the application of) v Legal Ombudsman [2014] EWHC 3726 (Admin).

CELL COMPANY. Stat. Def., Finance Act 2013 s.173.

CHARITABLE ACTIVITY. Stat. Def., Small Charitable Donations Act 2012 s.7.

CHARITABLE PURPOSE. Stat. Def., Small Charitable Donations Act 2012 s.18.

CHARITABLE PURPOSES. For discussion of the history and present meaning of this term see *Helena Partnerships Ltd v HM Revenue and Customs* [2012] EWCA Civ 569.

CHEATING.
"This is, as far as I know, the first case in which the question whether or not the conduct of a party to a gaming contract amounted to cheating has had to be determined in an English court. There is no commonly accepted view amongst those who play Punto Banco about whether edge sorting does or does not amount to cheating. . . . There are difficulties with the current English statutory definition. It appears to define deception and interference as cheating, but there is no attempt to define the overall concept of cheating as the explanatory notes make clear. It is not obvious whether *Ghosh* [1982] QB 1053 dishonesty is a necessary element of the offence, or if it is, how in the unusual circumstances of a casino it is to be measured. . . . The fact that the claimant is genuinely convinced that he is not a cheat and even that that opinion commands considerable support from others—see for example, Dr Jacobson—is not determinative of the question. It is necessary to analyse what the consequences are of what he did in relation to the game that he was playing. They were threefold. He gave himself an advantage, throughout the play of the sixth and subsequent shoes, which the game precludes—knowing, or having a good idea, whether the first card was or was not a 7, 8 or 9. That is quite different from the advantage which may accrue to a punter as a result of counting the cards, so that very near to the end of the shoe he may obtain a legitimate advantage by doing so. He did so by using the croupier as his innocent agent or tool by turning the 7s, 8s and 9s differentially. He was not simply taking advantage of an error on the part of the croupier or an anomaly produced by a practice of the casino for which he was not responsible. He was doing so in circumstances in which he knew that she and her superiors did not realise the consequence of what she had done at his instigation. Accordingly, he converted a game in which the knowledge of both sides as to the likelihood that player or banker will win—in principle nil—was equal into a game in which his knowledge is greater than that of the croupier and greater than that which she would reasonably have expected it to

be. This in my view is cheating for the purposes of civil law. It is immaterial that the casino could have protected itself against it by simple measures. The casino can protect itself by simple measures against cheating or legitimate advantage play. The fact that it can do so does not determine which it is. . . . What precisely is condemned as cheating by section 42 of the 2005 Act and what must be proved to make out the offence is not, in my view, clear and it would be unwise if it is unnecessary, as it is, for me to attempt to determine what that might be."
Ivey v Genting Casinos UK Limited [2014] EWHC 3394 (QB).

CHIEF OFFICER (POLICE). Stat. Def., Crime and Courts Act 2013 s.16.

CHILD IN NEED.
"The meaning of 'child in need' was considered by Lord Nicholls in *R(G) v Barnet LBC* [2004] AC at [30] in the following terms: . . . This was a minority speech in relation to the duty to meet needs. The majority held that the duty in section 17 was a 'target' duty which gives rise to a specific duty on the part of a local authority to assess a child's needs but no specific right to provision of the assessed services. Nevertheless it remains an authoritative statement that determining a child's statutory 'needs' is not an exercise in applying objective criteria to a simple binary test. 'Needs' are an elastic concept on which the value judgment of different persons may legitimately differ to a considerable extent."
SJ, R. (on the application of) v Surrey County Council [2014] EWHC 449 (Admin).

CIVIL AND COMMERCIAL MATTERS. See *British Airways Plc v Sindicato Espanol De Pilotos De Lineas Aereas* [2013] EWHC 1657 (Comm).

CIVIL LEGAL SERVICES. Stat. Def., Legal Aid, Sentencing and Punishment of Offenders Act 2012 s.8.

CIVIL PARTNERSHIP (SHAM CIVIL PARTNERSHIP). Stat. Def., Immigration and Asylum Act 1999 s.24 amended by Immigration Act 2014 s.55.

CIVIL PROCEEDINGS. Stat. Def., Legal Aid, Sentencing and Punishment of Offenders Act 2012 s.55.

CIVIL SERVANT. Stat. Def., "individual employed in the civil service of the State" (Legal Aid, Sentencing and Punishment of Offenders Act 2012; Public Service Pensions Act 2013 s.37).

CLAIM.
"12. The EAT held that those findings of fact were not susceptible to challenge on appeal and I agree. I should add that Ms Mallick criticised the

reference in the last line of para.472 to suspicion that the Claimant intended to bring a discrimination claim; suspicion that the person victimised intends to make an allegation is sufficient in law, even if there is no suspicion that a tribunal claim might be issued. So it is, but the word 'claim' is ambiguous, and the reference by the ET at the end of para.474, as well as in paras 494 and 497, to the absence of any suspicion on Prof Thompson's part that the Claimant might make a complaint of race discrimination demonstrates that this is not a point of substance."
Fraser v University of Leicester [2015] EWCA Civ 212.

CLAIMS.

"In my view there is no real prospect of persuading the court that the judge was wrong in his construction of the word 'claims'. There is nothing, as he said, to support the conclusion that the word was intended to refer only to fully formulated and sustainable legal claims, as opposed to claims which could reasonably be advanced, and there is much force in his observation that it would be surprising if it had been so limited."
Ackerman v Ackerman [2012] EWCA Civ 768.

CLEARLY.

"12. 'Clearly' and 'manifestly' unfounded mean the same and it was held in *Thangarasa and Yogathas* [2002] UKHL 36 that 'No matter what the volume of material submitted or the sophistication of the arguments deployed to support the allegation, the Home Secretary is entitled to certify if, after reviewing this material, he is reasonably and conscientiously satisfied that the allegations must clearly fail.'"
Kurtaj, R. (on the application of) v Secretary of State for the Home Department [2014] EWHC 4327 (Admin).

COAL. See CONCESSIONARY COAL.

COLLATERAL.

"I prefer the submission of Mr Harris which is that the kind of defence that could properly be described as a collateral defence is one where the burden of establishing the facts that would determine that issue would be on the defendant in the main action. To ascertain whether this is the position as regards any particular issue one must look at the totality of the pleaded case as the pleadings stand at the date of settlement."
W.H. Newson Holding Ltd v IMI Plc [2015] EWHC 1676 (Ch).

COLLECTIVE BENEFIT. Stat. Def., Pension Schemes Act 2015 s.8.

COMB HONEY. Stat. Def., "honey stored by bees in the cells of freshly built broodless combs or thin comb foundation sheets made solely of beeswax and sold in sealed whole combs or sections of such combs" (Honey (England) Regulations 2015 (SI 2015/1348) reg.2).

COMMERCIAL ACTIVITY.
"The first instance decision of Laws J in *Propend Finance Pty Ltd v Sing* (1997) 111 ILR 611 is the only domestic authority to have addressed the meaning of 'commercial activity' in article 31(1)(c). . . . I would hold that, as a matter of ordinary language, a contract for the provision of services which are incidental to family or domestic daily life is not 'commercial activity'."
Reyes v Al-Malki [2015] EWCA Civ 32.

COMMISSIONING.
"In my judgment the conclusion that I should reach is that commissioning in s.85 means that there must be an obligation on the part of the commissioned party to produce the work and an obligation on the part of the commissioning party to pay money or money's worth."
Trimingham v Associated Newspapers Ltd [2012] EWHC 1296 (QB).

COMMUNITY BUILDING. Stat. Def., Small Charitable Donations Act 2012 s.8.

COMMUNITY PLANNING. Stat. Def., Local Government Act (Northern Ireland) 2014 s.66.

COMPANY.
"'Company' is a word having potentially a wide signification. As the Appeal Tribunal correctly observed, companies existed long before the Companies Acts (the Joint Stock Companies Act 1844, applying only to England; and the Joint Stock Companies Act 1856 and subsequent legislation also applying to Scotland) were first enacted; corporate status being conferred by Act of Parliament, letters patent or Royal Charter: cf Partnership Act 1890 section 1(2)(b). Joint stock companies were reorganized, which were in effect large partnerships with transferable equity stock. These were usually statutory in origin, and Companies Clauses Acts, such as the Companies Clauses Consolidation (Scotland) Act 1845, were passed to facilitate their formation. . . . Therefore, there is nothing either in the statutory provisions or in the authorities to which we were referred which requires a narrower meaning of 'company' where it appears in section 1(6) of the 1970 Act than would be suggested by the ordinary use of language, having regard to the context. It respectfully appears to us that the ordinary meaning of the word was well expressed by Lord Hoffman in O'Neill. Construing section 1(6) by reference to that ordinary meaning of company is consistent with what we would see to be the purpose of the provision which is to determine who are the employees whose terms and conditions fall within what Mr Truscott referred to as the appropriate arc of comparison, these being the employees of employers one of whom is controlled by the other or both of whom are controlled by a third party. As Mr Mitchell on behalf of the first now respondents submitted, control is

the key concept; a company is a form of business organisation which in both a legal and a practical sense is capable of controlling and being controlled. It would be remarkable, to say the least, if by using the word 'company' Parliament intended to bring the employees of some business organisations having all or most of the characteristics of companies formed and registered under the 2006 Act and capable of controlling and being controlled, but not others. The restricted definition adopted by the tribunal would exclude, for example, an overseas company, such as a French sociètè anonyme which was carrying on business in the United Kingdom. Mr Truscott could not suggest any reason for Parliament wishing to do so.

[46] Once it is accepted that 'company' where it appears in section 1(6) of the 1970 Act is to be construed according to its ordinary meaning as set out by Lord Hoffmann in O'Neill, it would seem clear that an LLP must be included within that construction."

Glasgow City Council v Unison Claimants [2014] ScotCS CSIH 27.

COMPENSATION.

"16. I also agree with the judge that in any event the word 'compensation' in limb 1 of Clause 13 is apt to embrace recovery by Sellers of compensation for failure by the Buyers to pay the deposit, the measure of which, by analogy with the position at common law, will be at least the amount of the deposit itself."

Firodi Shipping Ltd v Griffon Shipping LLC [2013] EWCA Civ 1567.

COMPETITION LAW. Stat. Def., Civil Aviation Act 2012 s.6.

COMPRISING.

"It is well established that under English law the use of the word 'comprising' in the claim of a patent specification permits the addition of other elements. Thus, in Terrell on the Law of Patents 17th Ed. Para.9–127 it is stated: 'A requirement that a claim "comprises" certain elements does not mean that other elements may not be present: "comprising" does not mean "only consisting of".' A similar use is recognised in the Guidelines for Examination in the European Patent Office paragraph C-III/4.21 which states: 'While in everyday language the word "comprise" may have both the meaning "include", "contain" or "comprehend" and "consist of" in drafting patent claims legal certainty normally requires it to be interpreted by the broader meaning "include".'"

Medeva BV v Comptroller General of Patents [2012] EWCA Civ 523.

CONCERNED WITH.

"21. The judge said (para 30) that the words 'concerned with' in the phrase 'concerned with the administration of the scheme' cover 'those who, while having a lesser role than trustees, managers or the employer, have some

responsibility for running the whole or part of the scheme or some involvement beyond, here (sic), acts of administration'. It was a 'broad phrase'.
He accepted that the GAD did not run the whole of the scheme. But it was
'concerned with the scheme' because: 'GAD is under a duty imposed as
part of the structure of the scheme and indeed it is a duty necessary for the
proper operation of a part of the scheme commonly used. It is only GAD
which can perform that duty. [Counsel for the Ombudsman] placed decisive weight on the fact that it had a continuing duty to consider revising
the tables and, if necessary, then to revise them. It was GAD which had to
exercise that expert judgment as to whether it was necessary to revise the
tables at any particular juncture.' (para 31)

36. Whatever the precise meaning of a person 'concerned with the provision of benefits' may be, the existence of this category does not cause me to
doubt the correctness of the conclusion that I have reached as to the meaning of a person who is 'concerned with the administration of the scheme'. I
see no reason to give an expansive meaning to 'concerned with the provision of benefits' and a correspondingly narrow meaning to 'concerned
with the administration of the scheme'. Mr Swift has been unable to suggest any policy reason why Parliament would have intended to exclude
victims of maladministration by GAD from the Ombudsman's jurisdiction. In view of the central role played by GAD in the scheme and the fact
that it alone is responsible for the discharge of functions which are critical
for its proper and effective operation, it would be surprising (to say the
least) if Parliament had intended to limit the jurisdiction of the Ombudsman in this way. The fact that the gap in protection which was exposed by
the *Britannic* case was made good by the introduction of section 146(4A)
strongly suggests that Parliament did not consider that there was any policy justification for restricting the Ombudsman's jurisdiction."
*The Government Actuary's Department, R. (on the application of) v The Pen-
sions Ombudsman* [2013] EWCA Civ 901.

CONCESSIONARY COAL. Stat. Def., Small Business, Enterprise and
Employment Act 2015 s.158.

CONCLUDED CASES. See *Tesfay, R. (on the application of) v Secretary of
State for the Home Department* [2014] EWHC 2109 (Admin).

CONCURRENT.
"Thirdly, *Craies on Legislation 10th ed.*, (2012) supports the notion that
the concept of concurrent power to exercise functions has an established
meaning in legislation. At para.3.12.6, it is stated that '[w]here a function
is vested in two Ministers concurrently, either may perform it, acting
alone, on any occasion'. While no case law is cited in support of this proposition, such an unequivocal statement in a respected book on the subject
deserves respect, and is likely to be familiar to those responsible for drafting statutes."

Local Government Byelaws (Wales) Bill 2012—Reference by the Attorney General for England and Wales [2012] UKSC 53.

CONDITION.
"In many years of involvement with employment law I have rarely encountered the labels 'condition' and 'warranty'. Most obligations in an employment contract are, to use the classification set out in *Hong Kong Fir Shipping Co Ltd v Kawasaki Kisen-Kaisha Ltd* [1962] 2 QB 26, innominate terms. The duty not to be dishonest is an obvious exception. But it is not easy to think of others."
Crocs Europe BV v Anderson (tla Spectrum Agencies [2012] EWCA Civ 1400.

CONDUCIVE.
"Finally, I observe that the *Shorter Oxford English Dictionary* defines 'conducive' as 'tending to promote or encourage'. While mindful of the judicial observations on its meaning the starting point, it seems to me, and consistent with the Incorporated Council of Law Reporting op cit, is that this language of 'incidental or conducive to the attainment of the above objects' is not inconsistent with merely allowing the Society to engage in activities ancillary to its main and indisputably charitable objects. It may be that they would include the lobbying of the legislature in regard to the provision of housing to the aged of limited means. That would be ancillary. That would not, on a proper reading of these rules, at the time the Society came into existence, lead one to conclude that its objects were not exclusively charitable."
Charity Commission for Northern Ireland v Bangor Provident Trust Ltd [2014] NI Ch 19.

CONDUCT. Stat. Def., "includes a failure to act and unintentional conduct" (Civil Aviation Act 2012 s.72; Crime and Courts Act 2013 s.42).

CONNECTED (CHARITIES). Stat. Def., Small Charitable Donations Act 2012 s.5.

CONNECTED WITH.
"The phrase 'connected with', like 'in connection with', may be apt to denote things that are ancillary, i.e., connected with, something else. However, I agree with the judge that in the present connection, the natural meaning of 'expenses connected with his education' includes the major expense, namely the tuition fees."
Kebede, R. (on the application of) v Newcastle City Council [2013] EWCA Civ 960.

CONSERVATION AREA. See AREA.

CONSISTENT.
"The language of 'consistency' is very familiar in the context of injuries sustained in the course of a fight or struggle. Rarely can the nature of the injury determine precisely how it was caused."
Demetrio, R. (on the application of) v Independent Police Complaints Commission (IPCC) [2015] EWHC 593 (Admin).

CONSTABULARY.
"The Shorter Oxford English Dictionary defines 'constabulary' as 'an organised body of constables or police in an area'. I accept that some degree of organisation is required. A mere gathering of constables would not constitute a constabulary. On the other hand the degree of organisation required will depend upon the number of constables involved and the functions which they are performing. At one end of the scale the British Transport Police comprise a large number of constables with a wide range of responsibilities. The Redbridge Parks Police Service come at the other end of the scale. This comprised a small group of constables. Their function was to patrol the parks of Redbridge, making sure people behaved themselves and complied with the byelaws. The organisation of that body (two teams of five constables headed by two sergeants who reported to a chief officer) was quite sufficient. There was a proper chain of command and the officers all wore uniform when they were on duty. In my view the Redbridge Parks Police Service constituted a constabulary."
McKinnon v The London Borough of Redbridge [2014] EWCA Civ 178.

CONSULTANT LOBBYING. Stat. Def., Transparency of Lobbying, Non-Party Campaigning and Trade Union Administration Act 2014 s.2.

CONSUMER. Stat. Def., Consumer Insurance (Disclosure and Representations) Act 2012 s.1.

"52. Mr Hibbert sought to persuade me that, in English law, the word 'consumer' did not so much mean whatever it was defined in any particular statutory provision as meaning, but rather was almost a status people having which should be protected. That may be slightly over-stating Mr Hibbert's submission, but it is difficult to understand why he referred me to the decision in *Davies v Sumner* [1984] 1 WLR 1301, in which the issue was whether a false trade description was applied 'in the course of a trade or business', and the decision in *R&B Customs Brokers Co Ltd v United Dominions Trust Ltd* [1988] 1 WLR 321, in which the issue was whether the purchase of a motor car was on terms excluding the provisions of Sale of Goods Act 1979 s.14(3) or whether exclusion of that provision was negated by the Unfair Contract Terms Act 1977 s.12(1), unless I was being invited to accept some submission along those lines.
53. I have indicated my view of the proper construction of the definition of the expression 'consumer' in Regulation 2(1) of the 2008 Regulations

simply as a matter of interpretation of the English words used in the definition. However, actually it is not appropriate, in construing the relevant words, simply to look at the definition in Regulation 2(1). The 2008 Regulations were a re-implementation in English law of Council Directive 85/577/EEC. The English language text of that Directive also included a definition of the expression 'consumer', actually in exactly the same words as the definition in Regulation 2(1). Thus it is obvious that the intention of Parliament in enacting the 2008 Regulations was to apply the same definition of 'consumer' as had been used in the English language text of Council Directive 85/577/EEC.

. . .

59. In other words, in the circumstances of this case, in construing the definition of the expression 'consumer' in Regulation 2(1) of the 2008 Regulations, this court should interpret it consistently with the objective of Council Directive 85/577/EEC as construed and explained by the European Court of Justice, at least insofar as that is possible under English law. . . .

60. Happily, the interpretation of the definition of 'consumer' in Regulation 2(1) of the 2008 Regulations which commended itself to me without reference to the European jurisprudence is simply confirmed by that jurisprudence."
RTA (Business Consultants) Ltd v Bracewell [2015] EWHC 630 (QB).

Stat. Def., "an individual acting for purposes that are wholly or mainly outside that individual's trade, business, craft or profession" (Consumer Rights Act 2015 s.2).

CONSUMER INSURANCE CONTRACT. Stat. Def., Consumer Insurance (Disclosure and Representations) Act 2012 s.1.

CONSUMMATE.
"33. 'Consummated' is an ordinary word of the English language. As both sides accepted, it is not a legal word of art. It has no technical meaning. But it has a meaning. To consummate, means, as the Judge set out in a footnote, 'to bring to completion; to accomplish, fulfil, complete, finish'. Its most common use is in relation to marriage. A marriage is not consummated when the couple become engaged, even if their engagement is legally binding (and actions for breach of promise of marriage were once common). A marriage is not consummated when the couple's wedding ceremony takes place.

34. In order to determine when something is consummated, it is necessary to ask what it is that has to be consummated. In this case it is the Sale. The natural meaning of the words 'if any Sale is consummated' is 'if any Sale is completed', i.e. the relevant interest is transferred pursuant to an agreement for a Sale within the wide contractual definition. In my judgment, to say that a Sale is consummated when an agreement for a sale is

made, let alone when the major terms of a sale are agreed, is inconsistent
with the contractual language."
African Minerals Ltd v Renaissance Capital Ltd [2015] EWCA Civ 448.

CONTINUALLY.
"I do not consider that, in the circumstances of this case, anything turns
on the use of the word 'continually' as opposed to 'continuously' in Class
13. The two words often cause confusion. My resort to the *Concise Oxford
Dictionary* yields a definition of 'continual' as meaning 'always happening; very frequent and without cessation', whereas 'continuous' is defined
as 'connected, unbroken; uninterrupted in time or sequence'."
Winfield v Secretary of State for Communities and Local Government [2012]
EWCA Civ 1415.

CONTINUOUS.
"21.The usual meaning of 'continuous' (both in ordinary English usage
and in the context of conveyancing) is uninterrupted or unbroken. The
right or advantage claimed is a right to use the ways, not the ways themselves. Accordingly it is the use that must be continuous. In my judgment
in the context of clause 12.3.3 the reasonable reader would interpret the
word 'continuous' in its conventional sense. Given that there is a well-
defined category of easements which are 'continuous' I conclude, in agreement with the judge, that clause 12.3.3 should be interpreted as being
confined to easements of that category. The claimed rights of way are not
among them."
Wood v Waddington [2015] EWCA Civ 538.

CONTRACT. See TERMS.

CONTRACTED. See SUSTAINED OR CONTRACTED.

CONTROL SURVEY.
"By 'control survey', Mr Phillips means another survey run in parallel
where the interviewees are shown 'a different stimulus of known characteristics and performance'. The results of the control survey can then be
compared with the survey which used Enterprise's green logo to assess the
information so provided."
Enterprise Holdings Inc v Europcar Group UK Ltd [2014] EWHC 2498 (Ch).

COPE.
"Like 'stress' (see paragraphs 23–5 below), 'cope' has a variety of meanings in an employment context. At large, its meaning is 'to deal successfully' with something; but, in a work context, there are differing
parameters for 'success'. Where an employee has too much to do, the
usual consequence is that his performance of that work suffers: some of
the work does not get done, or there is a reduction in the quality of the

work that is done. In performance terms, such an employee is not 'coping' with his work. Most employees will on occasions be 'overworked', and will have problems in 'coping' with their work, in this sense. However, that does not mean that work necessarily poses a threat to that person's health. Indeed, even in those circumstances, it will rarely do so. Doing your work whilst maintaining your function and health is to use another legitimate marker of 'success' for the purposes of the definition of 'coping', but a marker that is quite different and distinct. When used in an employment context, 'cope' may have either meaning: but it is often used in reference to performance, rather than health."

MacLennan v Hartford Europe Ltd [2012] EWHC 346 (QB).

COPYRIGHT.

"At the time when the Electronic Commerce Directive was adopted, 'copyright' in the Annex to the directive must in my view have had its normal meaning, encompassing all aspects of the law of copyright under national laws, and cannot have had the elaborate meaning attributed to it by the appellants. At that time there was no harmonising directive at the Community level in the field of copyright protection. It would be unrealistic to impute to the Community legislature, at least in the absence of clear, express language to this effect, an intention to give 'copyright' a meaning related to provisions of a copyright directive that had not yet been adopted. But if 'copyright' did not have the appellants' meaning at the outset, I do not see how it can have come to acquire that meaning subsequently. The later adoption of the Copyright Directive cannot of itself have had the effect of changing the meaning of the expression. It would have needed an express amendment of the Electronic Commerce Directive to achieve that result, but no such amendment has ever been made."

British Telecommunications Plc, R. (on the application of) v BPI (British Recorded Music Industry) Ltd [2012] EWCA Civ 232.

COULD.

"Giving the word 'could' in Paragraph 16 of the national policy (set out at paragraph 13 above) its natural and obvious meaning in its context, it seems to me that the natural meaning is that a prisoner with SOTP as a current sentencing target but unready for SOTP solely as a result of denial, could be denied Enhanced status, but he might not be. The most natural reading of that sentence in my Judgment is that it would be permissible in appropriate circumstances to deny Enhanced status, but that it will depend on the circumstances. Thus there would need to be an informed decision as to whether a particular sex offending prisoner in denial and so unready for SOTP should be denied Enhanced status."

Shutt, R. (on the application of) v Secretary of State for Justice [2012] EWHC 851 (Admin).

COUPLE. Stat. Def., Welfare Reform Act 2012 s.39.

COURT. Stat. Def., "a tribunal with jurisdiction over criminal cases. It includes a judge, recorder, District Judge (Magistrates' Court), lay justice and, when exercising their judicial powers, the Registrar of Criminal Appeals, a justices' clerk or assistant clerk" (Criminal Procedure Rules 2013 r.2.2).

COURT OF PROTECTION.
"49. Looked at in this way, the question in the present case is whether Parliament in approving paragraph 44 intended the term 'Court of Protection' to refer only to the court which was then known as the 'Court of Protection' or to the court of that name existing on the date as at which it relevant to decide whether a capital sum falls within paragraph 44 ('the relevant date'). The term is capable of bearing either of these meanings. If required to decide between them, however, without reference to any later events, I prefer the second 'updating' interpretation. In reaching that conclusion, I think it significant that, at the time when paragraph 44 was introduced into Schedule 10 to the Income Support Regulations, Parliament had already enacted the 2005 Act. It was therefore in contemplation that, as soon as a commencement order was made and the relevant provisions of the 2005 Act were brought into force, the old Court of Protection would cease to exist and would be replaced by a new court which would exercise substantially similar (albeit not identical) functions and would also be called the 'Court of Protection'.

50. I see no reason to attribute to Parliament an intention that, when the 2005 Act came into force, there should be a change in policy regarding whether capital administered by the Court of Protection (or which can only be disposed of by order or direction of that court) is to be taken into account in the means testing of benefits. In saying that, I express no view about the desirability or otherwise of taking into account such capital sums. It is simply that I can see no difference between the regime for administering the property and affairs of people lacking in capacity under the 1983 Act and the regime under the 2005 Act which would betoken or justify a change in policy. If it was considered appropriate by Parliament to disregard capital administered by the Court of Protection under the 1983 Act—as it evidently was, I cannot identify any change made by the 2005 Act which made it any less appropriate to disregard capital administered by the (new) Court of Protection when the 2005 Act came into force. Nor has the Council sought to argue that the 2005 Act made any such material change.

51. In these circumstances, I do not think it reasonable to suppose that Parliament intended the reference in paragraph 44 to the 'Court of Protection' to be, in effect, self-limiting or self-repealing on whatever date sections 45 and 66 of the new Act were brought into effect, so that thereafter—unless the words were redefined or re-enacted—the term 'Court of Protection' would not refer to any existing body. It seems to me to make better sense to suppose that Parliament intended paragraph 44 to

remain applicable to capital funds administered by the new Court of Protection. I would therefore interpret the term 'Court of Protection' as meaning the body of that name which is in existence and has statutory responsibility for administering the property and affairs of persons lacking capacity at the relevant date. . . .

66. In the absence of any compelling indication to the contrary, it must therefore be assumed that when the 2005 Act was brought into force Parliament left paragraph 44 unchanged advisedly. That could only be because Parliament was proceeding on the basis that the term 'Court of Protection' in paragraph 44 remained apposite when the office of the Supreme Court with that name ceased to exist and was replaced by the new Court of Protection. In these circumstances, any ambiguity in paragraph 44 should be resolved by construing it in a way which accords with Parliament's presumed understanding of its meaning and which treats it as having current effect rather than as an empty legacy of an earlier regime which has been left uselessly on the statute book.

Conclusion

67. I conclude that the term 'Court of Protection' in paragraph 44 of Schedule 10 to the Income Support Regulations is apt to refer to the current Court of Protection."

ZYN, R. (on the application of) v Walsall Metropolitan Borough Council [2014] EWHC 1918 (Admin).

CREDIT.

"I take as a starting point that 'the ordinary and natural meaning of credit in the context of section 16 of the Act is "time to pay"' (Teare J). However the correct analysis is, in my judgment, that for which Mr Freedman QC leading counsel for the Claimant contends. Provision of a cheque in respect of a concurrent liability to pay a price suspends that liability until the cheque has been dishonoured, in which case the suspension ceases to have effect and the debt becomes immediately payable. But if the cheque is then redeemed before banking business hours, the initial giving of the cheque did not thereby become the provision of credit."

The Ritz Hotel Casino Ltd v Al Daher [2014] EWHC 2847 (QB).

CREDITOR.

"I agree with Mr Allen's interpretation of the meaning of creditor in the context of Article 3 of the Maintenance Regulation. The term 'creditor' is of course generally to be found where a debt is already in existence. However, I think a proper reading of the Article, particularly against the background of the case of *Farrell v Long* drives me to the conclusion that a maintenance creditor is someone who is an applicant in the sense of a potential creditor. I consider that the Regulation makes little sense unless that is the proper interpretation. Accordingly I find that the court does have jurisdiction to hear this claim."

M v W [2014] EWHC 925 (Fam).

CREDITORS. For discussion of the meaning of "creditors" in a range of commercial contexts see *Welcome Financial Services Ltd, Re Companies Act 2006* [2015] EWHC 815 (Ch).

CRIME. See ORGANISED CRIME GROUP.

CRIME OF VIOLENCE.
    "12. Various attempts have been made to define what is meant by the phrase 'a crime of violence' for the purposes of the schemes for compensation for criminal injury. . . . It would, I think, be more accurate to say that it is for the tribunal which decides the case to consider whether the words 'a crime of violence' do or do not apply to the facts which have been proved. Built into that phrase, there are two questions that the tribunal must consider. The first is whether, having regard to the facts which have been proved, a criminal offence has been committed. The second is whether, having regard to the nature of the criminal act, the offence that was committed was a crime of violence. I agree with Lord Carnwath for all the reasons he gives that it is primarily for the tribunals, not the appellate courts, to develop a consistent approach to these issues, bearing in mind that they are peculiarly well fitted to determine them. A pragmatic approach should be taken to the dividing line between law and fact, so that the expertise of tribunals at the first tier and that of the Upper Tribunal can be used to best effect. An appeal court should not venture too readily into this area by classifying issues as issues of law which are really best left for determination by the specialist appellate tribunals. 17. The question whether a criminal offence has been committed is a question for the tribunal, having informed itself as to what the law requires for proof of that offence, to determine as a matter of fact. The question whether the nature of the criminal act amounted to a crime of violence may or may not raise an issue of fact for the tribunal to determine. This will depend on what the law requires for proof of the offence. For example, some of the common law crimes known to the law of Scotland are quite loosely defined. The range of acts that fall within the broad definition may vary quite widely, so the question whether there was a crime of violence will have to be determined by looking at the nature of what was done. But in this case the words of the statute admit of only one answer. They speak for themselves."
Jones v First Tier Tribunal (Rev 1) [2013] UKSC 19.

    "17. It follows from *Ex parte Webb* that when deciding whether a crime is a 'crime of violence' it is necessary to have regard to the nature of the offence rather than its consequences. However, since some conduct may constitute an offence whether or not it is accompanied by violence, it is necessary to have regard to the facts of the offence itself in order to decide whether it amounts to a crime of violence: see *R (August) v Criminal Injuries Compensation Appeals Panel, R (Brown) v Criminal Injuries Compensation Appeals Panel* [2001] 1 Q.B. 774. That is so in the case of the offence created by section 3(1) of the Dangerous Dogs Act 1991."

Criminal Injuries Compensation Authority v First-Tier Tribunal (Social Entitlement Chamber) [2014] EWCA Civ 65.

CRIMINAL CAUSE OR MATTER.

"5. The phrase 'criminal cause or matter' appears in statutory provisions other than section 6 of the Act. Primarily, it occurs in statutory provisions concerned with appeals. Mr Chawla QC, quite properly, took me through a number of decisions in which the phrase has been considered in that context and/or when the court has found it necessary to consider whether proceedings are criminal or civil in nature. In particular he referred me to *R v Lambeth Magistrates Court ex parte McComb* [1983] 1 QB 551, *Bonalumi v Secretary of State for the Home Department* [1985] 1 QB 675, *Cuoghi v Governor of HMP Brixton No 1* [1997] 1 WLR 1346 and *B v Chief Constable of Avon and Somerset* [2001] 1 WLR 340.

6. It does not seem to me to be necessary or fruitful to seek to analyse those decisions, or indeed, to seek to reconcile them all if that is possible. I say that since in *R. (Guardian News and Media Limited) v City of Westminster Magistrates' Court and Another* [2013] QB 618 the Court of Appeal concluded that the phrase 'criminal cause or matter' need not have one meaning regardless of its statutory context but, rather, might be interpreted differently depending upon its statutory context—see, in particular, paragraphs 101 to 106 in the judgment of Hooper LJ and paragraph 110 in the judgment of Lord Neuberger of Abottsbury MR (as he then was). I must determine whether these proceedings fall to be described as a criminal cause or matter in the context of and set against the policy behind the 2013 Act.

7. In his written and oral submissions Mr Chawla QC argued persuasively that a purposive interpretation of section 6 of the Act compelled the conclusion that this judicial review should not be excluded from its ambit. I agree. It would be most unfortunate if cases of this kind were excluded from the ambit of section 6 of the Act just because they have a connection with criminal proceedings in another jurisdiction. I agree with Mr Chawla's point that in order to decide whether proceedings are civil or criminal in the context of the Act it is necessary to identify the core function to be performed by the court in the proceedings in question. In this case the court will be called upon to determine whether the Defendant lawfully exercised her discretion when she refused the requests made of her on the grounds of national security. The function of this court is a step removed from any proceedings which can properly be categorised as a criminal cause or matter."

Fawwaz v Secretary of State for the Home Department [2015] EWHC 468 (Admin).

CRIMINAL PROCEEDINGS.

"18. The Lord Advocate submits that, properly construed, extradition proceedings are not 'criminal proceedings' for the purposes of section 288AA(4) of the 1995 Act: see para 15 above, in which the definition of 'compatibility issue' for the purpose of that subsection is set out. This is because they do not involve the determination of any criminal charge. The Lord Advocate performs the functions that he is required to carry out in proceedings of this kind under section 191 of the 2003 Act, which states that he must conduct any extradition proceedings in Scotland. He accepts that he is constrained in what he can do by the fact that he is a member of the Scottish Government under section 57(2) of the 1998 Act, which provides that he has no power to act in a way that is incompatible with any of the Convention rights. But his position is that he does not perform these functions in his capacity as the public prosecutor.

19. In *Pomiechowski v District Court of Legnica, Poland* [2012] UKSC 20, [2012] 1 WLR 1604, para 31 Lord Mance said that an examination of the case law of the Strasbourg court shows that both the commission and the court have stood firm against any suggestion that extradition as such involves the determination of a criminal charge or entitles the person affected to the procedural guarantees provided in the determination of such a charge under article 6(1) or 6(3) of the Convention. In *BH v Lord Advocate*, para 33 it was noted that in *Goatley v HM Advocate* [2006] HCJAC 55, 2008 JC 1 and *La Torre v HM Advocate* [2006] HCJAC 56, 2008 JC 23 the Lord Advocate had conceded that devolution minutes were competent in proceedings under the 2003 Act. It seemed to me that this concession was properly made and that the High Court was right to give the concession its approval. The basis on which it was made was that the Lord Advocate and the Scottish Ministers were performing their functions under the 2003 Act as members of the Scottish Executive within the meaning of section 57(2) of the Scotland Act 1998, and that the Lord Advocate was not acting as head of the system of prosecution in Scotland: see *Goatley*, paras 13–14; *La Torre*, paras 46–47. A challenge to their proposed exercise of those functions by means of a devolution minute was to be seen as a parallel remedy to that afforded by section 87(1) of the 2003 Act.

20. The conclusion that these proceedings are not criminal proceedings for the purposes of section 288AA(4) of the 1995 Act which follows from the analysis in *BH v Lord Advocate* is reinforced by the fact that extradition is a reserved matter under section B11 of Schedule 5 to the Scotland Act 1998. Scots criminal law is devolved, unless it relates to a reserved matter: section 29(4) of that Act. The Lord Advocate and the Scottish Ministers are given a specific role under various provisions of the 2003 Act in relation to extradition proceedings in Scotland, as is the High Court of

Justiciary. These roles are not made part of, but are provided for separately from, those that they are required to perform under the 1995 Act."
Kapri v The Lord Advocate (representing The Government of the Republic of Albania) (Scotland) [2013] UKSC 48.

Stat. Def., Legal Aid, Sentencing and Punishment of Offenders Act 2012 s.14.

DAMAGE.

"The question as to whether indirect or secondary damage is sufficient to give jurisdiction to the English and Welsh courts is by no means tabula rasa so far as the present type of case is concerned. Indeed four High Court decisions have all answered in the affirmative. . . . The High Court cases have determined that the ordinary natural meaning of 'damage' includes physical and economic damage. (*Booth* paragraph 35, *Cooley* paragraph 32–34, 53) *Wink* (paragraphs 32–35). The Defendants submit that, given the legislative and European case law background, it is a perfectly proper and unforced interpretation of 'damage' to restrict it to direct damage only. The Defendants submit that ascertaining the legislative intention requires that the meaning to which previous judges have been attracted, as a matter of first impression, must yield to the appropriate context. . . . Absent the European context on which the Defendants rely, it seems to me clear that the previous decisions are correct. As Haddon-Cave J said in *Wink* at paragraph 33 'there are no limiting words in sub paragraph (a) which would justify such a narrow meaning and exclude indirect damage. The word "damage" is not modified or trammelled in any way. The ordinary and natural meaning of the word "damage" . . . is any damage flowing from the Tort. In the words of Teare J at paragraph [37] in *Booth*, "damage" in this context means any "physical or economic" harm, ie. direct or indirect.' For the reasons I give below, the context upon which the Defendants rely does not alter that view. Whilst it may be said that the decision in *Metall und Rohstoff* was not concerned with the question of whether indirect or secondary damage could found jurisdiction, I agree with Haddon-Cave J's statement in *Wink* [38] that 'the direction of travel of the Rules of Court was clearly to maintain a broad, rather than a narrow, construction of "damage" by discarding the definite article to make it clear, *selon Metall v Rohstoff* that not all of the damage must have been sustained within the jurisdiction.' 17. The Defendants point to the fact that English courts have always been cautious in asserting jurisdiction over foreigners. See *Metall und Rohstoff* (page 435, 437). If there is any doubt about the construction of the rule it must be resolved in favour of the foreigner. Tugendhat J in *Cooley* dealt with this at [47]–[49]. He concluded that the interpretation to be placed on the CPR rule is clear. I do not disagree with him."

Pike v The Indian Hotels Company Ltd [2013] EWHC 4096 (QB).

"43. The word 'damage', which appears four times in section 10, is in my view a reference to the actual damage which has been wrongfully caused to or inflicted upon C. C's right to recover costs from D is not part of C's 'damage'. It is an ancillary entitlement, subject to the discretion of the court.

44. The phrase the 'amount to be paid' which appears in the latter half of section 10(4) of the 1980 Act must be construed consistently with the opening words of that subsection. In my view it means the amount to be paid in respect of the actual damage caused to C. It does not refer to or include the amount of costs which D must pay to C, even though those costs can be the subject of a contribution claim."

Hampshire Constabulary v Southampton City Council [2014] EWCA Civ 1541.

DATA. See Traffic Data (Communications).

DAY (WORKING DAY). Stat. Def., "a day which is not a Saturday, Sunday or public holiday" (Licensing of Pavement Cafés (Northern Ireland) Act 2014 s.30).

DEBT.
"21. The word 'debt' can be used in a number of different senses. In terms of classification, a distinction is drawn between a claim in debt and a claim in damages. The distinction may be clear in terms of analysis, but it sometimes produces what seem to be odd distinctions in practice. For example whether a claim under a guarantee is in debt or in damages may depend on a close reading of the terms of the guarantee: see *McGuinness v Norwich and Peterborough Building Society* [2011] EWCA Civ 1286.

22. That distinction had to be addressed in that case because a bankruptcy petition must be based on a liability which is a debt for a liquidated sum: see Insolvency Act 1986 section 267(2)(a). In the case last mentioned it was held that the debtor's liability under the guarantee did create a debt, not merely a liability in damages."

Phillips & Co (a firm) v Bath Housing Co-Operative Ltd [2012] EWCA Civ 1591.

DEEP GEOTHERMAL ENERGY. Stat. Def., Infrastructure Act 2015 s.48.

DEFAULT. See In Default.

DEFINED BENEFITS SCHEME. Stat. Def., Public Service Pensions Act 2013 s.37.

DEFINED CONTRIBUTIONS SCHEME. Stat. Def., Public Service Pensions Act 2013 s.37.

DENTISTRY. Teeth whitening treatment is the practice of dentistry for the purposes of the Dentists Act 1984 s.37: *General Dental Council v Jamous* [2013] EWHC 1428 (Admin).

DEPENDANT.
"20. The focus of the debate before me was on the definition of 'dependant'. The diligent researches of Counsel, to which I have referred, demonstrate that there is no single definition of 'dependant' applicable in all circumstances: the definition of the term is largely context-specific. Mr Goatley rightly emphasised the difficulties and dangers of resorting to common sense usage or dictionaries when defining terms in a statutory context (see *Customs and Excise Commissioners v Top Ten Promotions Limited* [1969] 1 WLR 1163 at 1171 per Lord Upjohn); and, although a financial element is a common theme in such definitions, it is by no means the case that being dependant necessarily requires the presence of such an element in all usages of the word. Furthermore, where it is not specifically defined, 'dependant' in a statutory or other legal context displays the same ambivalence. For example, 'wholly or mainly dependant' generally in an immigration context has been held to mean primarily financial dependence, but where there is doubt as to that, other forms of dependency, such as emotional, may be taken into account and may tip the balance (*R v Immigration Appeal Tribunal ex parte Bastiampillai* [1983] 2 All ER 844). In a family law context, perhaps as to be expected, dependency has sometimes been given a wider scope: and so, in Australia, it has been held that provision from the estate of a deceased person to someone who is wholly or partly dependent on the deceased under section 6(1) of the Family Provisions Act 1982 (NSW) covers the situation where a deceased mother had provided typical maternal services to a child essential for their well-being, but not in money or money's worth (*Petrohilos v Hunter* (1991) 25 NSWLR 343). That is no doubt why, when the term is used in a statutory context, it is often expressly defined. For example, section 186 of the Housing Act 1996 defines 'dependant' in the context of an asylum-seeker as a person who is a spouse or child under the age of 18 years, and who does not have the right of abode or indefinite leave to remain in the United Kingdom. Section 1 of the Fatal Accidents Act 1976 has a wider and very specific definition, but to include a spouse or child.
    21. Therefore, as with so much else, so far as the definition of 'dependant' is concerned, context is everything. . . .
    30. Therefore, even in the statutory context (or a context in which the precise statutory wording had been adopted), there is no clear authority to the effect that 'dependant' necessarily implies financial dependency. . . . It is unnecessary for me to seek to construe 'dependants' in the statutory context to which I have referred, and I decline to do so."
Shortt v Secretary of State for Communities and Local Government [2014] EWHC 2480 (Admin).

DEPOSIT.

"5. This claim for Judicial Review is concerned with the question of whether, on the true interpretation of s. 33(1)(a) of the Act, the unintended escape of sewage amounted to a 'deposit' of the sewage in question on land by Thames. . . . Pulling the threads together, the answer to the question whether the unintended escape of sewage amounted to a 'deposit' within s.33(1)(a) of the Act, is not to be found in dictionary definitions. However, when construed in the context both of sub-section (1)(a) and s.33 as a whole, the preponderance of the argument favours and clearly so, the word 'deposit' including unintended escapes. The contrary argument, that this construction results in an unsatisfactory overlap with s.34 of the Act, falls to the ground because s.34 is inapplicable in such circumstances. Conscious though I am that s.33 gives rise to a penal provision, I am satisfied that the usual and strong presumption of a mens rea is here displaced. Having thus far approached the matter in stages, it must now be right to stand back and look at the question in the round. Doing so, I am left in no real doubt overall that the intention of the legislature was to impose strict liability under the first limb of s.33(1)(a), so that 'deposit' does include an unintended escape of sewerage from the sewerage undertaker's network."
Thames Water Utilities Ltd v Bromley Magistrates' Court [2013] EWHC 472 (Admin).

DETAINED.

"Although informal patients are not 'detained' and are therefore, in principle free to leave hospital at any time, their 'consent' to remaining in hospital may only be as a result of a fear that they will be detained. In *Principles of Mental Health Law and Policy* (2010 OUP) ed. Gostin and others, the authors have written in relation to admission at para.11.03: 'Since the pioneering paper by Gilboy and Schmidt in 1979, it has been recognised that a significant proportion of [informal] admissions are not "voluntary" in any meaningful sense: something in the range of half of the people admitted voluntarily feel coerced into the admission; it is just that the coercion is situational, rather than using legal mechanisms.'"
Rabone v Pennine Care NHS Foundation [2012] UKSC 2.

DEVELOPMENT.

"17. Section 55 of TCPA defines 'development' as being ' . . . the carrying out of building, engineering, mining or other operations in, on, over or under land, or the making of any material change in the use of any buildings or other land'. Thus in principle a change of use is as much development as the various forms of operational development identified in s.55.

18. The meaning of the word 'development' when used in the NPPF has the same meaning as that identified in s.55. This is the meaning adopted generally in a planning law context. No other meaning is suggested. This construction appears to be consistent with the view expressed by Ouseley J in *Europa Oil and Gas Limited v. SSCLG* (ante) at [53]. It follows that a

material change of use is capable of being inappropriate development within the meaning of Paragraph 87 of the NPPF."
Fordent Holdings Ltd v Secretary of State for Communities and Local Government [2013] EWHC 2844 (Admin).

DEVOLVED. Stat. Def., Public Service Pensions Act 2013 s.37.

DIAGNOSIS. Stat. Def., "'diagnosis' means a registered medical practitioner's identification (in writing, where it pertains to an employee) of—
   (a) new symptoms; or
   (b) symptoms which have significantly worsened" (Reporting of Injuries, Diseases and Dangerous Occurrences Regulations 2013 reg.2).

DIGITAL CONTENT. Stat. Def., "data which are produced and supplied in digital form" (Consumer Rights Act 2015 s.2).

DILATORY.
"The word 'dilatory' does not appear again in the following discussion, and it is not mentioned in the index. It has long since dropped out of the vocabulary of the Court of Session practitioner. It was preserved in section 40(1) as part of the process of consolidation of the previous Court of Session Acts. But it now looks rather odd, and thought might perhaps be given to rewording this part of the subsection at the next opportunity."
Apollo Engineering Ltd v James Scott Ltd (Scotland) [2013] UKSC 37.

DIRECT SUPPLIER. Stat. Def., Groceries Code Adjudicator Act 2013 s.22.

DISEASE. Stat. Def., "a clinical or non-clinical infection with one or more aetiological agents in fish" (Aquaculture and Fisheries (Scotland) Act 2013 s.63).

"45. If viewed in isolation, the term 'disease' is far from easy to interpret and apply, as demonstrated by the fact that Mr Hogan did not attempt to explain its meaning or to explain why NIHL is not a disease (other than by asserting that it is any injury). In isolation, the term does not provide the certainty as to the success fee due in injury and disease claims funded by a CFA that was plainly the legislative purpose of sections IV and V.

46. However, as set out above, the term 'disease' has been used in legislation relating to employers' liability claims and insurance since 1906, legislation which Mr Hogan accepts represents the origins of the terminology used in the relevant section of Part 45. That legislation has consistently used the term 'disease' to cover conditions (including 'injuries') which

have arisen by process rather than by accident. That exact distinction was adopted, only shortly before section IV and V were introduced, in the definition of 'disease' utilised in the Pre-Action Protocol for Disease and Illness claims. Pre-Action Protocols are published pursuant to a Practice Direction and their use is governed by provisions of the CPR and can have costs consequences: CPR 44.2(5)(a). . . .

50. In my judgment consideration of the legislative history in this case strongly indicates that Parliament intended the term 'disease' in sections IV and V of CPR 45 to include any illness (whether physical or physiological), disorder, ailment, affliction, complaint, malady or derangement other than a physical or physiological injury solely caused by an accident or other similar single event. The provisions of section IV are therefore restricted to injuries caused by accidents (or other single events), preserving the long-established distinction."

Dalton v British Telecommunications Plc [2015] EWHC 616 (QB).

DISPOSAL.

"2. The crucial word is 'disposal' in DL [40]. Its legal importance stems from the waste hierarchy set out in Article 4 of the EC's Waste Framework Directive, 2008/98/EC ('the Directive') as part of its aim of achieving more sustainable waste management. The waste hierarchy classifies activities and gives priority to waste prevention and management. 'Prevention' is at the top of the hierarchy, then 'preparing for re-use', 'recycling" and 'other recovery'. 'Disposal' is at the bottom of the hierarchy. The Directive was implemented by the Waste (England and Wales) Regulations 2011, SI No. 988/2011 ('the 2011 Regulations') and the relevant planning policies. The material part of the applicable statutory development plan is Policy 38 of the East Midlands Regional Plan 2009 ('RP Policy 38'). That (in line with the Directive) provides for the promotion of proposals resulting in the treatment of waste higher up the 'waste hierarchy' in DEFRA's Waste Strategy for England 2007 ('WS 2007').

3. There is no issue between the parties concerning the relevant legal principles or the policy framework. It is also not disputed that the proposed facility's operations would not initially qualify as 'recovery' within the Directive. At issue is the Inspector's treatment of the concepts of the 'disposal' and 'recovery' of waste. He stated that 'the proposed waste treatment facility on the appeal site lies higher in the hierarchy than disposal'. The question is whether this showed he erroneously categorised the proposed facility under consideration as a 'recovery' operation rather than as a 'disposal' operation, and whether, even if he did not so err, the reasoning in his decision letter is legally inadequate. . . .

28. To interpret the word 'disposal' as meaning that the Inspector characterised the activity as 'recovery' is untenable in the light of the express and correct direction only three paragraph earlier in DL [37]. The interpretation for which Mr Simons contends would require the conclusion

that, immediately after making his correct finding, the Inspector put it aside and made a different finding. Moreover, had the Inspector put aside the correct finding in DL [37] and concluded that the activities were 'recovery', his discussion in DL [37]–[39] of how the plant would operate in the future was entirely unnecessary. This was because, as Mr Moffett stated (skeleton argument, paragraph 44(3)) the facility would have been in accordance with PPS 10 and RP 38 in any event."

Skrytek v Secretary of State for Communities and Local Government [2013] EWCA Civ 1231.

DISPOSITION.

"The context of Sections 27 and 29 is the perceived need to protect private parties who buy a vehicle in good faith from the usual consequences of the 'nemo dat' rule (i.e. that the buyer cannot obtain a better title to a chattel than the seller). 'Sale' and 'contract for sale' are not defined and are not stated to have the same meaning as in the Sale of Goods Act. It is not therefore simply a question of applying Section 2 of that Act. Nevertheless the concept of sale of a chattel has at common law and in statute long been associated with a money transaction—see for example the extract from Westminster quoted above. In a context where there seems no need to stretch the definition to cover less conventional transactions, and thereby broaden the exception to the nemo dat rule, and given the careful wording of the section—particularly 'disposition (as so defined)'—I conclude that 'disposition' is limited to the specific types of transaction described in the section where the vehicle is transferred in return for money."

VFS Financial Services Ltd v JF Plant Tyres Ltd [2013] EWHC 346 (QB).

DISPUTE.

"While I am not sure that the word 'crystallised' adds anything (either there is or there is not a dispute), Mr Broome has failed to persuade me that the adjudicator's decision on this issue was wrong. It is true that discussions on various matters were ongoing, and that there were outstanding action points at the time of the referral to adjudication. But in my opinion none of that indicates the absence of a dispute or that no dispute had crystallised. Judges have been exhorted to give the term 'dispute', as it appears in section 108 of the 1996 Act, its normal meaning, and not to indulge 'opportunistic technicalities'—see for example the comments of May LJ in *Amec Civil Engineering Limited v Secretary of State for Transport* [2005] 1 WLR 2339. The facts in the present case point to the parties being in dispute at the date of the referral to adjudication in relation to the difference between the pursuers' valuation and the interim certificates. It is artificial and wrong to assert that a dispute arose only in the course of the adjudication. Long before then the parties were at issue as to the correct valuation of the work concerned."

J&A Construction (Scotland) Ltd v Windex Ltd [2013] ScotCS CSOH 170.

DISSUASIVE.

"Whether something is 'dissuasive' is on the face of it a question of fact and judgment."

Hemming (t/a Simply Pleasure Ltd), R. (on the application of) v Westminster City Council [2015] UKSC 25.

DOCUMENT.

Stat. Def., "anything in which information is recorded" (Civil Aviation Act 2012 s.72).

DOCUMENT (PRODUCTION OF).

Stat. Def. " . . . in relation to information recorded otherwise than in legible form, references to [a document's] production include references to producing a copy of the information in legible form or in a form from which it can readily be produced in visible and legible form." (Financial Services (Banking Reform) Act 2013 s.110).

DOMESTIC ABUSE.

Stat. Def. (implicit), Serious Crime Act 2015 s.76.

DOMICILE.

"'Domicile' for the purposes of the Judgments Regulation [EC No 44/2001] may not be what that word ordinarily means in English law, but neither is it necessarily the same as habitual residence. This was made clear, for instance, in the Jenard report (chapter IV.A.3). A party may, it seems, have more than one domicile for the purposes of the Regulation (Briggs and Rees at para.2.135). However, this case had not been argued under articles 9 and 13 and it appears that the Sherdleys had not advanced a case that, whatever their current habitual residence, they still retain a domicile in the United Kingdom."

Sherdley v Nordea Life and Pension SA (Societe Anonyme) [2012] EWCA Civ 88.

DOMINANT INFLUENCE.

"It was submitted that the concept of 'dominant influence' in the procurement regime is not the same as 'decisive influence' in the merger regime. However, insofar as there might be a difference between the two concepts, the term 'decisive influence' suggests to me a higher standard than 'dominant influence.' and the former expression is significantly employed as a definition of 'control', a term which by contrast does not feature in the procurement test at all. But since for the reasons I have set out I find that LCR as a result its veto rights meets the mergers test of decisive influence, it is unnecessary to decide what, if anything, might be the practical difference between the two terms. I conclude that LCR is in a position to exercise dominant influence over EIL. On that basis, EIL is a public undertaking, and therefore a 'relevant person' for the purpose of reg 3(1)."

Alstom Transport v Eurostar International Ltd [2012] EWHC 28 (Ch).

DOMINUS LITUS.
"A dominus litis is a person in control of, and with an interest in the out-come of a litigation."
Friends of Loch Etive v Argyll and Bute Council [2014] ScotCS CSOH 116.

DONATION. See SMALL DONATION.

DOWNSTREAM.
"26. Nothing turns on the CJEU's use of the words 'upstream' and 'down-stream'. *Bonik* may have been among the first cases in which the CJEU used these actual terms but, in *Kittel* at [43], [44], [45] and [49], the CJEU referred to transactions occurring prior and subsequent to the purchase giving rise to the input tax on which the trader relied, which comes to the same thing. Those words simply go to timing."
Fonecomp Ltd v HM Revenue and Customs [2015] EWCA Civ 39.

DRAG-ALONG RIGHTS. Stat. Def., "'drag-along rights', in relation to shares in a company, means the right of the holders of a majority of the shares, where they are selling their shares, to require the holders of the minority to sell theirs;" (Employment Rights Act 1996 s.205A as inserted by the Growth and Infrastructure Act 2013 s.35).

DRUG-CUTTING AGENT. Stat. Def., Serious Crime Act 2015 s.65.

DUE.
"The word 'due' is found in section 36(2) of ALDA, but, although ALDA and CEMA are to be construed together, the same word can have a slightly different meaning in different contexts in the same statute. Having said that, the way in which a word is used in one Act may be legitimately invoked to assist in deciding the meaning to be ascribed to the word when used in the other Act. Accordingly, it seems to me that there is a real case for saying that 'due' in section 137(4) of CEMA should have the same meaning as it has in section 36(2) of ALDA, and I think that that latter meaning is 'liable to be paid'. The expressions used in paras (a) and (b) of section 36(2) are in rather an odd order. Be that as it may, 'become due' was presumably intended to have a different meaning from 'charged', 'paid, or 'determined', and its natural meaning, in those circumstances, appears to me to be 'become liable to be paid'."
Carlsberg UK Ltd v HM Revenue and Customs [2012] EWCA Civ 82.

DUE REGARD. For discussion of the principles to be applied in giving "due regard" to guidance or other matters see *Redcar and Cleveland Borough Council* [2013] EWHC 4 (Admin).

DUTY OF FAIR PRESENTATION. Stat. Def., Insurance Act 2015 s.3.

DWELLING.

"The word 'dwelling' is not a technical word with a precise scientific meaning. Nor does it have a fixed meaning. Words such as 'live at', 'reside' and 'dwell' are ordinary words of the English language, as is 'home'. It is clear, as the respondent local authorities submitted, that the word 'dwelling' in the phrase, 'let as a dwelling' has been used in PEA 1977 in the same sense as that word was used in the phrase 'let as a separate dwelling' in the Rent Acts. Section 3 of PEA 1977 had its origin in section 32 of the Rent Act 1965 and section 5 in section 16 of the Rent Act 1957. There is no reason to think that Parliament intended the word 'dwelling' to have a different meaning in sections on protection from eviction from its meaning in provisions relating to rent restriction and security of tenure. In *Skinner v Geary* [1931] 2 KB 546, Scrutton LJ (at 564) said that the Rent Acts did not protect a tenant who was not in occupation of a house in the sense that the house was his home. More recently, in *Uratemp Ventures Ltd v Collins* [2002] 1 AC 301 the speeches in the House of Lords showed that the word 'dwelling' had different shades of meaning. Lord Bingham of Cornhill (at para.10) said that a 'dwelling-house' was 'the place where someone dwells, lives or resides'. Lord Steyn (at para.15) suggested that the court should not put restrictive glosses on the word which conveyed the idea of a place where someone lived. Lord Millett said (at para.30):

'The words "dwell" and "dwelling" are not terms of art with a specialised legal meaning. They are ordinary English words, even if they are perhaps no longer in common use. They mean the same as "inhabit" and "habitation" or more precisely "abide" and "abode", and refer to the place where one lives and makes one's home. They suggest a greater degree of settled occupation than "reside" and "residence", connoting the place where the occupier habitually sleeps and usually eats . . . '

In my view there is no strict hierarchy in terms of settled occupation between the words 'live at', 'reside' and 'dwell' and much may depend on the context in which the words are used. But there are nuances and as a general rule I agree with Lord Millett that 'dwelling' suggests a greater degree of settled occupation than 'residence'."

R. (on the application of N) v Lewisham LBC [2014] UKSC 62.

EARNINGS. For discussion of the term in the dual contexts of social security and income tax, and contrast with "emoluments", see *HM Revenue and Customs v Forde and McHugh Ltd* [2012] EWCA Civ 692.

Stat. Def., Public Service Pensions Act 2013 s.37.

Erratum: ignore the cross-reference to AVERAGE WEEKLY EARNINGS.

EASEMENT.
"An easement is a right benefiting land. As such it closely resembles the Roman law concept of 'servitude'. An easement is an incident to the land and not a personal right in the owner. Thus a grant of the sole and exclusive right of putting pleasure boats on a canal to a lessee of land on the canal's bank was held to confer a licence only in *Hill v Tupper* (1863) H& C121. Moreover in *Ackroyd v Smith* (1850) 10 CB 164 it was held that a grant of a right of way 'for all purposes' to the tenant of an estate and his successors in title permitted the right to be used for all purposes not necessarily connected with that estate and so it failed to create an easement."
McNulty v Ross [2015] NIQB 42.

ECONOMIC ACTIVITY.
"52. In the first place, the concept of 'economic activity' in VAT law is a very wide one. It has been translated into UK legislation as being 'engaged in a business'. It is the very opposite of being a final consumer. A person carrying on an economic activity is a taxable person, who has a right to recover input VAT incurred on taxable supplies in the course of that activity and, in so far as he is obliged, to charge output VAT."
BAA Ltd v HM Revenue and Customs [2013] EWCA Civ 112.

ELECTION MATERIAL. Stat. Def., Political Parties, Elections and Referendums Act 2000 s.143A inserted by Transparency of Lobbying, Non-Party Campaigning and Trade Union Administration Act 2014 s.23.

ELIGIBLE BISHOP. Stat. Def., Lords Spiritual (Women) Act 2015 s.1(4).

EMBRYO. See HUMAN EMBRYO.

EMOLUMENTS. See EARNINGS.

EMPLOYEE.
"It follows from the definition that all employees are workers, but not all workers are employees. The central feature of both concepts, however, is

that the worker should be employed pursuant to a contract. If there is no contract personally to perform work or services, then neither concept applies."
Ajar-Tec Ltd v Stack [2012] EWCA Civ 543.

"45. The words 'employee' and 'partner' are legal terms with a fairly clear meaning describing legal concepts. The strictness of the meaning of 'employee' and of the reference to 'working . . . fulltime' is only emphasised by the proviso which refers to the case of a person undergoing agricultural training. I do not see it as appropriate to read the word 'employee' in a broad way or to read the word 'partner' so as to extend to a sole trader in a different business to that apparently described by the sub-clause."
Creasey v Sole [2013] EWHC 1410 (Ch).

EMPLOYER. Stat. Def. (in relation to a pension scheme), Public Service Pensions Act (Northern Ireland) 2014 s.34.

EMPLOYER (IN PENSION CONTEXT). Stat. Def., Public Service Pensions Act 2013 s.37.

EMPLOYER'S LIABILITY INSURANCE. Stat. Def., Mesothelioma Act 2014 s.18.

EMPLOYMENT.
"4. In my judgment, for the reasons given below, the appellant was not an employee of WDF. The existence of the relationship of employment does not turn on whether the parties entered into a formal contract which would be recognised in domestic law as constituting employment but on whether it meets the criteria laid down by EU law. These criteria are capable of being applied even in the complex situation described in the preceding paragraph. The criteria include a requirement that the putative employee should agree personally to perform services, and a requirement that the putative employee should be subordinate to the employer, that is, generally be bound to act on the employer's instructions. In determining whether the relationship is one of employment, the court must look at the substance of the situation. In this case, the Employment Tribunal ('the ET') made clear findings of fact that the two criteria I have just set out were not satisfied. Accordingly, in my judgment, this appeal must fail. . . .

36. There is no doubt that section 83(2) of the EA 2010 must be interpreted so as to be compatible with EU law, as the Supreme Court interpreted it in *Hashwani*. Likewise there is no doubt that there is an autonomous meaning in EU law of the term 'employee', and Member States' domestic legislation cannot diminish this meaning. . . . Mr Diamond has not established that there is any incompatibility between section 83(2) of the EA 2010 and EU law. In those circumstances, I do not need to deal with Mr Diamond's application for this court to refer this case to the CJEU for a preliminary ruling on the requirements of EU law."

Halawi v WDFG UK Ltd (t/a World Duty Free) [2014] EWCA Civ 1387.

ENACTMENT. Stat. Def., "includes—
  (a) an enactment contained in subordinate legislation within the
      meaning of the Interpretation Act 1978;
  (b) an enactment contained in, or in an instrument made under, an
      Act of the Scottish Parliament;
  (c) an enactment contained in, or in an instrument made under, a
      Measure or Act of the National Assembly for Wales;
  (d) an enactment contained in, or in an instrument made under,
      Northern Ireland legislation." (Financial Services Act 2012 s.117.)

Stat. Def., Crime and Courts Act 2013 s.16.

ENDEAVOURS. See ALL REASONABLE ENDEAVOURS.

ENGLISH PLANNING OBLIGATION. Stat. Def., Town and Country
Planning Act 1990 s.106BA as inserted by the Growth and Infrastructure
Act 2013 s.7.

ENTERS AN APPEARANCE.
"20. We were not referred to any authority which lays down an autonomous definition of 'enters an appearance' in the first sentence of Article
24. I do not understand the ECJ to be saying in *Elefanten Schuh* that the
making of submissions on the substance of the action defines the entry of
an appearance within the first sentence of Article 24. Rather, the court is
explaining that after such submissions have been made, it is too late to take
advantage of the exception in the second sentence. Likewise, *Cartier-Par-
fums*, to the extent that it is concerned with Article 24 at all, is concerned
with the scope of the exception in the second sentence. ... The language of
CPR 11(8) is clear, and it is unlikely in the extreme that the draftsman
intended the words in paragraphs (5) and (8) to have different meanings.
The correct course for a defendant who has failed in a jurisdiction challenge and who wishes to appeal is to ask for an extension of time for filing
the acknowledgment of service sufficient to enable his application for permission to appeal, or his appeal, to be determined. It is quite unrealistic to
suppose that a sensible claimant, or if not the court, would refuse such an
extension when the effect of such a refusal would be to render the appeal
nugatory. It is unnecessary therefore to read qualifying words into paragraph 11(8).
36. In my judgment, the words 'he shall be treated as having accepted
that the court has jurisdiction to try the claim' in paragraphs (5) and (8) of
CPR Part 11 are to be given the same construction, namely that preferred
by this court in *Hoddinott*. The disinterested bystander test has no application to what I have called statutory submission to the jurisdiction. Thus,
where the conditions of those paragraphs are met, the defendant is to be

treated as having submitted to the jurisdiction. The rigour of such a construction is mitigated by the fact that it remains possible to withdraw an acknowledgment of service with the permission of the court: see CPR Part 10 PD 5.4. The effect of the withdrawal, if permitted, would no doubt be that there is no longer a submission to the jurisdiction. No such application was made at first instance in the present case, although, as I shall explain, one is informally launched in Mr Choo-Choy's skeleton before us.

37. I do not see that there is any impediment in Article 24 of the Convention to construing the rules in this way. Jurisdiction is conferred under that Article where the defendant enters an appearance. One of the ways in which this occurs under English procedural law is when the defendant returns a second acknowledgment of service after an unsuccessful challenge to the jurisdiction. The defendant is not compelled to return the acknowledgment of service in order to protect his position on the merits: he may apply for a stay or an extension of time if he wishes to continue his challenge. The operation of these rules is fully consistent with, and does not impair the operation of, the Convention."
Deutsche Bank AG London Branch v Petromena ASA [2015] EWCA Civ 226.

ENTRY DOCUMENT. Stat. Def., Specialist Printing Equipment and Materials (Offences) Act 2015 s.2.

ENVIRONMENTAL ACTIVITIES. Stat. Def., "activities that are capable of causing, or liable to cause, environmental harm," Regulatory Reform (Scotland) Act 2014 s.17.

ENVIRONMENTAL EMERGENCY. Stat. Def., Antarctic Act 2013 s.13.

ENVIRONMENTAL HARM. Stat. Def., Regulatory Reform (Scotland) Act 2014 s.17.

EQUIPMENT.
"Equipment is a word which should bear its meaning again depending on the context. There are a number of authorities which have dealt with what would be regarded as equipment and as I said, that is a matter or may be a matter for context. If it was necessary to decide whether a lawyer's equipment included books and law reports, I suspect the answer would be yes, of course it does. It should be regarded as equipment because it is something that he needs as equipment for carrying out his business. The question here is whether refreshment kiosks can properly be regarded as equipment of the show. . . . As I say, for the reasons I have indicated, it seems to me that in the circumstances and on the findings of fact in relation to Mr Kayes's use of the vehicle and more particularly the vehicle itself, this in the circumstances can properly be regarded as a vehicle permanently fitted with a special type of body forming part of the equipment of the show, the special type of body being the kiosks in question."

Vehicle & Operator Services Agency, R. (on the application of) v Kayes [2012] EWHC 1498 (Admin).

Stat. Def., "includes any device, machinery or apparatus and any wire or cable, together with any software used with it" (Specialist Printing Equipment and Materials (Offences) Act 2015 s.2).
    See WORK EQUIPMENT.

EQUITABLE.
    "The question for the court under section 33 is whether it 'would be equitable to allow the action to proceed', notwithstanding the expiry of the primary limitation period. That question is to be answered by having regard to all the circumstances of the case, including in particular the factors identified in section 33(3).
    59. Whether it is 'equitable' to allow an action to proceed is no different a question, in my judgment, from asking whether it is fair in all the circumstances for the trial to take place–the same question as the judge asked in the first part of the criticised paragraph 29 of the judgment. That question can only be answered by reference (as the section says expressly) to 'all the circumstances', including the particular factors picked out in the Act. No factor, as it seems to me, can be given a priori importance; all are potentially important. However, the importance of each of those statutory factors and the importance of other factors (specific to the case) outside the ones spelled out in section 33(3) will vary in intensity from case to case."
Ellam v Ellam [2015] EWCA Civ 287.

EQUITY SHARE CAPITAL. Stat. Def., Co-operative and Community Benefit Societies Act 2014 s.102.

ESCROW. See IN ESCROW.

ESTIMATES.
    "The word 'estimates' in the phrase 'estimates it will incur in the year in performing its functions' describes what the Council is doing at the budget-setting stage. It is estimating, but not determining, what will happen. As Mr Giffin says, the estimate is merely a means to the end of setting the budget and, therefore the council tax."
Buck, R. (on the application of) v Doncaster Metropolitan Borough Council [2013] EWCA Civ 1190.

ETC.
    "In my judgment the only reasonable reading of the word 'etc.' in the postcard is that it referred to everything else in the boxes. The message cannot properly be read as meaning: 'books, pictures, sculptures and anything else of a domestic nature but not the manuscripts of my compositions'.

Undoubtedly the message referred to the contents of the boxes, and showed that a gift was intended, not a mere temporary deposit for safe-keeping, and that the gift was to both children. It was of more than just the three categories of item mentioned specifically. It was of these 'and the rest'. It seems to me that 'the rest', here, can only mean everything else in the boxes."

Day v Harris [2013] EWCA Civ 191.

EXAMINATION.

"I turn, first, to consider whether the word 'examination' which appears on many occasions in the contract should be taken to mean 'full mouth examination'. What would the word 'examination' convey to a reasonable person having all the background knowledge which would reasonably have been available to the parties in the situation in which they were at the time of the conclusion of the contract. In my judgment the probability is that the reasonable person would conclude that the word did mean a 'full mouth examination'. I accept the submission of Mr Williams QC that the purpose of an examination, at least in the vast majority of cases, must be to facilitate an assessment of a patient's oral health overall. That can be done, effectively and efficiently, by the carrying out of a 'full mouth exam-ination' when a patient first visits the dentist. The carrying out of such an examination is not unduly time consuming and I can think of no sensible reason why an examination in the context of this contract should not extend to seeking to ascertain the true state of the patient's oral health overall at the first reasonable opportunity. As Mr Williams QC pointed out during the course of argument it would constitute an unsatisfactory state of affairs if the word examination was so interpreted so as to lead to the likelihood of 'successive examinations' limited to particular areas of the mouth in respect of individual patients. In my judgment it would be wrong to restrict the meaning of the word examination so that it meant no more than an examination of the particular point in the mouth about which a patient may complain."

Dusza v Powys Teaching Local Health Board [2014] EWHC 339 (Admin).

EXCEPT. The note on *Sowerby v Great Northern Railway* is misleading and should be disregarded.

EXCEPTIONAL.

"43. The word 'exceptional' is often used to denote a departure from a general rule. The general rule in the present context is that, in the case of a foreign prisoner to whom paras 399 and 399A do not apply, very compel-ling reasons will be required to outweigh the public interest in deporta-tion. These compelling reasons are the 'exceptional circumstances'."

MF (Nigeria) v Secretary of State for the Home Department [2013] EWCA Civ 1192.

EXCUSE.
"16. 'Reasonable excuse' is an ordinary expression requiring an evaluative judgment to be made by the jury. What may constitute a 'reasonable excuse' is qualified by the provisions of section 2(7), but it is for the jury to apply those qualifications, where relevant, to the facts as they find them. So, in the present case, it would have been for the jury to decide whether it was unreasonable to expect the appellant not to follow the agent's instructions to hand over his passport to the agent in Khartoum."
Asmeron v R. [2013] EWCA Crim 435.

EXPEDIENT.
"The discretion is given to make such directions as appear to him to be expedient. 'Expediency' is a term which fits Mr Tindall's characterisation of subjective and not hard edged. A quick examination of dictionary definitions gives the following meanings: 'convenient and practical', 'suitable or appropriate'. The *Oxford English Dictionary* states: 'conducive to advantage in general or to a general purpose, suitable to the circumstances of the case.' There is also a more deprecative sense of 'useful or politic as opposed to just or right' and also 'something that helps forward or that conduces to an object'."
McCormack, R. (on the application of) v St Edmund Campion Catholic School [2012] EWHC 3928 (Admin).

EXPENSIVE. See PROHIBITIVELY EXPENSIVE.

EXPLOITATION. Stat. Def., Modern Slavery Act 2015 s.3.

EXTRACTION. For the meaning of extraction in the Database Directive see *Football Dataco Ltd v Sportradar GmbH* [2012] EWHC 1185 (Ch).

FACILITATES.

"49. The Appellant relies on the OED definition of 'facilitates': 'to render easier the performance of an action, the attainment of a result; to afford facilities for, promote, help forward an action or process.' He submits that an act which facilitates causes that activity to be made easier and that an act which does not does not facilitate. . . .

52. Parliament did not find it necessary to provide a statutory definition and nothing before us persuaded us that the Judge should."
Ali, R. v [2015] EWCA Crim 43.

FACT. See FINDING OF FACT.

FAIR PRESENTATION. See DUTY OF FAIR PRESENTATION.

FAIRNESS.

"16. 'Fairness' is a concept which arises in many public law contexts and also in connection with the conduct of proceedings. There can sometimes be a fine line between fairness and unfairness depending upon the eye of the beholder. The essence of 'conspicuous unfairness' is that it does indeed leap from the page or, to put it another way, is plain as a pike staff."
Navaratnam v Secretary of State for the Home Department [2013] EWHC 2383 (QB).

FAMILY. Stat. Def. (in relation to a child), "includes any person who has parental responsibility for the child and any other person with whom the child has been living" (Social Services and Well-being (Wales) Act 2014 s.197).

FASTENINGS.

"With regard to clause 2.26, the word 'fastenings' is not obviously apt to refer to the Paintings. The word would, I should have thought, refer more naturally to an attachment than to the thing attached. On that basis, the chains used to secure Paintings might be 'fastenings' but the Paintings themselves would not be. Alternatively, it might be said that the meaning of 'fastenings' should be determined by reference to 'fittings' rather than the other way around. In any case, the 'furniture fixtures and fastenings' which are to be yielded up need not correspond precisely with the 'furniture fixtures and fittings' demised. It makes sense that the Earl should be obliged to yield up chattels in Savernake Lodge belonging to the landlords regardless of whether they were encompassed by clause 1."

Cardigan v Moore [2012] EWHC 1024 (Ch).

FEES AND EXPENSES.
"38. Mr Brown took the court to different examples of the use of the terms 'expenses' and 'disbursements' but it seems to me that the phrase 'fees and expenses' must be construed in the context of the legislation in which it appears. On the face of it, once it is conceded (as seems to me is inevitable) that the solicitor does not have to be in funds before incurring costs (such as the obtaining of a medical report), that cost has been borne by the solicitor (at least for the time being) and becomes an expense of providing advocacy or litigation services. To put it another way (which may be more relevant to the precise question which has to be answered), the cost may have to be the subject of an account to the client as a disbursement but the credit afforded to the client in respect of that cost is part of the service provided by the solicitor to his client."
Flatman v Germany [2013] EWCA Civ 278.

FINAL SALARY. Stat. Def., Public Service Pensions Act 2013 s.37.

FINAL SALARY SCHEME. Stat. Def., Public Service Pensions Act 2013 s.37.

FINANCIAL ASSISTANCE. Stat. Def., Financial Services Act 2012 s.67.

FINANCIAL CRIME. Stat. Def., Financial Services and Markets Act 2000 s.1H as inserted by Financial Services Act 2012 s.6.

FINANCIALLY MOTIVATED.
"29. Mr Butler does not criticise the committee's interpretation of the words 'financially motivated' at the outset of that passage. He accepts that failure to offer a refund for inadequate treatment may have been unprofessional, as was admitted, but submits that 'to allege that the registrant was financially motivated by the omissions is simply going too far'. He says, further, that there was no evidence that the replacement treatment was 'deliberate, repeated, large scale, highly organised and highly profitable'. All of that may be correct, but cannot be the test of whether the failures were financially motivated. At most it goes to the scale or gravity of the charge and the financial motivation.
   30. During the oral evidence counsel for the GDC went through the repeat treatments at Day 4–19 to Day 4–21, now bundle pages 276–278. It was quite clear and frankly admitted by Mr Booth that a number of treatments did have to be repeated, in one case three times. Mr Booth effectively admitted that he had double, or on one occasion treble, charged the patient, but could give no explanation why. In total he accepted at page 277 F–278 A that about £7,000 should have been refunded, but was not. In an answer at Day 4–22, now bundle page 279 D–E, he volunteered: 'It is

very difficult for me now because clearly . . . It is just indefensible, is it not? I mean, what can I say?'

31. In the light of that evidence it was, in my view, clearly open to the committee to conclude that Mr Booth had been financially motivated in the sense in which they had interpreted those words, namely putting his own financial interests before the best clinical and financial interest of his patient. He volunteered that his conduct had been indefensible and, frankly, could give no explanation for it. I am unable to conclude that the decision of the PCC on this point was wrong or not justified by the evidence."

Booth v General Dental Council [2015] EWHC 381 (Admin).

FINDING OF FACT.
"41. However, I do not accept Mr Davies's submissions regarding the conditions which have to be satisfied before a matter qualifies as a 'finding of fact' in regulations 11(2)(c) and (d). In my judgment, the meaning of that phrase is straightforward and accords with the ordinary meaning attached to those words. It covers any matter in a judgment in civil proceedings which, as a matter of ordinary language, is properly described as a finding of fact made by the court in the course of giving its judgment. The notion of a 'finding of fact', when used in reference to a judgment, is one which is very familiar, and there is no indication that the drafter of regulation 11 intended the phrase to bear any strained or unusual meaning when used in that provision. (I note in passing that the Divisional Court in *Constantinides v The Law Society* [2006] EWHC 725 (Admin), when considering a rule in the Law Society's disciplinary code which stated that 'the findings of fact upon which . . . a judgment is based shall be admissible as prima facie proof of those facts', appeared to have no difficulty in giving the term its ordinary meaning: see para.28 . . . 'There will be cases when a finding of fact, be it in a civil or criminal case, of dishonesty will be prima facie evidence of that dishonesty . . . .')"

Hollis, R. (on the application of) v Association of Chartered Certified Accountants [2014] EWHC 2572 (Admin).

FIRE AND RESCUE WORKERS. Stat. Def., Public Service Pensions Act 2013 s.37.

FISH FARMING. Stat. Def., "the keeping of live fish with a view to their sale or to their transfer to other waters; but only where such activity is required to be authorised as an aquaculture production business under regulation 6 of the Aquatic Animal Health (Scotland) Regulations 2009 (S.S.I. 2009/85)" (Aquaculture and Fisheries (Scotland) Act 2013 s.63).

FITTINGS.
"On balance, however, the preferable view is, I think, that the Paintings do not represent 'fittings'. The word 'fittings' is not a legal term of art (see

Woodfall, 'Landlord and Tenant', at paragraph 13.131). It is often used in combination with 'fixtures' (as in 'fixtures and fittings'). That was the case in *Berkley v Poulett* (see [1977] 1 EGLR 86 at 88), but no one appears to have considered the addition of 'fittings' important. Nor does reference to the *Oxford English Dictionary* suggest that the word 'fittings' extends the scope of clause 1 in a relevant way. The Dictionary defines 'fittings' as 'Fixtures, apparatus, furniture'. Clause 1 makes separate reference to 'fixtures' and 'furniture', and the Paintings would not normally be regarded as 'apparatus'. Further, the word 'fitted' would not naturally apply to the Paintings. A carpet or cupboard might be 'fitted'. The Paintings were surely hung rather than 'fitted'. The value of the Paintings is also, to my mind, of significance. Had the parties intended the Lease to extend to such valuable items, they might have been expected to refer to them specifically, not to rely on the somewhat vague word 'fittings'."
Cardigan v Moore [2012] EWHC 1024 (Ch).

FLAGRANCY.
"20. 'Flagrancy' has been defined by the ECtHR as 'a nullification or destruction of the very essence of the right guaranteed by [the relevant] article': *Mamutkulov and Askarov v Turkey* (2005) 41 EHRR 494, para OIII-14."
B, R. (on the application of) v Secretary of State for the Home Department [2014] EWCA Civ 854.

FLEECE.
"52. For this reason, in so far as the Advertisement includes the word 'fleece', I conclude that it is capable only of being understood as an expression of opinion, or a value judgment. . . .

55. There can be little doubt that the inclusion of the word 'fleece' would be disparaging of a person or company referred to by the Advertisement in the minds of prospective customers. But, as already noted, that would not suffice to make the Advertisement defamatory. A claimant has to satisfy the court that the disparagement would be in the minds of right thinking members of society generally."
Euromoney Institutional Investor Plc v Aviation News Ltd [2013] EWHC 1505 (QB).

FLEXIBLE BENEFIT. Stat. Def., Pension Schemes Act 2015 s.74.

FOR.
"In my judgment the meaning of clause G1(3) is clear and unambiguous in its context, notwithstanding the use of the word 'aggregate' (and indeed 'average'). Even without the more refined defining term in clause G1(1), on their plain and ordinary meaning, the words 'his pensionable pay for the year ending with the relevant date' do not mean his pensionable pay

received in the year in question; it means his pensionable pay referable to or relating to or in respect of his employment/work done in the year in question. To adopt the Appellants' interpretation would be to strain the language unnaturally in preference to the natural and obvious meaning of the words."

Stokes v Oxfordshire County Council [2014] EWHC 2177 (Ch).

FORBEARANCE.

"35. I agree with Morland J that it appears that the draftsman intended 'neglect', 'forbearance' and 'time . . . given' to mean different things; but as Sullivan LJ pointed out in the course of argument, each of these expressions takes colour from the other two as well as from the overall context. Neglect shades into forbearance which shades into giving time. Having regard to the context and purpose of the proviso, I consider that 'forbearance' connotes a decision by the landlord not immediately to enforce the observance or performance of a covenant against a tenant who is in breach of that covenant, but rather to tolerate the breach for the time being."

Topland Portfolio No 1 Ltd v Smiths News Trading Ltd [2014] EWCA Civ 18.

FORM.

"38. The starting-point is that it seems to me a natural use of English to describe the software format in which a copy (or digest) of the requested information is provided as an aspect of its 'form'. Mr Capewell sensibly eschewed the suggestion that there was a necessary verbal distinction between 'form' and 'format'; but the distinction which he advanced between the 'form' in which information is provided and the way in which it is 'arranged' does not seem to me to be any more clear-cut. Once it is accepted that an applicant can require provision of information in electronic form it seems to me only a small step to hold that he can also choose the format in which that electronic information is provided: the one naturally follows from the other. It is worth considering the case of information which will be embodied in text (i.e. rather than numbers): it would in such a case be rather unusual for an applicant to say 'can I have it in e-format?' rather than, say, 'can I have it as a Word document?'. It is true that a software format such as Excel is more than simply a means of presenting information: it enables the recipient of the information, if he or she himself has the appropriate software and licence, to do things with it. But I do not think that that feature means that the format cannot be described as an aspect of the 'form' of the information. After all, the same is true, even if the functions are more familiar (at least to lawyers), of word-processing software: if information is provided in the form of text embodied in, say, a Word document it can be edited and copied in a variety of ways which facilitate its use."

Innes v Information Commissioner [2014] EWCA Civ 1086.

FORTHWITH.
"The 'Oxford English Dictionary' defines forthwith as 'without delay'. In legislation such as this, words have to be given their natural ordinary meaning, so that is exactly what it means."
Licensing Bill 2002–03 Standing Committee D—Minister for Tourism, Film and Broadcasting (Dr Kim Howells): *http://www.publications.parliament.uk/ pa/cm200203/cmstand/d/st030410/pm/30410s12.htm*

FOSSIL FUEL. Stat. Def., Energy Act 2013 s.61.

FREEHOLD INTEREST.
"42. The phrase freehold interest is a legal term of art. It describes one of the two legal estates in real property. By defining ownership by reference to the person or persons holding the freehold estate in the relevant premises Parliament clearly intended that liability for council tax in respect of premises within Class C should fall upon the owner the legal estate in the premises i.e. the registered owner."
Soor v London Borough of Redbridge [2013] EWHC 1239 (Admin).

FRESHWATER FISH. Stat. Def., "any fish living in fresh water—
   (a) including trout and eels (and the fry of eels);
   (b) excluding salmon and any kind of fish which migrate between the
       open sea and tidal waters" (Long Leases (Scotland) Act 2012
       s.80).

FRIVOLITY.
"I think it very unfortunate that the expression 'frivolous' ever entered the lexicon of procedural jargon. To the man or woman in the street 'frivolous' is suggestive of light-heartedness or a propensity to humour and these are not qualities associated with most appellants or prospective appellants. What the expression means in this context is, in my view, that the court considers the application to be futile, misconceived, hopeless or academic. That is not a conclusion to which justices to whom an application to state a case is made will often or lightly come. It is not a conclusion to which they can properly come simply because they consider their decision to be right or immune from challenge. Still less is it a conclusion to which they can properly come out of a desire to obstruct a challenge to their decision or out of misplaced amour propre. But there are cases in which justices can properly form an opinion that an application is frivolous. Where they do, it will be very helpful to indicate, however briefly, why they form that opinion. A blunt and unexplained refusal, as in this case, may well leave an applicant entirely uncertain as to why the justices regard an application futile, misconceived, hopeless or academic. Such uncertainty is liable to lead to unnecessary litigation and expenditure on costs."
R. v North West Suffolk (Mildenhall) Magistrates Court Ex p. Forest Heath DC, April 30, 1997 [1998] Env. L.R. 9 Court of Appeal (Civil Division).

FUNCTION. Stat. Def., "Includes a power to do anything that is calculated to facilitate, or is conducive or incidental to, the exercise of a function." (Care Act 2014 s.79).

FUNCTIONS. Stat. Def., Crime and Courts Act 2013 s.16.

FUNCTUS OFFICIO.
"36. Functus officio means no more than that a judicial, ministerial or administrative actor has performed a function in circumstances where there is no power to revoke or modify it. It is a Latin tag still in universal use and usually abbreviated to the short statement that someone is 'functus'."
Demetrio, R. (on the application of) v Independent Police Complaints Commission (IPCC) [2015] EWHC 593 (Admin).

FURNISH.
"The court is not satisfied that the placing of material on a website, without something more, is sufficient to amount to the 'furnishing' of that material [in the Land Compensation (Scotland) Development Order 1975 Article 4] to another for the purposes of statutory interpretation. There may be circumstances in which such information may be furnished by, say, providing a hyperlink to a website, where it has been made available, or uploading the information to a particular website at the request of the intended recipient. Where a party does nothing, however, there is no act which might be construed as 'furnishing' the information to anyone. The first respondents cannot be expected to seek out the information required by article 4(3) on the basis that it may or may not be in the public domain. Aside from the uncertainty that would be created as a result, in relation to whether the appeals were being insisted upon, it would run entirely contrary to the logical and clearly expressed intention of Parliament that it is the appellants who are responsible for the furnishing of the documents under article 4(3) in order to proceed with their appeals."
Network Rail Infrastructure Ltd v The Scottish Ministers [2013] ScotCS CSIH 64.

G

GAAR ADVISORY PANEL. Stat. Def., Finance Act 2013 s.214, Sch.43.

GAMING MACHINE. See *HM Revenue and Customs v The Rank Group Plc* [2013] EWCA Civ 1289.

GENERAL ANTI-ABUSE RULE (Tax). Stat. Def., Finance Act 2013 s.206.

GEOTHERMAL ENERGY. See Deep Geothermal Energy.

GOOD CHARACTER.
"It may be that Mr Thursfield has been, in other respects, of what might be called good character, but so far as the litigation is concerned, including what little we know of the litigation in Michigan, and certainly in the UK proceedings, his failure to comply with orders has been persistent and protracted, and I find it impossible to regard him as being of 'good character' in that respect. Likewise what one might call 'attempts' to comply with the order were manifestly inadequate, as the judge observed, and his acknowledgement of such failure was belated and also in itself inadequate."
Thursfield v Thursfield [2013] EWCA Civ 840.

"11. The broad language of s. 63(3) of the Constitutional Reform Act 2005, which places on the JAC the obligation to be satisfied that a candidate for judicial office is of good character has been the subject of elaboration by the JAC doubtless not only to ensure consistent decision making but also to provide information to prospective candidates. The relevant guidance specifically in force at the time of this competition had been published on 1 November 2011 although it was revised by a version dated 10 July 2013 i.e. the date after the day upon which this competition was launched. . . .
22. It is beyond argument that the JAC may lawfully adopt principles in determining good character based, first, on the overriding need to maintain public confidence in the standards of the judiciary; and, secondly, on the fact that public confidence will only be maintained if judicial office holders and those who aspire to such office maintain the highest standards of behaviour in their professional, public and private lives. Mr Swift accepts that the JAC may adopt a policy with a view to ensuring a level of consistency in its approach to the good character decision under section 63(3).
23. He argues, however, that there is no logical connection between what is described as the six-plus points policy and the purpose of section 63(3),

namely the maintenance of public confidence in the standards of the judiciary. . . .

30. Any policy enunciated by the JAC is obviously subject to review on
public law grounds and this particular policy is hedged with a discretion
(reflected by the word 'normally'). It is sufficient to conclude that, in my
judgment, the JAC is entitled to take the view that public confidence in the
standards of the judiciary would not be maintained if persons who are
appointed to judicial office have committed motoring offences resulting in
penalty points at the level identified in the guideline within four years of
their appointment. Accordingly, I would reject the Claimant's challenge to
the material part of the JAC good character policy on the basis that it does
not rationally reflect the purpose pursued by section 63(3) of the 2005
Act. . . .

Mr Swift suggests that it defies logic for the JAC to conclude that the
maintenance of public confidence would not tolerate Mr Jones' appointment as a judge when he already sits as a judge in the same jurisdiction.

49. I would reject this submission. As I have sought to explain above, in
my view, there is a difference between permitting a person to continue to
sit as a part time judge (which falls to the Lord Chief Justice and Lord
Chancellor) and appointing that person to a full-time position (which is
the responsibility of the JAC).

50. Having concluded that the six-plus points policy is lawful and that it
was applied in a lawful manner, the Committee considered mitigation
relating to the particular offences and I do not consider that the decision
Mr Jones was not 'of good character' was irrational although, to be fair to
Mr Jones, it must be recognised that the context for this conclusion is the
legislation and that the phrase must be treated as a term of art."

Jones, R. (on the application of) v Judicial Appointments Commission [2014]
EWHC 1680 (Admin).

For discussion of "good character" see *Hiri v SSHD* [2014] EWHC 254
(Admin) and *SA, R. (on the application of) v Secretary of State for the Home
Department* [2015] EWHC 1611 (Admin).

GOOD FAITH.

"109. I turn next to the content of the duty to co-operate in good faith,
limited as it is by the two stated purposes. It is clear from the authorities
that the content of a duty of good faith is heavily conditioned by its context. In *Manifest Shipping Co Ltd v Uni-Polaris Insurance Co Ltd* [2001]
UKHL 1, [2003] 1 AC 469 insurers alleged that shipowners had failed to
observe 'utmost good faith' (as required by s. 17 of the Marine Insurance
Act 1906) in the presentation of a claim. The Commercial Court judge, the
Court of Appeal and the House of Lords all rejected that defence. Lord
Scott, with whom Lord Steyn and Lord Hoffmann agreed, held that in the
particular context the duty of utmost good faith required no more than

that the insured should act honestly and not in bad faith: see paragraph 111."
Compass Group UK and Ireland Ltd (t/a Medirest) v Mid Essex Hospital Services NHS Trust, March 15, 2013, Court of Appeal (Civil Division).

GOOD REASONS.
"We consider that 'good reasons' is wide enough to encompass a change of circumstances and nothing is to be gained in this case by resolving the dispute between the parties about whether 'change of circumstances' or 'good reasons' is to be considered."
SN v Secretary of State for the Home Department [2014] ScotCS CSIH 7.

GOODS.
"An 'establishment' is defined in article 2(h) as 'any place of operations where the debtor carries out a non-transitory economic activity with human means and goods.' 'Goods' is hardly a satisfactory English word to use in this context. It is apparent from the equivalent term in the other language versions that it means the same as 'assets' ('biens', 'Vermögen') in article 3(2)."
Olympic Airlines SA Pension and Life Assurance Scheme, Trustees of v Olympic Airlines SA [2015] UKSC 27.

Stat. Def., Consumer Rights Act 2015 s.2.

GOODWILL.
"44. Goodwill is not susceptible to precise definition. Like the judge, I have derived assistance from what Lord Macnaghten said (admittedly in a wholly different context) in *Commissioners of Inland Revenue v Muller and Co. Margarine Ltd* [1901] AC 217 at p.223:
'It is the benefit and advantage of the good name, reputation, and connection of a business. It is the attractive force which brings in custom. It is the one thing which distinguishes an old-established business from a new business at its first start. The goodwill of a business must emanate from a particular centre or source. However widely extended or diffused its influence may be, goodwill is worth nothing unless it has power of attraction sufficient to bring customers home to the source from which it emanates. Goodwill is composed of a variety of elements. It differs in its composition in different trades and in different businesses in the same trade . . . The goodwill of a business is one whole, and in a case like this it must be dealt with as such.'
45. The same idea was expressed by the ECtHR in *Van Marle* at para.41 (see para.28 above). A possession comprising the goodwill of a business is the product of past work: 'by dint of their own work, the applicants had built up a clientele'. Goodwill is the present value of what has been built up. It is to be distinguished from the value of a future income stream.

From an accountants' point of view, this distinction may make little practical sense. But it is the distinction that has been clearly drawn by the ECtHR for the purposes of A1P1."
Department for Energy and Climate Change v Breyer Group Plc [2015] EWCA Civ 408.

GOPHER.
"The evidence of Lyndsey Barrett (and others for the Claimant) was that Mr Makhari was a 'gopher' for the Defendant, namely not an officially appointed agent but someone who knew her well and could be relied upon to make practical arrangements for her, do things on her behalf, and indeed on occasion to alert the casino to the fact that she intended to visit. The Defendant resisted any such suggestion. Mr Makhari was someone whom she regarded as a fellow gambler, and a friendly acquaintance. Their visits to the Claimant casino, as with other casinos, were independent. It had been a shock to her to discover that the Claimant made payments to Mr Makhari by way of a percentage commission upon her own losses.

104. Mr Makhari himself, a man of evident charm, was unembarrassed to acknowledge that the Claimant 'looked after him' because of his acquaintance with the Defendant. As to his informal role, he engagingly and straightforwardly answered, 'If she asks anything of me, she asks; if she asks anything of me, I do it for her'. A schedule of the dates when respectively the Defendant, and Mr Makhari, visited the Claimant casino, with the times of entering and leaving, shows that on a great many occasions the two arrived within a minute or two of one another. The suggestion is not that Mr Makhari was an appointed agent for the Defendant but that he was a gopher for her. I am fully satisfied that he was."
The Ritz Hotel Casino Ltd v Al Daher [2014] EWHC 2847 (QB).

GOVERNMENT DEPARTMENT. Stat. Def., Justice and Security Act 2013 s.4.

GRADING. Stat. Def., "in relation to farmed fish, means separating and sorting the fish according to size" (Aquaculture and Fisheries (Scotland) Act 2013 s.4).

GRAPHIC.
"In the judgment about the form of order Arden LJ emphasised the use of word 'graphic' in the order, which she explained as follows:
'We take the word "graphic" to mean vividly descriptive. In judging what is vividly descriptive, we have borne in mind that the person to be protected is a vulnerable child. In these circumstances, we consider that what should be injuncted is that which we consider to be seriously liable to being understood by a child as vividly descriptive so as to be disturbing.'"
Rhodes v OPO [2015] UKSC 32.

GREEN INVESTMENT BANK. Stat. Def., Enterprise and Regulatory Reform Act 2013 s.2.

GREEN PURPOSES. Stat. Def., Enterprise and Regulatory Reform Act 2013 s.1.

GROCERIES CODE. Stat. Def., Groceries Code Adjudicator Act 2013 s.22.

HABITUAL RESIDENCE.

"As to the first point, James Turner QC, on behalf of the wife, was specifically invited to specify what he divined to be the necessary features of 'habitual residence' from the authorities. He did so in terms that there must be demonstrated in the subject matter's living arrangements in the location under consideration : (i) a permanence or stability, not temporary or intermittent; (ii) the centre of his/her interest; (iii) exclusivity of such circumstances; that is to possess but one habitual residence.

11. This accords entirely with the judge's identification of 'the common core of interpretation of the term habitual residence . . . broadly the centre of interests test' as 'distilled' from *Marinos* [2007] 2 FLR 1018 at paragraphs 21 to 25 which the judge considered 'persuasive and authoritative' and as applied previously and subsequently in respective relevant context by the authorities."

Tan v Choy [2014] EWCA Civ 251.

For discussion by Thorpe LJ on the meaning of the concept of habitual residence as used in relation to European Union obligations (and, in particular, the use of references to permanence) see paras 71 to 81 of his judgment in *DL v EL* [2013] EWCA Civ 865.

"The concept of 'habitual residence' has been extensively, and profoundly analysed and discussed in judgments of the Court, and by jurists, over many years. As it happens, only a matter of hours before this case came into my list on 9 September 2013, the Supreme Court delivered its judgment in the case of *Re A (Children)* [2013] UKSC 60. In delivering the Judgment of the majority of the Court, Baroness Hale helpfully discussed the English Court's current approach to the determination of habitual residence. She observed that the common law definition (used for the purposes of the 1986 Act and the Hague Convention on the Civil Aspects of International Child Abduction 1980) has been generally (though not entirely) thought to be different (in some respects) from the concept used by the Court of Justice for the European Union (CJEU). She, and the majority of her fellow justices, declared that it is highly desirable that there is a uniform test, and that if there is any doubt, for the purposes of applying the BIIR Regulation it should be that adopted by the Court of Justice for the European Union (§35)."

N v K [2013] EWHC 2774 (Fam).

"Dr Clive noted that the House of Lords had stressed that habitual residence is 'a simple concept' which should be applied 'by concentrating on the ordinary and natural meaning of the two words' and on the facts of the particular case. He contended that the two words 'are quite capable of doing all the work which is required of them without the addition of spurious legal propositions'. While this comment has attracted some criticism (see *Mozes*), it is in line with the general direction of much of the recent authoritative judicial consideration of the concept of habitual residence. In *A v A* [2013] UKSC 60, [2014] AC 1, the UK Supreme Court relied upon recent case law of the Court of Justice of the European Union. Baroness Hale of Richmond stressed that a person's habitual residence is a question of pure fact. Courts should be resistant to temptations to legalise the concept. She criticised as a 'legal construct' the 'rule' that one parent cannot change a child's habitual residence unilaterally (paragraphs 39–40), commenting that there is not a hint of this in the European jurisprudence. The Court of Justice decisions focused on whether the residence of a child in a member state reflected 'some degree of integration in a social and family environment in the country concerned'. An infant shares the social and family environment of the person or people upon whom he or she is dependent. Thus, if looked after by the mother, 'it is necessary to assess the mother's integration in her social and family environment'. Baroness Hale quoted the operative part of the judgment in *Mercredi v Chaffe* [2012] Fam 22:

'The concept of "habitual residence" . . . must be interpreted as meaning that such residence corresponds to the place which reflects some degree of integration by the child in a social and family environment. To that end, where the situation concerned is that of an infant who has been staying with her mother for only a few days in a member state—other than that of her habitual residence—to which she has been removed, the factors which must be taken into consideration include, first, the duration, regularity, conditions and reasons for the stay in the territory of that member state and for the mother's move to that state and second, with particular reference to the child's age, the mother's geographic and family origins and the family and social connections which the mother and child have with that member state' (paragraph 50).

Baroness Hale dismissed any notion, which might otherwise arise from the English translation of *Mercredi*, that for residence to be habitual there is a requirement of permanence. The French word used was 'stabilité'. Concluding that the Court of Justice's approach should be adopted and applied, her Ladyship referred to an essentially factual and individual inquiry which should focus on the social and family environment of the person upon whom the child is dependent."

AR, Re An Order Under The Child Abduction And Custody Act 1985 [2014] ScotCS CSIH 95.

"12. It is common ground that 'habitual residence', for the purposes of applying the Hague Convention and the Regulation, is to be determined in accordance with the guidance given by this court in the cases of *A v A*, *In re*

L and *In re LC (Children) (Reunite International Child Abduction Centre intervening)* [2014] UKSC 1; [2014] AC 1038. It is also common ground that that guidance is consistent with the guidance given by the Court of Justice of the European Union as to the application of the Regulation in Proceedings brought by *A* (Case C-523/07) [2010] Fam 42, *Mercredi v Chaffe* (Case C-497/10PPU) [2012] Fam 22, and *C v M* (Case C-376/14PPU) [2015] Fam 116."
AR v RN (Scotland) [2015] UKSC 35.

HEALTH CARE. Stat. Def., Health and Social Care Act 2012 s.255.

HEALTH SERVICE WORKERS. Stat. Def., Public Service Pensions Act 2013 s.37.

HEAR.
"14. The first rule of natural justice is that no judge should be a judge in his own cause or, as it is now more popularly known, the rule against bias is an elementary but highly important component of any developed system of justice. So is the second rule that each party must be heard, sometimes expressed in Latin as 'audi alteram partem'. It is sometimes also expressed in the form 'he who decides must hear'.

15. The word 'hear' cannot be taken completely literally since a tribunal will necessarily read a good deal of evidence as well as, literally, hear it. But if it is decided that a defendant or a witness will give oral evidence then that evidence will be 'heard' and it is important that each member of the tribunal should, if at all possible, 'hear' all that evidence. Reading a transcript is normally no substitute for hearing evidence from a live witness given orally. For a tribunal member or juror or judge to absent himself (without consent) while oral evidence is given and later take part in the ensuing decision will, therefore, usually be a breach of the second rule of natural justice. Authorities for this proposition begin with cases about magistrates' courts but include at least one case about disciplinary tribunals."
Hill, R. (on the application of) v Institute of Chartered Accountants In England and Wales [2013] EWCA Civ 555.

HEAVY GOODS VEHICLE. Stat. Def., HGV Road User Levy Act 2013 s.2.

HEDGING.
"In the context of commodity trading, we would agree that the term 'hedging' is generally used to describe in broad terms steps taken to reduce existing exposure to risks, usually the risk of market fluctuations, and increase certainty of outcome, usually of price, whereas 'speculation' is used to describe the act of entering into a new obligation in the hope of making a profit as a result of favourable movements in the market and

thereby at the same time incurring the risk of adverse market movements. That reflects the distinction drawn by the Citibank tribunal."
Standard Chartered Bank v Ceylon Petroleum Corporation [2012] EWCA Civ 1049.

HELD.
"Agreeing that an arbitration is 'to be held' in a particular country suggests that all aspects of the arbitration process are to take place there. That would include any supervisory court proceedings which might be required in relation to that process."
Shagang South-Asia (Hong Kong) Trading Co Ltd v Daewoo Logistics [2015] EWHC 194 (Comm).

HER MAJESTY'S GOVERNMENT. Stat. Def., Justice and Security Act 2013 s.4.

HEREDITAMENT.
"It is common ground that The Cannis is capable of constituting a dwelling: the issue is whether it constitutes such a hereditament as would have been a hereditament for the purposes of the General Rate Act 1967 if that Act remained in force. The answer to that otherwise incomprehensible question is provided by the authorities to which I have referred above and those authorities make it clear beyond question that there must not only be occupation of the kind described in the first three requirements first propounded by Mr Michael Rowe QC in John Laing but, fourthly, that the occupation has the character of permanence about it and that it is not too transient to be ignored. The need for this fourth requirement must be obvious: rateable occupation does not arise for a resident who is only occupying for a matter of days or weeks or even months (see Lush J. in St Pancras Assessment Committee). The occupier must have put down some roots which tie him to indefinite occupation and make him a settler in the property rather than a wayfarer passing by. The settler will have adopted the property for his residence for settled purposes as part of the regular order of his life for the time being. The wayfarer is an itinerant of no fixed abode."
Reeves v Northrop [2013] EWCA Civ 362.

HIGH HEDGE. Stat. Def., "a hedge . . . which—
   (a) is formed wholly or mainly by a row of 2 or more trees or shrubs;
   (b) rises to a height of more than 2 metres above ground level;
   (c) forms a barrier to light; [and] a hedge is not to be regarded as forming a barrier to light if it has gaps which significantly reduce its overall effect as a barrier at heights of more than 2 metres; [and]
in relation to a high hedge no account is to be taken of the roots of a high hedge." (High Hedges (Scotland) Act 2013 s.1.)

HOME.

"The expressions 'private life' and 'home' in article 8 have been interpreted very broadly. 'Home' may include a holiday home and a place of intended residence. The 'home' of a businessman includes his business premises. 'Home' can also include premises which are unlawfully occupied. So I have no doubt that in this case the site is 'home' to those who are living there. Their position is in that respect similar to the occupants of Roma camps in *Yordanova v Bulgaria* [2012] ECHR 758 paragraph 103. However, that is only the start of the inquiry."
Malik v Fassenfelt [2013] EWCA Civ 798.

"In my judgment 'home' should be construed as 'only or main home'. This interpretation, in my view, accords with the statutory purpose of the legislation. Home is a place to which a person has a degree of attachment both physical and emotional. The test as to whether a person occupies premises as their home is both qualitative and quantitative (see para 36 above)."
Walford, R. (On the Application Of) v Worcestershire County Council [2014] EWHC 234 (Admin).

"The comparison to be made here is between the situation of somebody who lives in a caravan and somebody who lives in a dwelling-house. The two situations are not analogous. Of course, neither a 'caravan' nor a 'dwelling-house' is in itself synonymous with a 'home'. And I accept that the concept of a 'home' is broader than merely the physical structure which forms a habitation. But when that concept is being considered there is, in my view, a material difference to be discerned between a caravan and a dwelling-house, and a material difference between the situation of someone who lives in a caravan and someone who lives in a dwelling-house. When a caravan dweller is compelled to move from a site where he has stationed his caravan he is able to take the caravan with him. It is mobile. By contrast, when a person who lives in a dwelling-house is displaced from it he leaves not only the location where he has made his home but also the house in which he has lived. It is immoveable. This is a practical difference, and in my view a significant one. It goes to the very heart of this case. It is aptly described by Mr Lask in this way: that someone in the claimants' situation is moving his home from one place to another, while the person with whom the claimants seek to compare themselves must actually move out of his home, and leave it behind when he goes."
Mahoney, R. (on the application of) v Secretary of State for Communities and Local Government [2015] EWHC 589 (Admin).

HONEY. Stat. Def., "In these Regulations 'honey' means the natural sweet substance produced by Apis mellifera bees from the nectar of plants or from secretions of living parts of plants or excretions of plant-sucking insects on the living parts of plants which the bees collect, transform by combining with specific substances of their own, deposit, dehydrate, store and leave in honeycombs to ripen and mature" (Honey (England) Regulations 2015 (SI 2015/1348) reg.2).

HONEYDEW HONEY. Stat. Def., "honey obtained mainly from excretions of plant sucking insects (Hemiptera) on the living part of plants or secretions of living parts of plants" (Honey (England) Regulations 2015 (SI 2015/1348) reg.2).

HONOUR OR DIGNITY.
"16. As a matter of ordinary language the conferring of a life peerage would in my judgment be the conferring of 'an honour or dignity'. Other descriptions might be chosen or, in some contexts, preferred. In oral submissions Dr Sampson argued that a life peerage is 'not simply an honour and a dignity but a public office in its own right'. Even if that submission is accepted, as well it might be, the peerage is, on the face of the submission, nonetheless an honour and a dignity.
17. Dr Sampson makes the point that if reference to a peerage had been intended then it would have been easy for the legislation to use the term itself. In my judgment the answer to the point is simply that paragraph 3(b) is seeking to deal concisely with a number of things by using the overall description 'any honour or dignity'.
18. I do not see any different meaning is achieved by reading the language restrictively, as Dr Sampson urged, even if it was appropriate to do so. I do not regard the language as ambiguous or uncertain. However if I am wrong in that judgment, the argument would still be concluded against Dr Ranger by reference to *Hansard*. There can be no question that the rule in *Pepper v Hart* [1993] AC 593 would render *Hansard* admissible in the context of an ambiguity.
19. *Hansard* records that in the course of debate in the House of Lords on 24 October 2000 Lord Falconer of Thoroton, then Minister for the Cabinet Office, stated expressly that the words 'or dignity' were proposed to be added to paragraph 3(b) by amendment to ensure 'that the exemption applies to the granting of peerages' (HL Debs, October 24, 2000, col. 314)."
Ranger v House of Lords Appointments Commission [2015] EWHC 45 (QB).

HORSE. Stat. Def., "includes a pony, donkey or mule or any other equine animal" (Control of Horses (Wales) Act 2014 s.9).

HOUSE.
"It is clear from all the authorities that the words 'reasonably so called' are intended to be words of limitation: *Lake v Bennett* [1970] 1 QB 663, 670 (Lord Denning M.R.), 672 (Salmon L.J.); *Tandon v Trustees of Spurgeon Homes* [1982] AC 755, 764 (Lord Roskill); *Malekshad v Howard de Walden Estates Ltd* [2002] UKHL 49 [2003] 1 AC 1013, 1028 (Lord Millett); *Prospect Estates Ltd v Grosvenor Estate Belgravia* [2008] EWCA Civ 1281

[2009] 1 WLR 1313, 1317 (Mummery L.J.). Their purpose is to exclude buildings that would otherwise come within the other parts of the definition. The mere fact that a building might be called something other than 'a house' is not sufficient to trigger the exclusion: *Tandon v Trustees of Spurgeon Homes*, 765 (Lord Roskill). As long as a building can reasonably be called 'a house' it is within the definition, even though it may also reasonably be called something else: *Tandon v Trustees of Spurgeon Homes*, 767 (Lord Roskill). Whether a building can reasonably be called 'a house' or can only reasonably be called something else is a question of appellation: *Malekshad v Howard de Walden Estates Ltd*, 1030 (Lord Millett). I agree with the judge that the question is not whether it is possible to call a building 'a house'; the question is whether it is reasonable to do so. In the present case the structure and use of the building have hardly changed since it was first erected. That being so the extensive historical research that the parties undertook, although of great interest, is in my judgment largely irrelevant. In the case of a building predominantly used for residential purposes, whether it can reasonably be called 'a house' will depend primarily on its external and internal physical character and appearance: *Hosebay Ltd v Day* [2010] EWCA Civ 748 [2010] 1 WLR 2317, 2330 (Lord Neuberger of Abbotsbury MR). . . . The clear consensus of judicial opinion is that a purpose built block of flats cannot reasonably be called 'a house'. It is true that some judges have referred to tower blocks and others to large purpose built blocks, but in my judgment the underlying principle is clear. It is also true that none of these observations is binding ratio, but such is the strength and consistency of the consensus that it would in my judgment be wrong for us to depart from it. As Lord Roskill himself said in *Tandon v Trustees of Spurgeon Homes* (at 766–7) it is imperative that there should be not only uniformity of principle in the approach of the courts but also a broad consistency in the conclusions reached. In the present case there is the added feature that the building is not a wholly residential building but also includes the three shops."
Magnohard Ltd v RH Charles Gerald [2012] EWCA Civ 594.

For discussion of the meaning of "house" in the Leasehold Reform Act 1967 see *Day v Hosebay Ltd* [2012] UKSC 41; also—
"3. Section 2(1) of the 1967 Act provides that: 'For the purposes of this Part of this Act, "house" includes any building designed or adapted for living in and reasonably so called, notwithstanding that the building is not structurally detached, or was or is not solely designed or adapted for living in, or is divided horizontally into flats or maisonettes . . . '
4. That rather short, tolerably clear, inclusive description of a 'house' in ordinary English has for 30 years generated enough legal analysis and judicial guidance to verify one of the satirical laws promulgated by C Northcote Parkinson in 1957. The latest weighty decision of our newest highest court was handed down (on 10 October 2012): *Hosebay Ltd v. Day* [2012] UKSC 41; [2012] 1 WLR 2884 (*Hosebay*). The unanimous decision

in *Hosebay* explained the earlier 3–2 decision of the House of Lords upon which the trial judge in this case had had to rely: *Tandon v. Trustees of Spurgeons Homes* [1982] AC 755 (*Tandon*). This court has received written and oral submissions from each side about the impact of *Hosebay* on *Tandon*."
Henley v Cohen [2013] EWCA Civ 480.

Stat. Def., "includes a dwelling that forms part of a building" (Self-build and Custom Housebuilding Act 2015 s.5).

See PREMISES.

HOUSING ACCOMMODATION. Stat. Def., Anti-social Behaviour, Crime and Policing Act 2014 s.20.

HUMAN EMBRYO.
"What is meant by the term 'human embryos' in Article 6(2)(c) of the Biotech Directive? In particular, what was meant by the CJEU in Brüstle by the expression 'capable of commencing the process of development of a human being'? Does that contemplate the commencement of a process which must be capable of leading to a human being? Or does it contemplate the commencement of a process of development, even though the process cannot be completed, so that it is incapable of leading to a human being? . . . I agree with ISCC that if the process of development is incapable of leading to a human being, as the Hearing Officer has found to be the case in relation to parthenotes, then it should not be excluded from patentability as a 'human embryo'.
56. Like the Advocate General in Brüstle, I consider that totipotent cells should be excluded from patentability, whereas pluripotent cells should not. I note that totipotent cells are expressly referred to in recital 38 as an example of cells which are obviously excluded from patentability. This would seem surprising, if the intention of the legislation is to exclude pluripotent cells as well.
57. Stem cells have the potential to revolutionise the treatment of human disease. Because of their capacity to differentiate into almost any type of adult cell, human stem cells open the door to a wide variety of new therapies and other medical applications. For instance, cardiac muscle cells could be used to alleviate ischaemic heart disease, pancreatic islet cells for treatment of diabetes, liver cells for hepatitis and neural cells for degenerative brain diseases such as Parkinson's. Other potential applications include the treatment of burns, strokes, eye disease, spinal cord injuries and certain forms of cancer.
58. The recitals to the Biotech Directive show that a part of its purpose is to encourage research in the field of biotechnology by means of the patent system. The balance between this objective and the need to respect the

fundamental principles safeguarding the dignity and integrity of the person may properly be struck by excluding from patentability processes of development which are capable of leading to a human being. However, to exclude processes of development which are incapable of leading to a human being does not, in my view, strike a balance at all. This is particularly so in the case of parthenotes, which are not the same as fertilised ova at any stage. It is more akin to a total exclusion from patent protection of the fruits of stem cell research, to the detriment of European industry and public health. . . .

59. The parties have suggested that the following question should be referred. In my judgment this succinctly identifies the issue. Subject to any further submissions, this is the question that I intend to refer: Are unfertilised human ova whose division and further development have been stimulated by parthenogenesis, and which, in contrast to fertilised ova, contain only pluripotent cells and are incapable of developing into human beings, included in the term 'human embryos' in Article 6(2)(c) of Directive 98/44/EC on the legal protection of biotechnological inventions?"

International Stem Cell Corporation v Comptroller General of Patents [2013] EWHC 807 (Ch).

HUMAN TRAFFICKING. Stat. Def., Modern Slavery Act 2015 s.2.

HUSBAND. Stat. Def., includes a man who is married to another man. Marriage (Same Sex Couples) Act 2013 Sch.3.

HYBRID BILL.
"57. It may be helpful at the outset to explain what is meant by hybrid bill procedure. A hybrid bill shares certain characteristics of a public bill and a private bill. The Speaker has defined a hybrid bill as 'a public bill which affects a particular private interest in a manner different from the private interests of other persons or bodies of the same category or class' (Hansard (HC Debates), 10 December 1962, col 45). This hybrid character influences the Parliamentary procedure: a hybrid bill proceeds as a public bill, with a second reading, committee report and third reading, but with an additional select committee stage after the second reading in each House, at which objectors whose interests are directly and specifically affected by the bill (including local authorities) may petition against the bill and be heard. Parliamentary standing orders make provision for those persons who have standing to lodge a petition."

HS2 Action Alliance Ltd, R. (on the application of) v The Secretary of State for Transport [2014] UKSC 3.

IDENTIFIES.

"54. In my view, as Mr Harris, Mr Elvin and Mr Katkowski submitted, the concept of identifying an area as one of significant change, in regulation 6(2)(a)(ii) of the 2004 regulations, means establishing the principle of such change in a particular, defined area. Once this principle has been established the identification is complete. If a document is to be an area action plan it must be the document that achieves the identification. It must make what Mr Elvin referred to as the 'primary identification', or, as Mr Harris submitted, the 'autonomous identification' of the area as one of significant change. The sense of the word 'identifies' in regulation 6(2)(a)(ii) is plainly the ordinary English meaning of the transitive verb 'to identify', namely to '[e]stablish the identity of; establish who or what a given person or thing is; recognize' (*The New Shorter Oxford English Dictionary* (1993).

55. To construe the word 'identifies' in regulation 6(2)(a)(ii) as if it meant 'confirms the identification of' or 'acknowledges' or 'provides policy or guidance for' would be to rob it of its true sense in its statutory context. It is clear from paragraphs (2)(a)(i) and (2)(a)(iii) of regulation 6 that the expression 'identifies that area as an area of significant change . . .' in paragraph (2)(a)(ii) must have been meant to connote something different from the expression 'relates to part of the area of the local planning authority' in paragraph (2)(a)(i), and different also from the expression 'contains the authority's policies relevant to areas of significant change . . .' in paragraph (2)(a)(iii).

56. I think the wider construction of paragraph (2)(a)(ii) urged by Mr Jones would have consequences that Parliament cannot have intended. It would seem to preclude the preparation of supplementary planning documents for areas of significant change already identified in a development plan document. This is because any document that contained guidance for development proposals within such an area would automatically be identifying an area of significant change. It would therefore have to be an area action plan (cf. *R. (on the application of RWE Npower Renewables Ltd.) v Milton Keynes Borough Council* [2013] EWHC 751 (Admin), at paragraphs 68 and 69)."

West Kensington Estate Tenants and Residents Association v London Borough of Hammersmith and Fulham [2013] EWHC 2834 (Admin).

"The word 'identifies' is an ordinary English word which, in the absence of any express or implied provision in the statute, should be given its ordinary meaning. . . .

41. It was—at least to a certain extent—common ground that to be 'identified' for the purposes of section 393 it was not necessary for a person to be referred to in the notice expressly by name. . . . A useful parallel as to what is normally regarded as necessary in common English usage to amount to the 'identification' of an individual in a written or oral statement is to be found in the authorities relating to defamation proceedings."

The Financial Conduct Authority v Macris [2015] EWCA Civ 490.

IDENTITY DOCUMENT. Stat. Def., Specialist Printing Equipment and Materials (Offences) Act 2015 s.2.

IMMIGRATION FUNCTIONS. Stat. Def., Specialist Printing Equipment and Materials (Offences) Act 2015 s.2.

IMMINENT.
"As for whether the risk was 'immediate', Miss Carss-Frisk submits that the Court of Appeal failed to take into account the fact that an 'immediate' risk must be imminent. She derives the word 'imminent' from what Lord Hope said in *Van Colle v Chief Constable of the Hertfordshire Police* [2009] 1 AC 225, para.66. In the case of *In re Officer L* [2007] 1 WLR 2135, para.20, Lord Carswell stated that an apt summary of the meaning of an 'immediate' risk is one that is 'present and continuing'. In my view, one must guard against the dangers of using other words to explain the meaning of an ordinary word like 'immediate'. But I think that the phrase 'present and continuing' captures the essence of its meaning. The idea is to focus on a risk which is present at the time of the alleged breach of duty and not a risk that will arise at some time in the future."
Rabone v Pennine Care NHS Foundation [2012] UKSC 2.

IMPECUNIOUS.
"A dictionary definition of impecunious is 'having no money; penniless; in want of money'. Hence a dictionary definition of impecuniosity is 'lack of money; pennilessness'. Legally when determining whether, through impecuniosity, a plaintiff is entitled to recover the credit hire rate as opposed to the basic hire rate impecuniosity has a more nuanced meaning. Lord Nicholls in *Lagden v O'Connor* [2004] 1 AC 1067 stated:
'There remains the difficult point of what is meant by "impecunious" in the context of the present type of case. Lack of financial means is, almost always, a question of priorities. In the present context what it signifies is inability to pay car hire charges without making sacrifices the plaintiff could not reasonably be expected to make.'
In the same case Lord Hope expressed the same test in somewhat different language as follows:
'The full cost of obtaining the services of a credit hire company cannot be claimed by the motorist who is able to pay the cost of the hire up front

without exposing himself or his family to a loss or burden which is unreasonable.'

Accordingly an individual who is not penniless, can still be impecunious, because as a question of priorities he is unable to pay car hire charges without making sacrifices he could not reasonably be expected to make. Lord Nichols described this test as having an open-ended nature."

South Eastern Health & Social Care Trust v Flannagan [2015] NIQB 30.

IMPROPER.

"28. As we have set out in the judgment given by the judge in this case he relied upon the definition of "improper" set out in the decision of the Divisional Court in *DPP v Denning*. Although we have determined that the order must be quashed as the judge had no jurisdiction to make it, it is important to draw attention to the later decision of the Court of Appeal in *Ridehalgh v Horsefield* [1994] Ch 205 where Sir Thomas Bingham, MR (as he then was), gave the following definition at page 232:

"'Improper" means what it has been understood to mean in this context for at least half a century. The adjective covers, but is not confined to, conduct which would ordinarily be held to justify disbarment, striking off, suspension from practice or other serious professional penalty. It covers any significant breach of a substantial duty imposed by a relevant code of professional conduct. But it is not in our judgment limited to that. Conduct which would be regarded as improper according to the consensus of professional (including judicial) opinion can be fairly stigmatised as such whether or not it violates the letter of a professional code.'"

Director of Public Prosecutions, R. (on the application of) v Sheffield Crown Court [2014] EWHC 2014 (Admin).

IN ACCORDANCE WITH THE LAW.

"For a measure to be 'in accordance with the law', the relevant law must be adequately accessible and foreseeable, i.e. formulated with sufficient precision to enable the individual, if need be with appropriate advice, to regulate his conduct; and to meet these requirements a law must indicate with sufficient clarity the scope of discretion conferred on the competent authorities and the manner of its exercise. In *S v United Kingdom*, having recited that test in somewhat fuller terms at para.[95], the court went on to express doubts as to whether s.64 of PACE was sufficiently precise to meet the test, in providing that retained samples and fingerprints 'shall not be used . . . except for purposes related to the prevention or detection of crime, the investigation of an offence or the conduct of a prosecution'. But it noted that the issue was closely related in that case to the broader issue of whether the interference was necessary in a democratic society, and in view of its analysis of that broader issue it did not find it necessary to decide whether the 'in accordance with the law' test was met."

RMC, R. (on the application of) v Commissioner of Police of the Metropolis [2012] EWHC 1681 (Admin).

"The regime contained in the DPA 1998, the Human Rights Act, and the 2007 Act constitutes a sufficiently accessible and predictable body of law. Accordingly, it satisfies the requirement that any disclosure of personal census data under section 39(4)(f) is 'in accordance with the law' for the purposes of Article 8(2) of the European Convention. The Board's policy to refuse to disclose personal census data unless compelled by a court provides an important additional safeguard. It means that, looking at the decision-making process as a whole, the interests of the data subject will be adequately protected. Accordingly, this part of the challenge must be dismissed."

Ali, R. (on the application of) v Minister for the Cabinet Office the Statistics Board [2012] EWHC 1943.

IN DEFAULT.

"The phrase 'in default' in section 106 of the 1984 Act means in breach of an obligation arising under the 1984 Act. The provision does not require the court or the arbitrator to conduct a wide ranging review of other legislation and the common law in order to see whether the claimant is in breach of any duties arising outside the 1984 Act."

Manolete Partners Plc v Hastings Borough Council [2014] EWCA Civ 562.

IN ESCROW.

"The term 'in escrow' is, at least historically, most precisely applied to the delivery of a deed to a third party when the execution is not intended to be complete but operative only in certain circumstances or on certain conditions (*Watkins v Nash* (1875) 20 Eq 262), but it is now used by analogy to the delivery of money, stocks and other property to a third party pending an event, most usually until contractual obligations are fulfilled. If a person holding money in escrow pays it over before the event, he—like a stakeholder (or being a stakeholder)—risks having to pay again himself. Thus, there is readily available a businesslike rationale for the provision in the last sentence of the further agreement other than to provide for arbitration: namely to provide that, if it pays the deposit to the lessors or the lessees, the Agent is not exposed to potential liability to the other: the Agent's decision is 'final and binding' in that regard. It is readily understandable that the Agent should be given this protection when the identity of the lessee was changed but liability for past damage deferred. I do not overlook that the second and third leases are governed by French law, but there is no evidence that French law materially differs from English law."

Crowther v Rayment [2015] EWHC 427 (Ch).

IN PARTICULAR.

"The words 'in particular' point to the provision being non-exhaustive."

KS (Burma) v Secretary of State for the Home Department [2013] EWCA Civ 67.

IN RELATION TO.

"It is common ground that the words 'in relation to' are capable of having a broader or a narrower meaning, depending upon the context in which they are used:"

Trust Special Administrator Appointed to South London Healthcare NHS Trust v London Borough of Lewisham [2013] EWCA Civ 1409.

IN USE.

"16. Both counsel were ultimately agreed that the change in language of the regulations in relation to the demolition deduction has not made any change in the nature of the use of the premises that must be shown in the qualifying period. The only relevant change is that the qualifying period of six months may now be at any time within the three years prior to the date of grant of planning permission whereas previously it had to be in the 12 months prior to that date. In particular, although the regulations as amended in 2014 now refer to an 'in-use building' such a building must be one which is 'in lawful use', which is the same phrase as was used in the regulations as they originally stood, and one whose meaning has not changed.

17. It is also agreed that there is no relevant legislative definition of 'in lawful use'. There is no such definition in the regulations themselves. Although there is a partial definition of 'use' in the Planning Act 2008, the definitions in that Act are expressly stated not to apply for the purposes of CIL regulations. Further, it is agreed that 'lawful use' means a use that is lawful for planning purposes. In these circumstances, the question is a normal one of statutory interpretation, starting with the ordinary meaning of the language used, considered in the context of the other provisions of the legislation itself, and the legislative purpose as shown by the terms of the legislation and such external material as it may be permissible for the court to have regard to.

18. In my judgment, all of these considerations point in a direction which supports the defendant's position. The words employed ('in lawful use' and 'in-use building') clearly suggest that something more is required than that a building has a use to which it may theoretically be put, i.e. that the building is actually being used for that purpose."

R. (on the application of Hourhope Ltd) v Shropshire Council [2015] EWHC 518 (Admin).

INCIDENTAL.

"The word 'incidental' has various meanings in English, according to context, some of which are clearly not relevant here, including the occurrence of one thing by chance in connection with another (such as 'the incidental catch of dolphins in the pursuit of tuna', to borrow an example from the *Oxford Dictionary of English* (2nd edn, OUP 2009). In a legal context the word 'incidental' is often contrasted with 'necessary', for example, in

para.13 of Schedule 1 to the Insolvency Act 1986, which enumerates the powers of an administrator or administrative receiver under sections 14 and 42, respectively, of the Insolvency Act 1986. Para.13 of Schedule 1 provides that an administrator or administrative receiver, as the case may be, has the power to make any payment 'necessary or incidental' to the performance of his functions. Both *Jowitt's Dictionary of English Law* (3rd edn, Sweet & Maxwell 2009) and *Osborn's Concise Law Dictionary* (12th edn, Sweet & Maxwell 2013), while not defining 'incidental' separately, define 'incident' as 'a thing appertaining to or following another'. Could it be said that the Capital Debt appertains to or follows from some aspect of the IDA? Just as the Capital Debt does not arise under the IDA, it is hard to see how the Capital Debt is 'incidental' to the IDA in any normal sense of the word 'incidental'. It is true that the Capital Debt was transferred to RBSIF under the IDA, but that does not, without more, make the Capital Debt incidental to the IDA."
Ace Paper Ltd v Fry [2015] EWHC 1647 (Ch).

See NECESSARY OR INCIDENTAL.

INCOMPETENT.
"It is apparent that in referring to Lord Stewart's decision as 'incompetent' the petition is not using that expression in its ordinary significance. It would seem that what is alleged is error of law. However, we do not find that made out by the petitioner's averments. In large part what appears in statements 13 to 19 is a reiteration, in a number of ways, of the petitioner's complaint that it is inequitable that he be prevented from pursuing the nuisance action. It does not appear that an argument was advanced to Lord Stewart under reference to the Convention on Human Rights. Even on the petitioner's averments it is entirely speculative as to whether the respondents have been guilty of breach of a duty of candour. The issues considered by Lord Stewart reflected the extensive submissions made to him many of which bore no direct relation to the issue before him, namely whether or not the respondents were entitled to summary decree. He was fully aware that the estate's liability had been incurred in proceedings for judicial review. Critically, the question to be determined by Lord Stewart in terms of Rule of Court 21.1 was whether any defence was disclosed to action A374/13. He was satisfied that there was none. There is nothing in the petition, and indeed nothing that was said to us by the petitioner, to challenge that conclusion. No relevant case has been put forward that Lord Stewart erred."
Richard N.M. Anderson as executor nominate of the late Mrs Patricia I. Anderson [2014] ScotCS CSIH 73.

INDIRECT SUPPLIER. Stat. Def., Groceries Code Adjudicator Act 2013 s.22.

INFORMATION.

"65. Having said that, clause 5 is concerned with Information as defined. It is not concerned with skill or experience. Knowledge is a bit more problematic because of the difficulty of identifying the source of any particular piece of knowledge. Mr Purvis also pointed out that the definition of 'Information' in clause 5 a is primarily concerned with information in tangible form; and that that reading is consonant with clause 5 g which required Aerolab to destroy 'Information' (as defined) on request and automatically on termination of the contract. As Mr Purvis said, Aerolab could not destroy what was in an employee's head. I accept that submission up to a point.

66. In *Terrapin Ltd v Builders' Supply Company (Hayes) Ltd* [1967] RPC 375, 391 Roxburgh J said in a similar case: ' . . . when I use the word "information", I mean something that can be traced to a particular source and not something which has become so completely merged in the mind of the person informed that it is impossible to say from what precise quarter he derived the information which led to the knowledge that he is found to possess.'

67. In my judgment that is an eminently sensible approach to interpreting a covenant that deals with confidential information. The judge appears to have considered both at [268] and [284] that if the CAD files contained a precise dimension that was 'memorable' then that dimension could be regarded as part of the employees' skill, knowledge and experience. I disagree. An identified piece of confidential information does not cease to be confidential simply because it is memorable."

Force India Formula One Team Ltd v Aerolab SRL [2013] EWCA Civ 780.

"33. As already noted, the entitlement under section 1(1) relates to recorded information but 'information' is not further defined. It is an ordinary English word and there is nothing to suggest that it is being used in an unusual or narrow sense. In *Common Services Agency v Scottish Information Commissioner* [2008] UKHL, [2008] 1 WLR 1550, a case under the materially identical Freedom of Information (Scotland) Act 2002, Lord Hope said that:

'[t]here is much force in Lord Marnoch's observation in the Inner House . . . that, as the whole purpose of the 2002 Act is the release of information, it should be construed in as liberal a manner as possible' (paragraph 4).

He went on to state that that proposition must not be applied too widely, observing that:

'while the entitlement to information is expressed initially in the broadest terms that are imaginable, it is qualified in respects that are equally significant and to which appropriate weight must also be given. The scope and nature of the various exemptions plays a key role within the Act's complex analytical framework.'

As it seems to me, the very fact that detailed exemptions are provided within the complex analytical framework of FOIA shows that 'information' itself does not need to be narrowly construed: on the contrary, there is no reason why effect should not be given in this respect to the purpose of the statute by construing it in as liberal a manner as possible. It is, moreover, common ground that 'information' is not limited to words and figures but extends to visual and aural information (photographs, drawings, CCTV or audio footage, etc). . . .

41. The dividing line between the record itself and the information recorded on it may not be susceptible of precise definition, but it is not difficult to identify examples falling either side of it. I accept that the physical properties of the medium on which information is recorded, such as the weave or weight of paper or the technical specifications of the medium on which an electronic copy of a document is stored, are features of the record itself, not of the recorded information, and fall outside the scope of section 1(1). An obvious example on the other side of the dividing line is that of the words and figures transcribed by IPSA from the invoices that were the subject of Mr Leapman's request: nobody doubts that they were recorded information. The material in dispute in this case is plainly closer to the dividing line but in my view it was rightly found by the Commissioner and the tribunals to fall on the recorded information side of that line. . . .

45. The fact that material is capable of informing an inquiry into the genuineness of a document is in my view relevant to the assessment of whether it constitutes information. I should, however, stress that the utility of a document for the purposes of forensic inquiry is not the touchstone of entitlement under section 1(1) (see, for example, paragraph 48 of the opinion delivered by Lord Reed in the Glasgow City Council case) and that the actual motive or purpose of the applicant in making the request for information is irrelevant: as Mr Coppel put it, the entitlement to information is generally 'purpose blind'. But I do not think that the Commissioner or the tribunals fell into material error in what they said about the use to which the additional recorded information contained within the invoices might be put."

Independent Parliamentary Standards Authority v Information Commissioner [2015] EWCA Civ 388.

INFRASTRUCTURE COMPANY. Stat. Def. (in context of financial services), Financial Services (Banking Reform) Act 2013 s.112.

INJURY. See NON-ACCIDENTAL INJURY.

INJURY BENEFITS. Stat. Def., Public Service Pensions Act 2013 s.37.

INSOLVENCY. Stat. Def., Financial Services and Markets Act 2000 s.2J as inserted by Financial Services Act 2012 s.6.

INSTRUCTION.

"In the first place, the Court of Appeal's decision does not amount to an 'instruction' to the Government to demand Mr Rahmatullah's return. Its judgment merely reflects the court's conclusion that there were sufficient grounds for believing that the UK Government had the means of obtaining control over the custody of Mr Rahmatullah. On that basis the court required the Secretaries of State to make a return to the writ. The essential underpinning of the court's conclusion was that there was sufficient reason to believe that the Government could obtain control of Mr Rahmatullah. It might well prove that the only means of establishing whether in fact it could obtain control was for the Government to ask for his return but that remained a matter for the ministers concerned. The Court of Appeal's judgment did not require the Secretaries of State to act in any particular way in order to demonstrate whether they could or could not exert control. What it required of them was that they show, by whatever efficacious means they could, whether or not control existed in fact."

Secretary of State for Foreign and Commonwealth Affairs v Rahmatullah [2012] UKSC 48.

"123. There was a dispute at the hearing as to the meaning of the word 'instruction' which was in danger of descending into a debate about semantics. I prefer to focus on what actually happened. I have no doubt that the actual decision not to run the advertisement was made by Mr Everitt on behalf of TfL. He notified Mr Weston who in turn notified CBSO. The decision was made in the course of a conversation with Mr Harri who told Mr Everitt that Mr Johnson had expressed a strongly-held opinion that the advertisements were offensive and that TfL should not run them on London buses. Mr Everitt was strongly influenced by Mr Johnson's views and wishes in reaching his decision that TfL would not run them."

Core Issues Trust Ltd, R. (on the application of) v Transport for London [2014] EWHC 2628 (Admin).

INSURANCE.

"8. It does not appear that any rules have been made pursuant to the power in Dentists Act 1984 s.26A(2). Consequently, for the purposes of that section there is no definition of the expression 'adequate and appropriate insurance'. However, it is plain from the definition of 'insurance' in Dentists Act 1984 s.26A(10) that what has to be 'adequate and appropriate' is arrangements for indemnity 'for liabilities which may be incurred in carrying out work as a dentist', that is to say liabilities which a dentist may incur as a result of providing dental treatment, rather than, for example, liabilities which a dentist may incur as a result of employing other people to provide dental treatment. . . . I think that it was common ground before me that the benefits conferred by clause 3(E) of the Memorandum of MPS satisfied the definition of 'insurance' in Dentists Act 1984 s.26A(10). However, as I shall explain, there was a significant difference between the position adopted on behalf of Mr. Whetstone and the position adopted on behalf of MPS as to what, on proper construction, the benefits of that insurance were."

Whetstone (Trading As Whelby House Dental Practice) v Medical Protection Society Limited (Sued As Dental Protection Limited) [2014] EWHC 1024 (QB).

INSURANCE COMPANY. Stat. Def., Finance Act 2012 s.65.

INSURED (PERSON). Stat. Def., Insurance Act 2015 s.1.

INSURER. Stat. Def., Insurance Act 2015 s.1.

INTERESTS OF JUSTICE.
"We shall focus on the statutory language, as interpreted in the authorities, to identify the principle appropriate to this application. The single question is whether the interests of justice make a further inquest either necessary or desirable. The interests of justice, as they arise in the coronial process, are undefined, but, dealing with it broadly, it seems to us elementary that the emergence of fresh evidence which may reasonably lead to the conclusion that the substantial truth about how an individual met his death was not revealed at the first inquest, will normally make it both desirable and necessary in the interests of justice for a fresh inquest to be ordered. The decision is not based on problems with process, unless the process adopted at the original inquest has caused justice to be diverted or for the inquiry to be insufficient. What is more, it is not a pre-condition to an order for a further inquest that this court should anticipate that a different verdict to the one already reached will be returned. If a different verdict is likely, then the interests of justice will make it necessary for a fresh inquest to be ordered, but even when significant fresh evidence may serve to confirm the correctness of the earlier verdict, it may sometimes nevertheless be desirable for the full extent of the evidence which tends to confirm the correctness of the verdict to be publicly revealed. Without minimising the importance of a proper inquest into every death, where a national disaster of the magnitude of the catastrophe which occurred at Hillsborough on 15 April 1989 has occurred, quite apart from the pressing entitlement of the families of the victims of the disaster to the public revelation of the facts, there is a distinct and separate imperative that the community as a whole should be satisfied that, even if belatedly, the truth should emerge."

Attorney General v Coroner of South Yorkshire (West) [2012] EWHC 3783 (Admin).

INTIMIDATING.
"22. I agree with the appellants that it is important not to diminish the

force of the word intimidate. It is a forceful word indicating, in its Latin root, the notion of putting someone in fear. It is to be contrasted with the other intentions identified within the section, namely, an intention to obstruct or an intention to disrupt, both of which indicate more moderate intentions than the intention to intimidate. It seems to me far better merely to consider the word used in the section in the context of the contrast between that word and the intention to obstruct, or an intention to disrupt.

23. I doubt whether, with respect to the District Judge, help is to be gained from the dictionary. Indeed, there is a danger in its use since by lighting on a dictionary definition, the force of the word used in the section is diminished. Looking up the dictionary to find synonyms does not assist in understanding the meaning of the word 'intimidating' in the context of s.68(1). I share Lord Upjohn's view that it is highly dangerous, if not impossible, to attempt to place an accurate definition upon a word in common use; 'you can look up examples of its many uses if you want to in your *Oxford Dictionary*, but that does not help on definition' (*Customs & Excise Commissioners v Top Ten Promotions Limited* [1969] 1 WLR 1163 at 1171)."

Bauer v The Director of Public Prosecutions [2013] EWHC 634 (Admin).

INTRODUCTORY TENANCY.

"Introductory tenancies are creatures of the Housing Act 1996. Their characteristic feature is that they operate for a trial period and only ripen into secure tenancies at the end of that period. By section 124(1) of the 1996 Act a Local Housing Authority or a Housing Action Trust may elect to operate an introductory tenancy regime. Usually, the trial period is one year (section 125(2)) but it can be extended by six months (section 125A). This case is concerned with the statutory procedure for terminating an introductory tenancy. By section 127(1) the landlord may only bring an introductory tenancy to an end by obtaining a court order."

Camden LBC v Stafford [2012] EWCA Civ 839.

INVIOLABLE.

"Quite apart from the fact that the weight of opinion is against the professor's view, it seems to us that it does not sit well with the object and purpose of the 1961 Convention. The purpose of the immunity conferred by articles 24 and 27.2 is to 'ensure the efficient performance of the functions of the diplomatic missions'. This idea has been articulated and applied in some of the cases: see, for example, *Rose v The King* (para 47 above) and *Iraq v Vinci* (para 55 above). Even if inviolability can in principle extend to inadmissibility of documents in some circumstances, it should not do so where the inadmissibility cannot promote or contribute to the efficient performance of the functions of a mission. The protection against the disclosure and use of the archives and documents of a mission can unquestionably promote and contribute to the efficient performance of a mission's functions in some cases. But it cannot do so where any damage that is done to a mission by the disclosure of an archive or document has already been done by their disclosure by a third party for which the party who wishes to adduce the evidence has no responsibility. In our judgment, it makes no sense for the concept of inviolability of the mission to be extended to prevent a document that is in the worldwide public domain from being admitted in proceedings in England and Wales, simply because it emanated from a diplomatic mission in the UK. Had the document emanated from the US embassy in Paris, we doubt whether the argument would have got off the ground. There is the further relevant point, derived from *Rose v The King*, that the US Government has not objected to the use of the cable in these proceedings."

Bancoult, R. (on the application of) v Secretary of State for Foreign & Commonwealth Affairs [2014] EWCA Civ 708.

IRRATIONALITY.

"64. The language of 'irrationality' carries with it pejorative overtones which may obscure the nature of the review called for. A decision will be vulnerable to being quashed where the reasoning is so flawed that it 'robs the decision of logic', as Sedley J put it in *R v Parliamentary Commissioner for Administration ex parte Baldwin* [1998] 1 PLR 1. That formulation has been repeated since, for example in *R. (Norwich and Peterborough Building Society) v Financial Services Ombudsman Ltd* [2002] EWHC 2379 (Admin)."

Demetrio, R. (on the application of) v Independent Police Complaints Commission (IPCC) [2015] EWHC 593 (Admin).

J

JOINT FAMILY.

"I take 'in a joint family' to mean 'with her in-laws'."
Gupta, Re Application for Judicial Review [2015] ScotCS CSOH 9.

JUDGMENT.

"38. . . . I add these few words only because the argument as originally presented to us proceeded, I think, upon the basis of what is perhaps an understandable confusion between two uses of the word 'judgment' in an area of law and procedure which it is not easy for non-lawyers to understand. I offer the following very short explanation in what I hope will be found to be non-technical language but I stress that it is not intended to alter established legal principles.

39. To many people, the word 'judgment' signifies the oral or written judgment given at the end of proceedings in which the judge explains in a narrative form what he has decided and why. What I am now saying is a judgment in this sense. In contrast, the word is used in a different sense in, for example, CPR 40.12 and CPR 52.10(2)(a) which refer to 'a judgment or order' meaning, to use lay language, the end product of the proceedings. The end product of this appeal is that the appeal is dismissed and that is what will be encapsulated in a formal order in due course. The end product of Judge Horowitz's 2011 hearing was the financial orders that he then made.

40. The correction that the father wished Judge Horowitz to make to his judgment was not 'an accidental slip or omission in a judgment or order' within the slip rule contained in CPR 40.12. It was not a correction of the judge's order or of the 'judgment' in the sense in which that word is used in CPR 40.12. The father was seeking a correction (in his eyes) of the contents of Judge Horowitz's judgment in the other sense.

41. The slip rule not being available, and the judge having concluded his function in relation to the February 2011 decision, as Patten LJ says in §22 of his judgment, the only possible route of challenge to what the judge said was by way of an appeal against the 'order or judgment made or given' by him (CPR 52.10(a)). Here again 'judgment' has a restricted meaning as Patten LJ has explained and I am doubtful that it includes the aspects of Judge Horowitz's judgment that the father sought to challenge. However, even if it did, it is a very great deal too late for an appeal to be launched now. It follows that there is no role for this court. That is why the first appeal must be dismissed."
A (A Child) [2014] EWCA Civ 871.

JUDICIAL. As to what amounts to a "judicial authority" for the purposes of the Extradition Act 2003 s.2, see *Assange v The Swedish Prosecution Authority* [2012] UKSC 22.

> "If (as I consider) 'judicial' is in the context of the Framework Decision a concept with autonomous content, then sections 2(2) and 2(7) must clearly be read (as they can be) as preserving and reflecting its autonomous meaning. How restricted the boundaries are of that autonomous meaning is a different matter. Bearing in mind the diversity within member states of judicial systems and arrangements, they may be quite relaxed. The *Assange* case witnesses to this. I will return to this aspect, after considering the second ground of challenge to the requests for surrender."

Bucnys v Ministry of Justice [2013] UKSC 71.

JUDICIAL ACTS; JUDICIAL CAPACITY; JUDICIAL FUNCTIONS.

> "147. As the above summary of the parties' submissions demonstrates questions as to what is meant by 'judicial acts', 'judicial capacity' and 'judicial functions' may arise in a wide variety of factual and legal contexts. Not surprisingly what is said in one context to be an important or even conclusive factor may not necessarily be an important or conclusive factor in another context. . . .
>
> 169. It is in my judgment clear that Parliament intended that there should be an absolute prohibition on the making of DRO in circumstances where the conditions in Part 1 of Schedule 4ZA are not met. This is therefore in my judgment an example of precisely the kind of situation which illustrates the policy lying behind Parliament's intention that the section 149 duty should not apply to the exercise of a judicial function. If the duty under section 251C had been imposed on a judge rather than an OR there can in my judgment be no question but that the making of a decision to revoke on the basis that the judge was not satisfied that the conditions in Part 1 were met would be the exercise by the judge of a judicial function to which by reason of paragraph 3 of Schedule 18 of the 2010 Act the section 149 duty did not apply. . . .
>
> 206. For all these reasons I am satisfied that the answer to the question posed by the first issue is that when deciding whether to revoke the DRO the OR was exercising a judicial function within the meaning contemplated by paragraph 3 of Schedule 18 to the 2010 Act and that accordingly in making that decision she was not subject to the public sector equality duty under section 149 of that Act."

Howard, R. (on the application of) v The Official Receiver [2013] EWHC 1839 (Admin).

JUDICIARY. Stat. Def., Public Service Pensions Act 2013 s.37.

KNEW OR HAD REASON TO BELIEVE.

"Notwithstanding different contentions advanced in the Defence and Reply, by the time of the trial it was common ground between the parties that 'knew or had reason to believe' in section 151(4) means 'knew' either in the sense of actual knowledge or in the sense of blind eye knowledge, that is to say suspicion accompanied by a deliberate refraining from asking questions. This reflected a contention made by Mr Worthington QC on behalf of Tradex that Tradex had to show that Ian had information from which he actually drew the conclusion that Anthony did not have permission to drive the Range Rover or from which he actually drew the conclusion that Anthony might well not have permission to drive it but deliberately refrained from asking questions lest his suspicions should be confirmed. He accepted that the words 'had reason to believe' add nothing to the requirement of knowledge. . . . In my judgment there is no reason to suppose that the word 'knew' as it appears in the exception in Article 2(1) of the Second Directive was intended to have a different meaning to the word 'knew' as it appears in the exception in Article 1(4) when the body can prove that the passenger knew that the vehicle was uninsured. To the contrary the reasons which led Lord Nicholls to interpret the word 'knew' in Article 1(4) in the way he did in my judgment apply equally to the word as it appears in Article 2(4). Moreover, as I have already pointed out, that reasoning was couched by Lord Nicholls in terms which suggest that he considered it to apply to the word 'knew' in Article 2(4) as well as in Article 1(4). In my judgment it also follows both from Lord Nicholls's obiter dicta in *White v White* and the dicta of the Court of Appeal in Churchill Insurance that the Marleasing principles require the English court to construe the exception in section 151(4) so far as possible to fulfil its obligations in the exception in Article 2(4) of the Second Directive. That being so in my judgment the parties were right to agree that the state of mind required to be proved by Tradex was actual or blind eye knowledge, that is to say that Ian had information from which he either actually drew the conclusion that the prescribed fact was in fact the case or actually drew the conclusion that it might well be the case and, suspecting that it was, deliberately refrained from asking questions so as to avoid confirmation that it was."

Stych v Dibble [2012] EWHC 1606 (QB).

KNEW OR OUGHT REASONABLY TO HAVE KNOWN.

"24. The expression 'knew or ought reasonably to have known' is a common expression in English law and does not require to be glossed. A person who is responsible for an animal carries out the physical element (actus reus) of an offence under section 4(1) if he causes the animal to suffer unnecessarily, whether by act or omission. For the conduct to constitute an offence, the prosecution have to prove additionally that the defendant knew or ought to have known that his act or omission would, or was likely to, have that consequence. (To digress for a moment, it could be argued as a matter of strict grammar that the prosecution need only prove that the defendant knew or ought reasonably to have known that the act or omission would cause the animal to suffer, and not that the suffering would be unnecessary. That linguistic argument could be advanced because the 'knew or ought reasonably to have known' requirement is placed between paragraph (a) (causation of suffering) and (b) (unnecessary nature of the suffering), whereas paragraph (d) should more appropriately have come after paragraph (a) and before paragraph (b). However, it cannot have been the legislature's intention to criminalise an act done with realisation that it would cause the animal pain but in the honest and reasonable, albeit mistaken, belief that it was necessary for the animal's welfare. In the present case the judge directed himself that the prosecution had to establish that the defendant knew or ought reasonably to have known both that his or her act or failure would cause an animal to suffer and that the suffering was unnecessary. In my judgment he was right.)"

Gray, R. (on the application of) v Crown Court Aylesbury [2013] EWHC 500 (Admin).

LAND. Stat. Def., "includes anything held or which, by its nature, may be held as a separate tenement" (Long Leases (Scotland) Act 2012 s.80).

LANDFILL. Stat. Def., "a disposal of material is a disposal of it by way of landfill if it is deposited on the surface of land or on a structure set into the surface, or it is deposited under the surface of land" (Landfill Tax (Scotland) Act 2014 s.5).

LARGE.
"37. Mr Berlin, for the Crown, suggests that an organisation should be treated as being 'very large' if its turnover exceeds £150 million per year on a three-yearly average. We do not think there is any advantage to be gained by such a definition. In the case of most organisations, it will be obvious that it either is or is not very large. Doubtful cases must be resolved as and when they arise."
Thames Water Utilities Ltd, R. v [2015] EWCA Crim 960.

LARGE RETAILER. Stat. Def., Groceries Code Adjudicator Act 2013 s.22.

LAW. See POINT OF LAW.

LAW ENFORCEMENT AGENCY. Stat. Def., Crime and Courts Act 2013 s.16.

LAWFUL AUTHORITY. See WITHOUT LAWFUL AUTHORITY.

LAWFUL USE. See IN USE.

LAWFULLY.
"The context in which the word 'lawfully' appears in article 32 is important too. The phrase in which it appears contemplates that the refugee is not merely present in the territory of the contracting state, but that he is there lawfully. This implies that his presence is not just being tolerated. On the contrary, it is to be assumed that he has a right to be there. As to the source of that right, the power to admit, exclude and expel aliens was among the earliest and most widely recognised powers of the sovereign state: Roma Rights, para.11. The Convention itself shows that it has come to be recognised that there is a right and indeed a duty in sovereign states

to give refuge to aliens who are fleeing from persecution and to refuse to surrender them to the authorities in their home states. But states the world over consistently have exhibited great reluctance to give up their sovereign right to decide which persons will, and which will not, be admitted to their territory and be given a right to settle there: Hyndman, "Refugees under International Law with a Reference to the Concept of Asylum" (1986) 60 ALJ 148, 153, in a passage quoted by Lord Bingham in the Roma Rights case, para.19. . . . For these reasons, I am not persuaded that there are sound grounds for departing from my provisional view that the word 'lawfully' in article 32(1) must be taken to refer to what is to be treated as lawful according to the domestic laws of the contracting state. I think, in agreement with the Court of Appeal and with Lord Dyson, that this is what the framers of the Convention intended by the use of this word in this context."

ST Eritrea, R. (on the application of) v Secretary of State for the Home Department [2012] UKSC 12.

LAYERING.

"4. The Tribunal accepted the FSA's definition of layering in the following terms:- 'layering' consists of the practice of entering relatively large orders on one side of an exchange's (in this case the LSE's) electronic order book ('the order book') without a genuine intention that the orders will be executed: the orders are placed at prices which are (so the person placing them believes) unlikely to attract counterparties, while they nevertheless achieve his objective of moving the price of the relevant share as the market adjusts to the fact that there has been an apparent shift in the balance of supply and demand. The movement is then followed by the execution of a trade on the opposite side of the order book which takes advantage of, and profits from, that movement. This trade is in turn followed by a rapid deletion of the large orders which had been entered for the purpose of causing the movement in price, and by repetition of the behaviour in reverse on the other side of the order book. In other words, a person engaged in layering attempts to move the price up in order to benefit from a sale at a high price, then attempts to move it down in order to buy again, but at a lower price, and typically repeats the process several times.

This is no doubt a useful definition of 'layering', although it must be remembered that the question for the Tribunal was not so much whether Swift Trade engaged in layering as such but whether the business in which they were engaged (whatever it might be called) constituted market abuse within section 118 of the 2000 Act."

7722656 Canada Inc v The Financial Conduct Authority [2013] EWCA Civ 1662.

LEGAL AID. Stat. Def., Legal Aid, Sentencing and Punishment of Offenders Act 2012 s.1.

LEGAL PROCEEDINGS.
"I add that in my judgment Nomihold's original application brought by application notice was by way of legal proceedings within the meaning of section 9 [of the Arbitration act 1996]. I acknowledge that not all forms of legal process are legal proceedings in that sense: see *Best Beat Limited v Rossall*, [2006] EWHC 1494 (Ch), in which Park J. considered that a winding up petition was not covered by the section although it was 'a species of legal proceedings'. Although the expression 'legal proceedings' is qualified in section 9 by the parenthesis '(whether by claim or counterclaim)', that qualification, I think, is intended only to make clear that a party to an arbitration agreement who has himself brought court proceedings is not thereby precluded from invoking the section. However that may be, I cannot accept that section 9 can be circumvented by a party who has agreed to arbitration seeking a court injunction by an application notice rather than by a claim form. That interpretation of the section would unnecessarily create an anomalous loophole in the legislation."
Nomihold Securities Inc v Mobile Telesystems Finance SA [2012] EWHC 130 (Comm).

Stat. Def., "proceedings before a court or tribunal" (Legal Aid, Sentencing and Punishment of Offenders Act 2012 s.42).

LEGAL SERVICES. Stat. Def., Legal Aid, Sentencing and Punishment of Offenders Act 2012 s.8.

LEGISLATION. Stat. Def., Recall of MPs Act 2015 s.22.

LIABILITIES.
"There is no definition of the word 'liabilities' in the 1973 Act or in SI 1975 No. 629. I was invited to take account of the history and purpose of the statutory enactments dealing with local government since 1889. The submission was made that as the definition of liabilities, to which I have referred in the 1889 Act and the 1929 Act, were still extant at the relevant date in 1975, the definition of liabilities in the 1889 Act applied to the 1973 Act and to SI 1975 No. 629. Accordingly I was invited to interpret the word 'liabilities' as meaning not only liabilities which existed at the relevant date, but liabilities to which 'any authority are or would be, but for the passing of this Act liable or subject, whether accrued due at the date of the transfer by this Act, effected or subsequently accruing . . . In summary, I consider that the meaning of the word 'liabilities' in the context of the 1975 regulations is not the same as 'obligations'. It has a wider meaning. I have no difficulty in construing the word to include contingent liability in the contractual sense. I do not think that there is a recognised use of the words 'contingent liability' in delict as the analysis is not usually made in these terms. But I consider that the concept of potential liability in delict has a comprehensible meaning in a situation where it is well established in

law that loss, injury and damage may occur separate in time from injuria. I also consider that the word 'liabilities' has a wide meaning which is certainly wide enough in scope to cover potential liabilities."
Anton v South Ayrshire Council [2012] ScotCS CSOH 80.

LIABILITY ATTACHING TO.
"33. As a matter of natural interpretation, a 'liability attaching to' a contract would be understood as a reference to a liability that is directly connected with, or emanates from, the contract itself, arising after that contract has come into existence. It would not readily be understood as referring to a liability for an actionable wrong which preceded or gave rise to the contract. In the context of a statutory novation of a book of insurance contracts, the natural interpretation makes sense, as it is consistent with the passing of insurance liabilities to the transferee, who is replacing the original insurer as the other contracting party."
PA(GI) Ltd v GICL 2013 Ltd [2015] EWHC 1556 (Ch).

LIFE ASSURANCE BUSINESS. Stat. Def., Finance Act 2012 s.56.

LIKELY.
"Thirdly, Mr McCracken would seek permission to appeal on the basis that the judge misinterpreted the word 'likely' as used in the EIA directive and the Habitats Directive as interpreted by the case of *Waddenzee* [2005] Env. LR 14, paragraph 44, but 'likely' is an ordinary word and it does not seem to me that the judge made any error in that regard, nor indeed did the Inspector."
Hargreaves v Secretary of State for Communities & Local Government [2012] EWCA Civ 241.

"112. It is common ground that in the ordinary course of its operation there is no prospect of HPC being 'likely to have significant effects on the environment' of another EEA state. The claimant's case is premised on the basis of a severe accident occurring. Because the effect of such an event will be significant the claimant submits that a broad interpretation should be given to the word 'likely' in Article 7 of the Directive and in Regulation 24. . . .
114. In my judgement the claimant's approach is not consistent with the scheme or language of the Directive or the 2009 Regulations. Regulation 24 applies when the Secretary of State is of the view that the development is 'likely to have significant effects' on the environment of another EEA state. That wording is materially the same as Article 7 of the Directive. That raises the question as to whether there is any linguistic divergence that requires one to look at the different language versions at all. I deal with that argument below. What is clear is that Article 7, in the material part, is identical in its wording to Article 2 in considering projects 'likely to have significant effects' on the environment."

An Taisce (The National Trust for Ireland), R. (on the application of) v The Secretary of State for Energy and Climate Change [2013] EWHC 4161 (Admin).

"In the absence of any conflict between the parties at the trial as to what the word 'likely' meant it was, in our view, unnecessary for the sheriff to define a word in common usage."
Doonin Plant Ltd & Gary Doonin v. Her Majesty's Advocate [2014] ScotHC HCJAC 26.

"33. The next point to consider is what is meant by 'likely'. Fortunately this was not an issue before me. Mr Price submits, and Mr Tomlinson is content to accept, that 'likely' serious harm will, generally, only be established where the court is satisfied that it is more probable than not that it will occur in the future. It is not necessary to decide in this case whether Mr Price is right to concede that 'in accordance with *Cream Holdings Ltd v Banerjee* [2005] 1 AC 253, there may be circumstances involving the threat of a future publication by the defendant with potentially very serious consequences, where a lesser degree of likelihood could suffice'."
Cooke v MGN Ltd [2014] EWHC 2831 (QB).

"53. The word 'likely' in s.1 is also undefined. As is well-known, this is a word capable of various meanings. Neither party identified any Parliamentary materials which could assist as to what it means in this context. The word appears in another statutory context relevant to publication cases: s.12(3) of the Human Rights Act 1998 prohibits the court from restraining the exercise of freedom of expression before trial unless it is 'satisfied that the claimant is likely to establish that publication should not be allowed'. In that context the ordinary meaning of 'likely' is 'more probable than not', though a lower standard of likelihood may be required in some circumstances, as where there is a slight risk of very serious damage: *Cream Holdings v Banerjee* [2005] 1 AC 253, [22].

54. Parliament must be taken to have known this, and it may be for that reason that in *Cooke* it was common ground that serious harm will, generally, be 'likely' within the meaning of s.1 only if it is more probable than not, and the defendant conceded that the lower *Cream* threshold would apply in comparable circumstances: [33]. Bean J did not expressly decide that issue. Ms Page submits that the term should be interpreted flexibly, as setting a standard of sufficient likelihood to justify continuation of the claim. I am inclined to think that Counsel in *Cooke* were right but the point has not been argued fully on this application and for reasons that appear later in this judgment I do not need to decide which approach is correct."
Ames v Spamhaus Project Ltd [2015] EWHC 127 (QB).

LIMITED WEIGHT.
"127. I turn to consider the irrationality argument. I would make the preliminary observation that expressions such as 'substantial weight', or for that matter 'limited weight', do not have some uniform meaning, or even carry some numerical evaluation. Their significance depends upon the particular context in which they have been used. They often represent no more than a summary expressing how the decision-maker has pulled together a number of judgmental factors. It is difficult to see how in the present type of case a rationality challenge could succeed merely on the basis that a decision-maker has decided to give 'substantial weight' to a policy. Instead, the challenge ought to be directed to the process of reasoning which has been adopted."
Luton Borough Council, R. (on the application of) v Central Bedfordshire Council [2014] EWHC 4325 (Admin).

LIVE. See DWELLING.

LIVE LINK. Stat. Def., "'live link' means an arrangement by which a person can see and hear, and be seen and heard by, the court when that person is not in court" (Criminal Procedure Rules 2013 r.2.2).

LIVING TOGETHER. Stat. Def., A reference to persons who are not married but are living together as a married couple is to be read as including a reference to a same sex couple who are not married but are living together as a married couple. Marriage (Same Sex Couples) Act 2013 Sch.3.

LONG WAVES.
"23. Kashima, like many other Japanese and other ports bordering the Pacific, is on infrequent occasions subject to the impact of 'long waves'. 'Long' in this context connotes the period of time which elapses between the full height of one wave and the next; typically there is a period of between 30 seconds to 5 minutes between the height of one long wave and the next. Long waves are different from normal waves created by the wind and prevailing conditions; long waves are usually much smaller in vertical height than the latter. Long period swells are not technically the same as long waves (although on occasions the judge appears to have used the expressions interchangeably [9]). Long period swell is part of the primary wave spectrum, where that spectrum has a period of up to about twenty seconds between waves. Long waves can penetrate the harbour and the swell from such waves can cause problems to moored vessels at the Raw Materials Berths and, in particular, can disrupt the discharging of cargo."
Gard Marine & Energy Ltd v China National Chartering Co Ltd (Rev 1) [2015] EWCA Civ 16.

LORDS. See MEMBER OF THE HOUSE OF LORDS.

LORDS SPIRITUAL. See ELIGIBLE BISHOP.

LUCY BOX.
"The term 'lucy box' was used in evidence: but none of the witnesses could say why a lucy box is called a lucy box. A lucy box, according to senior counsel for the pursuer, quoting, she said, from Wikipedia, is a metal cabinet, usually about one metre in height, typically located on the roadside, housing switch gear. The name derives from the fact that earlier, cast iron boxes were manufactured by W Lucy & Co of Jericho, Oxford. The name has become generic. Switch gear for 'assets' belonging to Scottish Water, the defenders, is housed in lucy boxes. In this case the contents of the lucy box were described as 'electronic controls'."
Smith v Scottish Water [2014] ScotCS CSOH 140.

MACRO-PRUDENTIAL MEASURE. Stat. Def., Bank of England Act 1998 s.9L as inserted by Financial Services Act 2012 s.4.

MANIFEST.
"46. However it is impossible in my view to say that that reasoning is manifestly erroneous. To my mind Walton's submissions are classic examples of every mistake becoming 'manifest' when it is discovered. Manifest is a word which gives a very limited window of opportunity to challenge. The examples given in the various authorities above show that it is something like an arithmetical error, or a reference to a non existent building and the like. There is nothing 'manifestly wrong' about the decision of Mr Tanney. This is well demonstrated by the fact that the competing arguments put forward in this case were in my view very strong on both sides. This is not merely a situation where a dispute is created so as to lead to a suggestion that it cannot be manifestly wrong. There was merit and is merit in both sides' arguments. The parties by the Agreement gave the Surveyor the power to determine that Decision in law and in fact. I do not see that his reasoning provided as set out above is manifestly erroneous. It might be wrong if one was pressed to argue it but that as I have said that is not sufficient. It does not look obvious when reading his analysis. It is not obvious that he is disentitled from looking to the factual matrix outwith the four corners of the Agreement. It is not manifestly erroneous for him to do that because the limited construction put forward by Walton produces a commercially absurd result. It is not manifestly erroneous for him to apply the principles in *Chartbrooke* and apply that to the words 'the Permission' and come up with a wording which reflects the intent namely that the parties were to share equally the planning gain obtained in respect of this site. It was not intended for the planning gain to be largely pocketed by Walton which is the logical conclusion of the application of the literal wording in the Agreement. As Lord Hoffman said something must have gone wrong. These are perfectly acceptable reasons for his conclusion. They are not manifestly erroneous."
Walton Homes Ltd v Staffordshire County Council [2013] EWHC 2554 (Ch).

"100. In neither EU nor domestic law is there an articulation of what is understood by 'manifest'. The phrase is defined in dictionaries as something which is: readily perceived, clear, evident, clearly apparent, obvious or plain. The etymology is from the Latin 'manifestus'—palpable or manifest. These definitions are helpful only to a degree. What has to be 'manifest' is the inappropriateness of a measure. There are two broad types of case where inappropriateness is put in issue. First, where it is said that a measure is vitiated by a clearly identifiable and material error. These are the relatively easy cases because the error can be identified and determined and its materiality assessed. The error may be a legal one, e.g. the measure is on its face discriminatory on grounds of nationality (as in *R. v Secretary of State for Transport ex Parte Factortame* [1991] ECR I-3905). It may be a glaring error in logic or reasoning or in process. But even here there are complications since whilst it is true that an error which is plain or palpable or obvious on the face of the record may easily be termed 'manifest' that cannot be the end of the story. An error which is clear and obvious my nonetheless not go to the root of the measure; it might be peripheral or ancillary and as such would not make the disputed measure manifestly inappropriate. Equally an error which is far from being obvious or palpable may nonetheless prove to be fundamental. For instance a decision or measure based upon a conclusion expressed mathematically might have been arrived at through a serious error of calculation. The fact that the calculation is complex and that only an accountant, econometrician or actuary might have exclaimed that it was an 'obvious' error or a 'howler', and even then only once they had performed complex calculations, does not mean that the error is not manifest. An error in the placing of a decimal point may exert profound consequences upon the logic of a measure. This suggests that manifest in/appropriateness is essentially about the nature, and, or centrality/materiality of an error. An error will be manifest when (assuming it is proven) it goes to the heart of the impugned measure and would make a real difference to the outcome.

101. But a measure might also be manifestly inappropriate, not because it is possible to pinpoint errors in reasoning or process, but simply because the end result fails the proportionality test to a sufficient degree to warrant the grant of relief. In these cases determining when the measure crosses the Rubicon and becomes manifestly inappropriate is a much more illusive process."

Gibraltar Betting & Gaming Association Ltd v Secretary of State for Culture, Media & Sport [2014] EWHC 3236 (Admin).

MANIFESTLY.
"12. 'Clearly' and 'manifestly' unfounded mean the same and it was held in *Thangarasa and Yogathas* [2002] UKHL 36 that:
    'No matter what the volume of material submitted or the sophistication of the arguments deployed to support the allegation, the Home Secretary is entitled to certify if, after reviewing this material, he is reasonably and conscientiously satisfied that the allegations must clearly fail.'
Kurtaj, R. (on the application of) v Secretary of State for the Home Department [2014] EWHC 4327 (Admin).

MARKET AREA. Stat. Def., Licensing of Pavement Cafés (Northern Ireland) Act 2014 s.30.

MARKET VALUE.
"104. In relation to this approach, it may be helpful to say a word about the concept of 'market value', which has been employed in some of the authorities (eg *BP Exploration Co (Libya) Ltd v Hunt (No 2)* [1979] 1 WLR 783, 840; *Sempra Metals*, para 103). It is an expression which can be used in more than one way, but the definition used by the Royal Institution of Chartered Surveyors captures the essence of the concept: 'The estimated amount for which an asset or liability should exchange on the valuation date between a willing buyer and a willing seller in an arm's length transaction after proper marketing and where the parties had each acted knowledgeably, prudently and without compulsion.'

105. So understood, market value is specific to a given place at a given time. That point can be illustrated by the episode in Vanity Fair in which Becky Sharp sells her horses during the panic which grips the British community in Brussels after the battle of Waterloo, when rumours reach the city that Napoleon has defeated Wellington and that his army is approaching. The circumstances create a market in which horses are exceptionally valuable, and Becky obtains a price which is far in excess of the ordinary value. It is, nevertheless, the value of the horses in the market in which they are sold.

106. That example illustrates the general point that market value depends critically on the identification of the relevant market, since there are different markets for many types of goods and services. That is reflected, for example, in the variability in the price of a haircut, or the cost of a meal in a restaurant, or the fees charged by solicitors, or the salaries of professional footballers, depending on the market in which they are operating."
Benedetti v Sawiris [2013] UKSC 50.

MARRIAGE. Stat. Def., a reference to marriage is to be read as including a reference to marriage of a same sex couple, and any related reference (such as a reference to a marriage that has ended) is to be read accordingly (Marriage (Same Sex Couples) Act 2013 Sch.3).

Stat. Def., Marriage and Civil Partnership (Scotland) Act 2014 s.4(1): "References (however expressed) in any enactment to—
   (a) marriage (including a marriage that has ended),
   (b) a person who is (or was) married to another person, and
   (c) two people who are (or were) married to each other,
are references to marriage whether between persons of different sexes or persons of the same sex and to a party (or former party), or as the case may be the parties (or former parties), to such a marriage."; and see other provisions of and under s.4;

Stat. Def., Marriage and Civil Partnership (Scotland) Act 2014 s.4.

MARRIAGE (of same sex couples). Stat. Def., a marriage between two men, or a marriage between two women, Marriage (Same Sex Couples) Act 2013 Sch.3.

MARRIAGE (Sham marriage). Stat. Def., Immigration and Asylum Act 1999 s.24 amended by Immigration Act 2014 s.55.

MARRIED. Stat. Def., a reference to a person who is married is to be read as including a reference to a person who is married to a person of the same sex (Marriage (Same Sex Couples) Act 2013 Sch.3; Marriage and Civil Partnership (Scotland) Act 2014 s.4).

MARRIED COUPLE. Stat. Def., a reference to a married couple is to be read as including a reference to a married same sex couple (Marriage (Same Sex Couples) Act 2013 Sch.3).

MATERIAL. Stat. Def., "Material of all kinds, including objects, substances and products of all kinds" (Landfill Tax (Scotland) Act 2014 s.39).

MATERIAL CONSIDERATIONS. For discussion of the meaning of material considerations in relation to planning law see *Tewkesbury Borough Council v Secretary of State for Communities and Local Government* [2013] EWHC 286 (Admin).

MAY.
"If Parliament had intended that a direction should be given in all cases, it would have used the word 'shall'. That is the obvious way of giving effect to an intention to impose an obligation. As a matter of ordinary language, the word 'may' connotes the existence of a discretion."
Gallastegui, R. (on the application of) v Westminster City Council [2013] EWCA Civ 28.

MEANING.
"51. To the English company lawyer's eye, 'merger' is a word usually given a restrictive meaning and the words 'issue to members of shares' denote that the members of the transferor company must actually be registered in respect of the consideration shares (for that is what, at least according to English company law, 'issue' ordinarily means) in exchange (that is what is stated) for the transfer to the transferee. As a matter of English company law, shares are only 'issued' when the allottee is entered in the company's register of members in respect of the new shares for which he has subscribed: *National Westminster Bank plc v Inland Revenue Commissioners* [1995] 1 AC 119. . . .
54. Further, it seemed to me that the definition of 'merger' in Article 2(2) of the Directive should be treated as autonomous: Member States

were not given the freedom to define a 'merger' by reference to their national laws. On that basis, the real question is not what an 'issue . . . of securities or shares' would mean as a matter of English company law but, instead, what this term means in a European context."
Olympus UK Ltd [2014] EWHC 1350 (Ch).

MEMBER OF THE HOUSE OF LORDS. Stat. Def., House of Lords Reform Act 2014 s.6.

MENACE.
"It is elementary, and unsurprisingly there was no dispute before us, that the offence of which the appellant was convicted cannot be proved unless the content of the message was of a 'menacing character'. Given that there is 'disappointingly little coherence in English law's approach to threat offences' (*Smith and Hogan's Criminal Law*, 13th edition, at p.951) we do not think that an analysis of the numerous other offences based on threats, including blackmail, takes the interpretation of this statutory provision any further. We were told that the word 'menace' is defined in the shorter *Oxford dictionary* as 'a thing threatening danger or catastrophe; a danger-ous or obnoxious thing or person; a great inconvenience', and that as an intransitive verb, to 'menace' was to 'utter menaces; be threatening'. Mr Smith submitted that no more, and no less, was needed than the applica-tion of ordinary language to the context in which any particular message was expressed and to all the relevant circumstances. Mr Cooper suggested that for a message to be of a menacing character it must, on an objective assessment, contain a threat of such a nature and extent that the mind of an ordinary person of normal stability and courage might be influenced or made apprehensive. Our attention was drawn to *DPP v Collins*, in the Divisional Court, while considering the meaning to be given to 'grossly offensive' within the section, Sedley L.J. identified the four different classes of message proscribed by s.127(1)(a). In the context of a menacing message he observed: 'fairly plainly, is a message which conveys a threat—in other words, which seeks to create a fear in or through the recipient that something unpleasant is going to happen'."
Chambers v Director of Public Prosecutions [2012] EWHC 2157 (Admin).

MICAWBERISM.
"No factual or legal basis for this assertion is pleaded. Nor was any factual or legal basis for it identified by counsel for the Claimants in his submis-sions. Instead, he submitted that the claim against OCBC should not be struck out because something might turn up on disclosure. This is blatant Micawberism. In my judgment the claim against OCBC should be struck out pursuant to CPR rule 3.4(2)(a) on the ground that the Particulars of Claim disclose no reasonable grounds for bringing the claim."
Chopra v Bank of Singapore Ltd [2015] EWHC 1549 (Ch).

MISCARRIAGE OF JUSTICE.
"4. 'Miscarriage of justice' is a concept which, as a matter of general language, has a number of legitimate meanings, and can have a wide meaning.
It is the fundamental concept in Article 14(6) and section 133 [of the Criminal Justice Act 1988] and it has been accepted that in this specific context
it has an autonomous meaning which is narrower than the way it can be
understood in other contexts. There is a history of disagreement between
senior judges about the meaning of the statutory concept in section 133
and the way qualifying 'miscarriages of justice' are to be formulated. The
differences can be seen in the decisions of the House of Lords in *Re
McFarland* [2004] UKHL 17 and *R (Mullen) v Home Secretary* [2004]
UKHL 18, and that of the Supreme Court in the *Adams* cases."
Ali, R. (on the application of) v Secretary of State for Justice [2013] EWHC
72 (Admin).

MISCONDUCT. For discussion of the natural meaning of misconduct in a
professional context see *Aga v General Medical Council* [2012] EWHC 782
(Admin).
    Stat. Def. (in context of financial services), Financial Services and Mar-
kets Act 2000 ss.66A and 66B inserted by Financial Services (Banking
Reform) Act 2013 s.32.

MIXING. For discussion of the meaning of "mixing" in relation to asbestos
see *McDonald v National Grid Electricity Transmission Plc* [2014] UKSC 53.

MODIFY. Stat. Def., "includes amend, repeal or revoke" (Legal Aid, Sentencing and Punishment of Offenders Act 2012 s.42).

MP. Stat. Def., Recall of MPs Act 2015 ss.2(5), 22.

MUTUAL INSURER. Stat. Def., Mutuals' Deferred Shares Act 2015 s.3.

NECESSARY.

"23. In another context, that of permission to instruct an expert in care proceedings, the Court of Appeal in *Re H–L (Expert Evidence: Test for Permission)* [2013] EWCA Civ 655 [2013] 2 FLR 1434 considered the proper approach to determining whether expert evidence was 'necessary to assist the court to resolve the proceedings'. 'Necessary' said Sir James Munby P, 'means necessary'. It has 'a meaning lying somewhere between "indispensable" on the one hand and "useful", "reasonable" or "desirable" on the other hand', having 'the connotation of the imperative, what is demanded rather than what is merely optional or reasonable or desirable'. It is useful to have this explanation of what is meant by 'necessary' in mind in the present context too."

Lindner v Rawlins [2015] EWCA Civ 61.

"The key issue, in my view, is the scope to be attributed to the words 'when necessary' in clause sixth. I accept the tenant's alternative submission that there may be circumstances where re-erection of a building is 'necessary' even though an existing building is still standing on the site. These might include (i) where the existing building is obsolete and unsuitable for any reasonable use, regardless of cost of repair; or (ii) where the cost of repair is excessive in relation to what it would cost to demolish and rebuild premises similar to the existing building. In each of these cases (and I note that the tenant offers to prove in the present case that both of those descriptions apply), I consider that it is in accordance with commercial common sense to describe re-erection as 'necessary'. It must follow, as a matter of practicality, that demolition of the existing obsolete and/or uneconomic building is also 'necessary' in order to allow re-erection to proceed."

Malin v Crown Aerosols UK Ltd [2015] ScotCS CSOH 58.

For discussion of the meaning of "necessary" in the context of Condition 6 of Schedule 2 to the Data Protection Act 1998 see *South Lanarkshire Council v The Scottish Information Commissioner* [2013] UKSC 55.

NECESSARY OR INCIDENTAL.

"119. Para 13 of Schedule 1 entitles an administrator to make any payment which is 'necessary or incidental' to the performance of his functions. I do not see how that can entitle him, let alone the court to direct him, to treat an unprovable debt as a provable debt (unless, conceivably, there was resulting benefit which would redound for the benefit of the

proving creditors, although even then it would be problematic). It can scarcely be said to be 'incidental' or 'necessary' to a person's statutorily prescribed functions to do something inconsistent with those functions."
Nortel Companies, Re [2013] UKSC 52.

NECTAR HONEY. Stat. Def., honey "obtained from the nectar of plants" (Honey (England) Regulations 2015 (SI 2015/1348) reg.2).

NEEDS.
"64. As a matter of the ordinary use of words, the idea that there is a 'need' to establish a new school imports a stronger sense of a compelling requirement for a new school to be established than simply thinking that it would be beneficial for a new school to be established."
The British Humanist Association v London Borough of Richmond Upon Thames [2012] EWHC 3622 (Admin).

NEGLECT.
"35. I agree with Morland J that it appears that the draftsman intended 'neglect', 'forbearance' and 'time . . . given' to mean different things; but as Sullivan LJ pointed out in the course of argument, each of these expressions takes colour from the other two as well as from the overall context. Neglect shades into forbearance which shades into giving time. Having regard to the context and purpose of the proviso, I consider that 'forbearance' connotes a decision by the landlord not immediately to enforce the observance or performance of a covenant against a tenant who is in breach of that covenant, but rather to tolerate the breach for the time being."
Topland Portfolio No. 1 Ltd v Smiths News Trading Ltd [2014] EWCA Civ 18.

NEGOTIATING A BET.
"The meaning of 'negotiating' a bet is less obvious. However, what was meant by negotiating a bet may be seen from the judgment of the Criminal Division of the Court of Appeal in *R v Gambrell* (unreported, 18 March 1981). The appellants had been charged with conspiracy to evade the payment of general betting duty, a duty payable by bookmakers on bets made with them. Giving the judgment of the Court, O'Connor L.J. said:
'[*Stone*] ran an old established business as an agency for placing bets, that is, to act as agent for punters who chose to use him. They were required to deposit a float of money with him. He waived this requirement as far as Gambrell was concerned. He earned his money by getting commission from bookmakers with whom he dealt; there was no evidence of these arrangements. He was clearly *negotiating bets* and therefore a bookmaker within the definition. His case was that no bet was made with him by punters using his services as it made no difference to

him whether the bet won or lost and therefore he was not liable for general betting duty. The bet only arose when he placed it with a bookmaker and it was that bookmaker who was liable for general betting duty. The learned judge rules as a matter of law that when Stone accepted instructions a bet was being made with him as bookmaker and general betting duty became chargeable. He was wrong so to do. He misdirected himself by examining the provisions of the Act which make general betting duty chargeable on bets made through the totalisator. (See Section 1(1)(b) and (c) and Section 14 of the Betting, Gaming and Lotteries Act 1963.) He became further confused by considering the definition of "betting transaction" in Section 55 of the Betting, Gaming and Lotteries Act. He ended up by in effect construing the words "on any bet which is made with a bookmaker" as if they read "on any betting transaction to which a bookmaker is a party." This will not do, for it would make general betting duty chargeable on "any bet made with 'or by' a bookmaker" and there are no possible grounds for reading these words into Section 1(1) (a) or Section 2(1) (a) of the 1972 Act. The effect of this ruling was to prevent Stone from putting forward one main plank of his defence. To a lesser extent, but nonetheless to an important extent, it had the same effect on the cases against Gambrell, Pavion and Zimmerman. On their behalf the contention was that they were professional punters, that is, Gambrell and Pavion, and that in so far as the evidence showed betting instructions coming in to them, they were not accepting bets but merely acting as conduit pipes like Stone.'

The italics are mine. The distinction between bets made with a bookmaker and bets made by a bookmaker is to be noted, but I can otherwise leave aside the concept of negotiating a bet, since the Claimant disclaims any reliance on it."

William Hill Organization Ltd, R. (on the application of) v The Horserace Betting Levy Board [2012] EWHC 2039 (Admin).

NEWSPAPER. Stat. Def., Local Government Act (Northern Ireland) 2014 s.52.

NEWS-RELATED MATERIAL. Stat. Def., Crime and Courts Act 2013 s.42.

NON-ACCIDENTAL INJURY.
"19. The term 'non-accidental injury' may be a term of art used by clinicians as a shorthand and I make no criticism of its use but it is a 'catch-all' for everything that is not an accident. It is also a tautology: the true distinction is between an accident which is unexpected and unintentional and an injury which involves an element of wrong. That element of wrong may involve a lack of care and /or an intent of a greater or lesser degree that may amount to negligence, recklessness or deliberate infliction. While an analysis of that kind may be helpful to distinguish deliberate infliction

from, say, negligence, it is unnecessary in any consideration of whether the threshold criteria are satisfied because what the statute requires is something different namely, findings of fact that at least satisfy the significant harm, attributability and objective standard of care elements of section 31(2).

20. The court's function is to make the findings of fact that it is able on the evidence and then analyse those findings against the statutory formulation. The gloss imported by the use of unexplained legal, clinical or colloquial terms is not helpful to that exercise nor is it necessary for the purposes of section 31(2) to characterise the fact of what happened as negligence, recklessness or in any other way. Just as non-accidental injury is a tautology, 'accidental injury' is an oxymoron that is unhelpful as a description. If the term was used during the discussion after the judgment had been given as a description of one of the possibilities of how the harm had been caused, then it should not have been; it being a contradiction in terms. If, as is often the case when a clinical expert describes harm as being a 'non-accidental injury', there is a range of factual possibilities, those possibilities should be explored with the expert and the witnesses so that the court can understand which, if any, described mechanism is compatible with the presentation of harm.

21. The threshold is not concerned with intent or blame; it is concerned with whether the objective standard of care which it would be reasonable to expect for the child in question has not been provided so that the harm suffered is attributable to the care actually provided. The judge is not limited to the way the case is put by the local authority but if options are not adequately explored a judge may find a vital piece of the jigsaw missing when s/he comes to look at all the evidence in the round."

S (A Child), Re [2014] EWCA Civ 25.

NORMAL PENSION AGE.   Stat. Def., Public Service Pensions Act 2013 s.10.

O

OCCUPATION.

"46. There is, so far as we are aware, no statutory definition and no authoritative determination of what may amount to occupation for the purposes of s. 18(1). In our view, the facts as summarised above do not, without more, demonstrate that ZH occupied the premises within the meaning of the subsection. We reach this view by reference to the context in which the word 'occupied' is used: the scheme established by PACE enables searches to be made of property where there are reasonable grounds for believing that evidence of an indictable offence will be found there. Section 18 specifically links the authorising of the search to the reasonable belief that there will be evidence on the premises of the indictable offence for which the arrested person has been arrested. The arrested person's occupation of the premises must therefore be such as to support the belief that it will have caused or contributed to the presence of such evidence.

47. This approach suggests no fixed duration or quality of the arrested person's presence at the premises such as would allow a formulaic approach to the meaning of 'occupied' in the subsection. We can imagine circumstances in which even a short stay might give rise to or support a reasonable belief that evidence relating to an arrested person's indictable offence may be there: drug offences or homicide are obvious examples. In the present case, however, nothing in the disclosed facts suggests that ZH's overnight stay would support a belief that evidence relating to the offence for which he was arrested would be found at the premises."

AB, R. (on the application of) v Huddersfield Magistrates' Court [2014] EWHC 1089 (Admin).

OFFER. See AWARD.

OR.

"Coming fresh to the provision, and on a straightforward reading of Class N, I consider the more natural interpretation is that the word 'or' bears the usual disjunctive meaning that it has in common parlance. That is how I read Class N when pre-reading for the hearing. . . . I accept that the interpretation offered by Mr Glover is a possible meaning, as a matter of English usage, but I do not think it is the most natural reading of the phrase in the context in which it appears. My first impression is reinforced by a number of contextual factors and aspects of the scheme of the Council Tax regime. I consider that reading the relevant phrase with the word 'or' bearing its more natural, disjunctive sense, is particularly appropriate in the context of interpretation of tax legislation such as this."

London Borough of Harrow v Ayiku [2012] EWHC 1200 (Admin).

ORDINARILY EMPLOYED.

"The requirement (which I have assumed in favour of the claimant to have been satisfied) that the assured was and would remain an employee of PFEL is fundamental to the policy, so that the interpretation of the phrase 'ordinarily employed in the United Kingdom' must proceed on that basis. The mere fact of being employed by a company based in the United Kingdom cannot therefore suffice to establish that the assured was employed in this country. Nor would it in my view correspond to normal linguistic usage.

29. In my view, the phrase poses a simple factual question: where, ordinarily, did the employee perform the acts which constituted his work for the employer? Sometimes, if perhaps rarely, the answer may not be straightforward, as in the so-called 'base cases', where an employee resident in United Kingdom spends much or even all of his working hours in trips to various destinations abroad, e.g. to carry out audits or surveys, service machinery, or fly aircraft [13]. The employee's working time may also sometimes be divided between two different places of work and his duties performed in both to an extent sufficiently substantial to justify the description 'ordinarily'—for example, the CEO of a multinational company who is required to be regularly present in its offices in both London and New York, often maintaining residences in both cities for this purpose. No such difficulty arises in the present case. Everything done—and, more pertinently, everything ordinarily done—by Mr Rai for his employer was performed in India."

Rai v Legal & General Assurance Society Ltd [2015] EWHC 170 (Comm).

ORDINARY RESIDENCE.

"'Ordinary residence' is not defined in the 1948 Act. The words are simple but the case law in this and other contexts shows the meaning of the concept is not and that the determination of ordinary residence is an intensely fact-sensitive process. It will be necessary to consider the approach of the courts and, in particular the decision of the House of Lords in *Barnet LBC v Shah* [1983] AC 309 and that of Taylor J. in *R v Waltham Forest LBC, ex p. Vale*, 25 February 1985. Shah's case is notable for Lord Scarman's definition (at 343) that ordinary residence refers to a person's 'abode in a particular place or country which he has adopted voluntarily and for settled purposes as part of the regular order of his life for the time being, whether of short or of long duration'. It has been described by one commentator (Bradley (2007) Solicitors Journal 1146) as 'canonical' but it did not consider how the 'ordinary residence' of a person who lacks the mental capacity to decide where to live is to be determined.

6. The determination of the 'ordinary residence' of a person who lacks the mental capacity to decide where to live was considered in Vale's case.

That case has been relied on in two later decisions and has influenced the formulation of the Department of Health's guidance (as to which see [24]) on determining 'ordinary residence'. Taylor J. set out two approaches, which are referred to as 'test 1' and 'test 2' in the Departmental Guidance. 'Test 1' applies where the person is so severely handicapped as to be totally dependent upon a parent or guardian. Taylor J. stated that such a person (in that case it was a 28-year-old woman) is in the same position as a small child and her ordinary residence is that of her parents or guardian 'because that is her base'. The second approach, 'test 2' considers the question as if the person is of normal mental capacity, taking account of all the facts of the person's case, including physical presence in a particular place and the nature and purpose of that presence as outlined in Shah, but without requiring the person himself or herself to have adopted the residence voluntarily. . . . Drawing the threads together, 'ordinary residence' is a question of fact and degree, and if the Secretary of State gets the law right, the determination of a person's ordinary residence is for the Secretary of State, subject only to *Wednesbury* unreasonableness. In the present case PH's connections with Cornwall differed from Judith's connections with Waltham Forest in Vale's case. In one sense PH's connections were more transitory because Judith had come to stay with her parents in Waltham Forest until appropriate arrangements were made for her whereas by December 2004 arrangements had been made for PH to be placed in a home in Somerset. But, in *North Yorkshire CC v Wiltshire CC* [1999] Fam. 323 at 334 Holman J. stated that 'the court is entitled to take into account matters other than where [the person himself or] herself was living during the specified period', and Potts J. in *R v Redbridge LBC, ex p. East Sussex CC* did not appear to have placed any weight on whether there was a physical presence by the twins in Redbridge during the period in which the court found they were ordinarily resident there."

Cornwall Council, R. (on the application of) v Wiltshire Council (Rev 1) [2012] EWHC 3739 (Admin).

"37. In my judgment, the dicta of Lord Scarman in Shah's case explained clearly the rationale for implying a requirement of lawfulness into the residence upon which 'ordinary residence' is based. There is no need to amplify what Lord Scarman said. It is that understanding of the words used in this area of legislation and that rationale which has been accepted as implicit in successive regulations. When the draftsman used those words in the 2009 Regulations he must, to my mind, be taken as having intended to import that settled understanding of the phrase 'ordinarily resident'. There was no need, in my view, to make the express provision which, perhaps wisely in the light of the arguments in this case, was inserted into the Regulations by the 2012 Amendment Regulations."

Arogundade, R. (on the application of) v Secretary of State for Business, Innovation and Skills [2013] EWCA Civ 823.

"'Ordinary residence' is an expression used historically in a number of statutes. It is not, however, a legal term of art (see Lord Scarman in *Reg. v Barnet LBC, ex. p. Shah* [1983] 2 A.C. 309 at 340). On the contrary, when it has fallen to be considered by the courts, they have sought to ascertain and elucidate the natural and ordinary meaning of the words, subject only to any variation or overtone which might be required by the context in which they were found: *ex p. Shah* at 340. That is little different from the approach required where the words (or the adjectival 'ordinarily resident') are included in a contract, and the authoritative judicial statements as to their natural and ordinary meaning thus provide, as the parties recognised in their submissions before me, important assistance in the present case."
Rai v Legal & General Assurance Society Ltd [2015] EWHC 170 (Comm).

ORGANISED CRIME GROUP. Stat. Def., Serious Crime Act 2015 s.45.

OUTCOME.
"'Outcome' is an ordinary word, an unpretentious and unsophisticated member of the English language. Purely in the abstract, one can readily conceive of several synonyms for the word 'outcome'—consequence, score, upshot, result and end product being prominent examples. While mindful of the importance of a contextualised approach, I observe that this simple exercise lends some weight to the Plaintiff's case, since none of these synonyms would be conventionally considered a precise equivalent. I accept that, in an imperfect world, there is no objective gold standard of clarity to be applied by the court in determining this issue. Ultimately, I consider the question to be one of degree: objectively, is the meaning of Selection Criterion No. 1 sufficiently clear? Would all reasonably well informed and normally diligent tenderers have construed it uniformly? On balance, I resolve this issue in the Plaintiff's favour. I conclude that, in this context, the Department's expectation that compliance with this criterion would require the provision by all bidders of data relating to achievements, success rates and destinations into positive outcomes arising out of previously delivered programmes is expressed with insufficient clarity in the criterion as a whole and in the word 'outcomes' in particular. I further reject the Department's claim that the word 'outcomes' has a well recognised meaning in the industry concerned. Mr. McVeigh's claim to this effect was, ultimately, bare and unsupported assertion. I find that it is unsubstantiated and is confounded by several aspects of the evidence: the Department's briefing publication (paragraph [5], supra); the terms of the equivalent selection criterion in two other comparable selection exercises; the formulation of an earlier draft of Selection Criterion No. 1; the extensive internal debate amongst four presumed experts generated by this aspect of the Plaintiff's tender; the detailed and elaborate terms in which the Department has seen necessary to explain and define the word 'outcomes' in this context; and the panel's need to resort to CPD for advice on the discrete issue of whether it could properly reject the Plaintiff's tender

for non-compliance with this criterion. The phraseology of this criterion, in my view, gave rise to an unacceptable degree of doubt and uncertainty. While I take into the evidence bearing on this issue in its totality and acknowledge that there are factors pointing in both directions, the balancing exercise which I have performed clearly favours this conclusion for the reasons explained. To summarise, Selection Criterion No. 1 fails the test of sufficient clarity."
Clinton (t/a Oriel Training Services) v Department for Employment & Learning [2012] NIQB 2.

OVERAGE. For discussion of the meaning of "overage" see *BP Oil International Ltd v Target Shipping Ltd* [2013] EWCA Civ 196.

OWNER. Stat. Def., "in relation to any land, means the person who has right to the land whether or not such person has completed title (and, where more than one person comes within that description, the person who most recently acquired that right)" (Long Leases (Scotland) Act 2012 s.80).

Stat. Def. (in relation to land in Scotland), Regulatory Reform (Scotland) Act 2014 s.34. Stat. Def. (in Northern Ireland), Local Government Act (Northern Ireland) 2014 s.126.

PAEDOPHILE MANUAL. Stat. Def. (implicit), Serious Crime Act 2015 s.69.

PARENT. For discussion of the modern concept of parenthood see *AB v CD* [2013] EWHC 1418 (Fam).

PARTICIPATE. For the meaning of the concept of participation in medical treatment in the context of abortion see *Doogan, Re Judicial Review* [2012] ScotCS CSOH 32.

PARTNER.
"45. The words 'employee' and 'partner' are legal terms with a fairly clear meaning describing legal concepts. The strictness of the meaning of 'employee' and of the reference to 'working . . . fulltime' is only emphasised by the proviso which refers to the case of a person undergoing agricultural training. I do not see it as appropriate to read the word 'employee' in a broad way or to read the word 'partner' so as to extend to a sole trader in a different business to that apparently described by the sub-clause."
Creasey v Sole [2013] EWHC 1410 (Ch).

PATHOGEN. Stat. Def., "an organism that causes or contributes to the development of a disease" (Aquaculture and Fisheries (Scotland) Act 2013 s.63).

PATIENT.
"28. The question whether or not someone is 'a patient' is prosaic rather than sophisticated. It does not turn on fine definitions. The answer depends on the factual evidence, i.e. how the actors said to be in a 'clinician-patient' relationship conducted themselves and the view taken by the fact-finding tribunal of the documentary and witness evidence as a whole.

29. There is no suggestion that the HCPC Panel convened in the present case (see above) was inexperienced or not perfectly well able to recognise a 'clinician-patient' relationship when they saw one. The definition test of 'a patient' proffered by Mr Garnham QC, namely 'a person receiving clinical treatment', merely states the obvious. There was no need for the Panel to state the obvious. Their task was to spot the elephant rather than spend time trying to describe it."
Levett v The Health And Care Professions Council ("The HCPC") [2014] EWHC 994 (Admin).

PAYMENT.
"Against the foregoing factual background, I am clearly of opinion that the transfer of shares in a money box company to an employee was a 'payment' within the meaning of section 203(1) of the Taxes Act. The word 'payment' is not defined for the purposes of section 203. It seems clear that the word has no single settled meaning but takes its colour from the context in which it is found: *Garforth v Newsmith Stainless Ltd*, 1978, 52 TC 522, at 528 per Walton J, following Jenkins LJ in *Re Vestey's Settlement*, [1951] Ch 209, at 222. In the construction of tax legislation, in particular, it has been emphasized that payment is a practical commercial concept: *DTE Financial Services Ltd v Wilson*, [2001] EWCA Civ 455, at paragraph 42 per Jonathan Parker LJ. In the latter case it was further pointed out that for the purposes of the PAYE system payment ordinarily means actual payment, in the form of a transfer of cash or its equivalent. For this purpose, the notion of an equivalent of cash may be important."
Aberdeen Asset Management Plc v HM Revenue and Customs [2013] ScotCS CSIH 84.

PAYMENT SYSTEM. Stat. Def., Financial Services (Banking Reform) Act 2013 s.41.

PEER. Stat. Def., House of Lords Reform Act 2014 s.6.

PENALTY.
"47. That discussion makes clear that the notion of 'penalty' in Article 7(1) [of the European Convention on Human Rights] has an autonomous meaning. The starting point in determining whether something is a penalty is whether the measure in question is imposed following conviction for a criminal offence. Significantly, there is a distinction to be drawn between a measure that constitutes in substance a 'penalty' and a measure that concerns the 'execution' or 'enforcement' of the 'penalty'. At paragraph 98 the Court concluded that where the nature and purpose of the measure relates to the remission of a sentence or a change in a regime for early release, this does not form part of the 'penalty' within the meaning of Article 7(1)."
Hall v Parole Board of England & Wales [2015] EWHC 252 (Admin).

PENSION. See NORMAL PENSION AGE.

PENSION BUSINESS. Stat. Def., Finance Act 2012 s.58.

PENSIONS PROMISE. Stat. Def., Pension Schemes Act 2015 s.5.

PERSON WHO PUBLISHES.
"1. Is a newspaper editor a person who publishes the contents of the newspaper? Most media law specialists would be likely to respond to the question with puzzlement. In civil claims for libel or misuse of private

information editors are often sued as publishers of articles that are com-
plained of. The law attributes responsibility for what is published to a wide
variety of those involved in the process, and editors are usually involved
enough for responsibility to attach. In this appeal by case stated, however,
the question arises in the context of a criminal charge of contravening a
reporting restriction imposed under s.39 of the Children & Young Persons
Act 1933. The issue is whether Parliament intended when enacting s.39
that a newspaper editor should be exposed to criminal liability under the
section. . . .

40. In my judgment the natural, ordinary and most obvious interpretation of the phrase 'any person who publishes' is that it refers to any person,
natural or legal, who takes such a part in the process of publishing the
matter that contravenes the direction or prohibition that it can properly be
said of them that they 'publish' the matter. As a matter of practice, and
using language in its ordinary sense, the commercial publisher of the newspaper will invariably be one such person, but it does not by any means
follow that such a publisher is the only person who will qualify. Nor does
the wording used in the subsection so indicate. On the contrary, in my view
it is a natural and not a forced reading of the expression 'any person who
publishes' to regard it as encompassing others responsible for bringing
about the publication of the particular matter in question, including
(assuming the particular facts of the case justify this conclusion) the editor
in charge of the newspaper at the relevant time, and the journalist who
wrote the matter. . . .

51. I have asked myself whether there might be a meaningful distinction
to be drawn between holding a person responsible for publication and
describing them as a 'person who publishes'. However, I do not consider
that there is any such distinction, in this legal context. In my judgment it is
clear that principles of common law which were long-established by 1933
held that editors and, I would add, proprietors were within the range of
persons responsible for the publication of what appeared in their newspapers, and who would aptly be described as persons who published such
content. . . .

68. For the reasons I have given, my answer to the question posed by the
case stated is that the editor of a newspaper does not as a matter of law fall
outside the scope of the expression 'any person who publishes' in s.39(2) of
the 1933 Act. I put it that way because, in contrast to most of the other
statutory provisions we have examined in the course of this case, the 1933
Act does not deem an editor to be guilty of an offence if his newspaper
publishes in contravention of its provisions. To make out the offence under
s.39 against any person the prosecution would need to prove so that the
magistrates were sure that the defendant's conduct on the particular occasion was such that he published the matter that creates the contravention."

Aitken v Director of Public Prosecutions [2015] EWHC 1079 (Admin).

PERSONAL CHATTELS. Stat. Def., Administration of Estates Act 1925 s.55(1)(x) amended by Inheritance and Trustees' Powers Act 2014 s.3.

PERSONAL INJURY. Stat. Def., "Includes any impairment of a person's physical or mental condition" (Energy Act 2013 s.112).

PERSONAL OR OTHER RELATIONSHIP.

"21. The question raised by the first issue is whether the alleged conduct of which complaint is made in these proceedings is conduct to which Part II of RIPA applies, on the footing that the conduct is the establishing and maintaining of a 'personal or other relationship' within the meaning of section 26(8)(a) [of the Regulation of Investigatory Powers Act 2000]. If an intimate sexual relationship is not a personal or other relationship, the IPT has no jurisdiction to entertain the human rights claims and they must, therefore, be determined by the court. What is meant by 'personal or other relationship'? These are ordinary words. A personal relationship is a relationship between persons. As a matter of ordinary language, a sexual relationship is an example of such a relationship. At first sight, it seems obvious that the IPT has jurisdiction to deal with the human rights claims. We must therefore examine the reasons given by Ms Kaufmann as to why a personal or other relationship does not include an intimate sexual relationship. . . . The phrase 'personal or other relationship' in section 26(8)(a) forms part of the definition of the type of conduct which can be authorised under section 27 and which, if it is carried out in 'challengeable circumstances', may be the subject of human rights proceedings before the IPT under section 65. In its plain and ordinary meaning, it includes intimate sexual relationships. In the principle of legality cases, there was a general power which was capable of being used for many purposes. There was doubt as to whether Parliament intended that it should be capable of being used so as to override fundamental rights. In the present context, there is no doubt that, in enacting RIPA, Parliament intended to override fundamental human rights subject to certain protections. Most pertinently, these include the requirement for necessity and proportionality. It can fairly be said that Parliament may not have foreseen in precisely what way those human rights might be overridden and there is certainly nothing to suggest that Parliament contemplated that surveillance by a CHIS might be conducted by using the extraordinary techniques that are alleged to have been used in the present case. But none of that matters. To give 'personal or other relationships' its ordinary meaning so as to include intimate sexual relationships does not produce any startling or unreasonable consequences which Parliament cannot have intended. That is why we do not consider that the principle of legality requires the words to be given a narrower meaning than they naturally bear."

AJA v Commissioner of Police for the Metropolis [2013] EWCA Civ 1342.

PERSONAL SERVICE. See SERVICE.

PETITION OFFICER. Stat. Def., Recall of MPs Act 2015 s.22.

PLAGIARISM. For discussion of what amounts to plagiarism see *Mustafa, R. (on the application of) v The Office of the Independent Adjudicator for Higher Education* [2013] EWHC 1379 (Admin).

PLAN.
"The words 'plan' and 'project' are not defined within the 2010 Regulations, nor are they defined in the Habitats Directive. However, there was no dispute between the parties that a 'project' concerns a concrete proposal whilst a 'plan' is something at a more general level. That is consistent with the approach in ODPM Circular 06/2005 (Biodiversity and Geological Conservation—Statutory Obligations and their Impact within the Planning System) concerned with earlier regulations (the Habitats Regulations 1994). 'Other projects' extended beyond those requiring planning permission to 'a current application for any kind of authorisation, permission, licence or other consent' (see paragraphs 14 and 16)."
Forest of Dean Friends of the Earth v Forest of Dean District Council [2014] EWHC 1353 (Admin).

PLANT AND MACHINERY. For discussion of the history and application of the phrase "plant and machinery" see *HM Revenue and Customs v The Executors of Lord Howard of Henderskelfe* [2014] EWCA Civ 278.

POINT OF LAW.
"18. Section 289(2) enables the Claimant to appeal against the Inspector's decision but only on a 'point of law'. Essentially that expression embraces established public law grounds of challenge (*Ashbridge v Minister of Housing and Local Government* [1965] 1 WLR 1320, 1326)."
Distinctive Properties (Ascot) Ltd v Secretary of State for Communities and Local Government [2015] EWHC 729 (Admin).

POLICE FORCE. Stat. Def., Crime and Courts Act 2013 s.16.

POLICIES FOR THE SUPPLY OF HOUSING.
"51. The natural meaning of the words 'policies for the supply of housing' is policies which make provision for housing. There are many such policies in local plans. Paragraph 49 could have been worded so as to read 'policies which may restrict housing development' or 'policies affecting housing development' in which case it would have been broader in scope. The adjective 'relevant' is attached to the word 'policies', and means policies which are relevant to the site in question. It does not have the meaning suggested to me in court, namely, policies 'relevant to the supply of housing'. That is an impermissible re-writing of the sentence."
Cheshire East Borough Council v Secretary of State for Communities and Local Government [2015] EWHC 410 (Admin).

POLICING BODY. Stat. Def., Crime and Courts Act 2013 s.16.

POLITICAL EXPRESSION.
"The protection goes to 'political expression'; but that is a broad concept
in this context. It is not limited to expressions of or critiques of political
views (*Calver* at [79]), but rather extends to all matters of public administration and public concern including comments about the adequacy or
inadequacy of performance of public duties by others (*Thorgeirson* at [64]:
see also *Calver* at [64] and the academic references referred to therein). The
cases are careful not unduly to restrict the concept; although gratuitous
personal comments do not fall within it."
Heesom v Public Services Ombudsman for Wales [2014] EWHC 1504
(Admin).

POSSESSION.
"The expression 'possession and control' indicates that the individuals
concerned needed to have had 'actual control of the goods' (or possession
of them), the test applied by the Court of Appeal in *R v Kousar* [2009]
EWCA Crim 139; [2009] 2 Cr.App.R. 5. Although that case concerned
'possession, custody or control' of an item by a principal for the purposes
of the Trade Marks Act 1994 in the context of a marriage, it is to be noted
that the Court of Appeal expressly disavowed the suggestion that an 'ability to control' was sufficient to establish liability, certainly in the context of
that case."
Montague, R. v [2013] EWCA Crim 1781.

"49. It was common ground that concluded contracts could be a possession for the purposes of A1P1. The most authoritative guidance on that
topic is the decision of the Court of Appeal in *Murungaru v Secretary of
State for the Home Department* [2008] EWCA Civ. 1015. There, the Court
of Appeal dismissed the claimant's claim that his contract with a private
health provider for medical treatment in England was a possession protected by A1P1. In the judgment of Lewison J (as he then was) the court
made plain that, in certain circumstances, contractual rights could
amount to possessions under A1P1. He said:
   '48. The Strasbourg jurisprudence establishes that the mere fact that
   rights are contractual does not disqualify them from counting as property or possessions . . . But the converse: viz. that all contractual rights
   are property or possessions, does not follow. Mr Rabinder Singh QC
   accepted that the logic of his argument entailed that conclusion.
   49. As Mr Rabinder Singh QC pointed out, a claim may count as a
   possession even though no court has yet adjudicated on its validity. But
   a claim justiciable in domestic law can amount to a possession for the
   purposes of A1 P1 only if it is sufficiently established to be enforceable.
   By contrast, a claim may amount to an assignable chose in action in
   domestic law, even if it is not established. Indeed it may be a speculative

claim, but it would still be classified, domestically, as a chose in action. In my judgment this demonstrates that there is no necessary coincidence between the autonomous Convention concept of property or possessions and the domestic concept of property . . .

58. In the present case, Dr Murungaru's contractual rights have none of the indicia of possessions. They are intangible; they are not assignable; they are not even transmissible; they are not realisable and they have no present economic value. They cannot realistically be described as an "asset". That is the touchstone of whether something counts as a possession for the purposes of A1 P1. In my judgment Dr Murungaru's contractual rights do not.'

50. The other authority principally relied on in this connection was the decision of the ECtHR in *Paeffgen GmbH v Germany* [AP 25379/04, Decision 18/09/07]. There, the applicant company had registered thousands of domain names and concluded contracts with the registration authority which granted them exclusive use of those names. In Germany the courts had allowed claims by those with the proper title to use those domain names. The applicant company brought a claim under A1P1. The ECtHR said:

'In the instant case, the contracts with the registration authority gave the applicant company, in exchange for paying the domain fees, an open-ended right to use or transfer the domains registered in its name. As a consequence, the applicant could offer to all internet users entering the domain name in question, for example, advertisements, information or services, possibly in exchange for money, or could sell the right to use the domain to a third party. The exclusive right to use the domains in question thus had an economic value. Having regard to the above criteria, this right therefore constituted a "possession", which the court decisions prohibiting the use of the domains interfered with.'

The court then went on to reject the underlying claims on the basis that any interference with the possessions represented by the contracts with the registration authority was justified.

51. On the basis of the Assumed Facts, it would seem that the concluded contracts in this case (examples of which I have set out in paragraph 48 above) had all of the indicia of possessions in accordance with Lewison J's analysis in *Murungaru*. They were tangible; they were assignable; on the face of it they had a present economic value. Of course I accept that, if there are arguments about particular contracts, those can only be dealt with on the facts but, as a matter of general impression, I would conclude that the signed/concluded contracts in this case were assets, and therefore possessions under A1P1."

Breyer Group Plc v Department of Energy and Climate Change [2014] EWHC 2257 (QB).

"On several occasions the European Court of Human Rights has held that a person's right to live in a particular property which he does not own does not, in itself, constitute a 'possession' (see, for example, *Kukalo v Russia, Application no. 63995/00*; *H.F. v Slovakia, Application no. 54797/00*; *Kovalenok v Latvia, Application no. 54264/00*; and *J.L.S. v Spain, Application no. 41917/98*). But even if the claimants were able to say that their licences to station caravans on pitches on the Eleanor Street site should be regarded as 'possessions' within article 1 of the First Protocol, I cannot see how they could say that such 'possessions' were in any way affected by the operation of section 33(2)."

Mahoney, R. (on the application of) v Secretary of State for Communities and Local Government [2015] EWHC 589 (Admin).

"23. The following principles can be extracted from the case law: (i) loss of future income is not a possession protected by A1P1; (ii) loss of marketable goodwill may be a possession protected by A1P1; (iii) a number of factors may point towards the loss being goodwill rather than the capacity to earn future profits: these include marketability and whether the accounts and arrangements of the claimant are organised in such a way as to allow for future cash flows to be capitalised; (iv) goodwill may be a possession if it has been built up in the past and has a present day value (as distinct from something which is only referable to events which may or may not happen in the future): and thus (v) if there is interference which causes a loss of marketable goodwill at the time of the interference, and if that can be capitalised, then it is prima facie protected by A1P1. . . .

43. The well-established distinction between goodwill and future income is fundamental to the Strasbourg jurisprudence. The consistent line taken by the ECtHR is that the goodwill of a business, at any rate if it has a marketable value, may count as a possession within the meaning of A1P1, but the right to a future income stream does not. I agree with Rix LJ that the distinction is not always easy to apply and it seems that the ECtHR has not addressed the difficulties. . . .

49. As I have said, the distinction between goodwill and loss of future income is not always easy to apply. But in my view, the judge was right to see a clear line separating: (i) possible future contracts and (ii) existing enforceable contracts. Contracts which have been secured may be said to be part of the goodwill of a business because they are the product of its past work. Contracts which a business hopes to secure in the future are no more than that."

Department for Energy and Climate Change v Breyer Group Plc [2015] EWCA Civ 408.

POWER OF ENTRY. Stat. Def., Protection of Freedoms Act 2012 s.46.

PRACTICABLE.
"In my judgment, it was not 'practicable' (within the meaning of section 15(6)(b)) to specify the items within the computers and mobile telephones

to which the search under section 8 Police and Criminal Evidence Act 1984 related. As Simon J observed in *Glenn* at [63]:

'the question of where the balance lines in an individual case will not be answered by reference to authority, since each case is likely to turn on particular facts. It will be answered by considering whether the warrant has identified the articles sought "so far as practicable" in the circumstances.'

It was not feasible to provide greater specificity in this case, and it was unrealistic to expect the officers to take away any relevant material from a computer (or other storage device) in paper form or on memory sticks. Furthermore, for the reasons set out above, I am unable to accept Mr Jones's contention that it is impermissible to order the seizure of electronic storage devices or their contents in circumstances such as these without invoking sections 19 or 20 of the Police and Criminal Evidence Act 1984 or section 50 Criminal Justice and Police Act 2001, and the protections provided thereunder. Finally, I reject the submission that the expression 'cash representing the proceeds of criminal activity' failed to identify, so far as is practicable, the articles sought or that it should only have been seized under the powers contained in section 19(2) Police and Criminal Evidence Act 1984."

Cabot Global Ltd v Barkingside Magistrates' Court [2015] EWHC 1458 (Admin).

PREMISES.

"I am quite unable to say that in using the word 'premises' rather than 'house' the parties have made a clear mistake. Nor do I accept that the clause in its present form is commercially nonsensical."

Campbell v Daejan Properties Ltd [2012] EWCA Civ 1503.

Stat. Def., Protection of Freedoms Act 2012 s.46.

Stat. Def., "Includes any land or other place (whether enclosed or not), and any outbuildings that are, or are used as, part of premises" (Anti-social Behaviour, Crime and Policing Act 2014 s.92).

Stat. Def., "Includes land, buildings, moveable structures, vehicles and vessels" (Immigration Act 2014 s.37).

Stat. Def., "includes any place and any vehicle, vessel, stall or moveable structure" (Tobacco Retailers Act (Northern Ireland) 2014 s.22). "Includes any place other than a public area, and any stall, moveable structure, vehicle or vessel" (Licensing of Pavement Cafés (Northern Ireland) Act 2014 s.30).

Stat. Def. (very wide), Serious Crime Act 2015 s.65.

PREMISES (RELIGIOUS). Stat. Def., "premises which are used solely or mainly for religious purposes, or have been so used and have not subsequently been used solely or mainly for other purposes" (Marriage and Civil Partnership (Scotland) Act 2014 s.21).

PRESCRIBED BY LAW. For illustrative analysis of what amounts to a scheme "prescribed by law" see *Gallastegui, R. (on the application of) v Westminster City Council* [2013] EWCA Civ 28.

> "56. Any interference will be prescribed by law where it has a basis in national law, the law is accessible and it is formulated with sufficient precision to enable an individual to foresee, to a degree that is reasonable in the circumstances, when the law will or might be applied: *Sunday Times v UK* (1979) 2 EHRR 245 at paras 47 and 49."

Core Issues Trust, R. (on the application of) v Secretary of State for Culture, Media and Sport and Minister for Women and Equalities [2014] EWCA Civ 34.

PRIMARY LEGISLATION. Stat. Def., Welfare Reform Act 2012 s.39; Public Service Pensions Act 2013 s.37.

Stat. Def. (in context of Northern Ireland), "Northern Ireland legislation or any provision of an Act of Parliament of the United Kingdom that would be within the legislative competence of the Assembly were that provision contained in an Act of the Assembly" (Public Service Pensions Act (Northern Ireland) 2014 s.34).

PRIORITY. *The reference to Dependent should be to Dependant.*

PRIVATE LEGAL INSTRUMENT. Stat. Def., Marriage (Same Sex Couples) Act 2013 Sch.4.

PRIVATE PERSON. For discussion of the concept of 'private person' in the context of the Financial Services and Markets Act 2000 s.150 see *Bailey v Barclays Bank Plc* [2014] EWHC 2882 (QB).

PROCEEDING.
> "The question to the opinion of the High Court is: were we correct in law to interpret the words 'proceeding in the same direction' as used in regulation 24(1)(a) of the Zebra, Pelican and Puffin Pedestrian Crossing Regulation 1997 to include a vehicle which was stationary whilst waiting in a queue of standing traffic. . . . This question should be answered 'no'. The magistrates were not correct in law to interpret the words of regulation 24(1)(a) in that manner. A stationary vehicle is not a vehicle 'proceeding' in the same direction."

Brooks v Blackpool Borough Council [2013] EWHC 3735 (Admin).

PROCEEDINGS.
"The word 'proceedings' is a word apt to cover all issues raised in legal proceedings and is a term with a meaning wider than simply the claims being brought by a claimant (or, indeed, the claims being brought by any party) in those proceedings. It is a term which includes defences raised in the proceedings as well. The width of the concept of 'proceedings' in the context of the UK proceedings and the US proceedings is reinforced by the terms of clause 1.1, which make it clear that the UK proceedings and US proceedings may include a significant number of claims beyond simply the claims made by the Claimant against the Defendant. In my view, it is also reinforced by clause 6.1 relating to disposal of the proceedings and the terms of the consent order annexed to the Settlement Agreement, which in paragraph 1 refers to 'all further proceedings in this action' being stayed, i.e. covering all aspects of the issues in dispute in the litigation between the parties."
Stretchline v H&M (UK) [2014] EWHC 3605 (Ch).

PROCUREMENT (DEFENCE). Stat. Def., Defence Reform Act 2014 s.1.

PROHIBITIVELY EXPENSIVE.
"It is my view that 'prohibitively expensive' can only be construed in relevant terms. What may be prohibitively expensive to one person who is in receipt of the minimum wage will not be so to another person who earns a six figure salary. I also consider that account should be taken of the difference between someone who brings an application such as Mr Garner in *R (Garner) v Elmbridge BC* (2011) Env LR 10 for entirely altruistic reasons and in the public interest and someone who is motivated primarily by private interest, although the application may have the necessary public interest dimension. Also the approach to Government departments funded by the taxpayer will be necessarily different to commercial organisations dependant on private finance and individuals who have to rely on their own resources."
The Alternative A5 Alliance, Re Judicial Review [2012] NIQB 97.

PROJECT.
"The words 'plan' and 'project' are not defined within the 2010 Regulations, nor are they defined in the Habitats Directive. However, there was no dispute between the parties that a 'project' concerns a concrete proposal whilst a 'plan' is something at a more general level. That is consistent with the approach in ODPM Circular 06/2005 (Biodiversity and Geological Conservation—Statutory Obligations and their Impact within the Planning System) concerned with earlier regulations (the Habitats Regulations 1994). 'Other projects' extended beyond those requiring planning

permission to 'a current application for any kind of authorisation, permission, licence or other consent' (see paragraphs 14 and 16)."
Forest of Dean Friends of the Earth v Forest of Dean District Council [2014] EWHC 1353 (Admin).

PROMOTE.

"The word 'promote' may carry various shades of meaning. Mr. Shepherd submitted that it is used here in the general sense of 'advance' and is apt to cover any steps designed to lead to the growth of Jet2's business. Mr. Leggatt submitted that it has the narrower meaning of 'market' and points to the use of the expressions 'promotional facilities', 'promotions' and 'promoting' in clauses 2(c) and (d), both of which are concerned with advertising and marketing. He submitted that the parties are likely to have used the word in the same sense in clause 1. I am not particularly impressed by the argument from consistency of use. This was a document apparently drafted by the parties themselves, probably without the benefit of legal advice. Clause 1 is worded in broad terms, as Mr. Leggatt often reminded us, and was intended to express the parties' intentions on a broad scale. In those circumstances I do not think that the narrower meaning of the word is to be preferred. The fact that the same or similar words are used in a narrower sense in the context of the more specific provisions of clauses 2(c) and (d) does not point strongly to an intention to adopt the same narrower meaning in the rather different context of clause 1. Although clause 1 no doubt looks forward to clause 2, its horizons are in my view much wider. I think the judge was right in his construction of the word 'promote' and that in this instance it bears the broader meaning of 'advance'."
Jet2.com Ltd v Blackpool Airport Ltd [2012] EWCA Civ 417.

PROOF.

"20. 'Proving' a debt is a technical term in the Insolvency Rules. It is dealt with by rule 4.73. In the case of a winding up by the court 'a person claiming to be a creditor of the company and wishing to recover his debt in whole or in part' must submit his claim in writing to the liquidator. In the case of a voluntary winding up the liquidator may require 'a person claiming to be a creditor of the company and wishing to recover his debt in whole or in part' to submit his claim in writing. Rule 4.73(3) says:

'A creditor who claims (whether or not in writing) is referred to as "proving" his debt; and a document by which he seeks to establish his claim is his "proof".'"
Joint Administrators of LB Holdings Intermediate 2 Ltd v Lehman Brothers Holdings Inc [2015] EWCA Civ 485.

PROPERTY.

"Applying the test enunciated by Lord Wilberforce in *NPB v Ainsworth*, in my judgment, an EUA [European Union Allowance] is 'property' at common law. It is definable, as being the sum total of rights and entitlements conferred on the holder pursuant to the ETS. It is identifiable by third parties; it has a unique reference number. It is capable of assumption by third parties, as under the ETS, an EUA is transferable. It has permanence and stability, since it continues to exist in a registry account until it is transferred out either for submission or sale and is capable of subsisting from year to year. . . . Thus in my judgment, applying the three fold test identified by Morritt L.J. in *In re Celtic Extraction* leads to the conclusion that an EUA is certainly 'property' and intangible property under the statutory definition there in place. First, there is, here, a statutory framework which confers an entitlement on the holder of an EUA to exemption from a fine. Secondly, the EUA is an exemption which is transferable, and expressly so, under the statutory framework. Thirdly the EUA is an exemption which has value: see paragraph 49 above. Whilst the cited case law concerned the meaning of 'property' as specifically defined in various statutes, in my judgment, the reasoning of Morritt L.J. applies equally to the characteristics of property at common law. Indeed, Morritt L.J. himself relied upon *National Provincial Bank v Ainsworth*. Moreover the terms used in statutory definitions are themselves derived from common law concepts—for example in *In re Celtic*, the s.436 statutory definition refers to 'things in action' and 'every description of property'; the meaning of these terms, in turn, must be derived from the common law notion of 'property'. Further, applying the reasoning of Jacob J. in *Swift v Dairywise*, an EUA is also capable of forming the subject matter of a trust and thus something in which equitable ownership can be held. There is a close analogy between the exemption conferred by milk quota and the exemption conferred by an EUA. Accordingly an EUA constitutes 'property' and it is 'intangible property'. The final issue here is whether an EUA is to be regarded as a 'chose in action' or, instead, some form of other intangible property. Armstrong suggests it may be a 'chose in action'; Winnington contends strongly that it cannot be a chose in action. On the one hand, in *Nai-Keung*, the Privy Council concluded that the quota there was not a chose in action, but rather fell within the term 'other intangible property' as that term appeared in the statutory definition in that case. On the other hand, in *In re Celtic Extraction*, the statutory definition in question did not have such an additional category of property, but was confined to 'things in action' and 'every description of property'. Morritt L.J. did not specify into which of these two categories the waste management licence fell. In my judgment, strictly an EUA is not a chose in action in the narrow sense, as it cannot be claimed or enforced by action. However to the extent that the concept encompasses wider matters of property, then it could be so described. For reasons set out below, ultimately I do not consider that it matters whether an EUA is a chose in action or merely some form of 'other intangible property'."

Armstrong DLW GmbH v Winnington Networks Ltd [2012] EWHC 10 (Ch).

"47. Everybody knows that 'property' differentiates between things that are mine and things that are not mine. The law lays down criteria for determining the boundary between, on the one hand, those rights that are only enforceable against particular persons and, on the other hand, those rights attaching to things that are capable of being vindicated against the whole world. The claim to property in intangible information presents obvious definitional difficulties, having regard to the criteria of certainty, exclusivity, control and assignability that normally characterise property rights and distinguish them from personal rights."
Fairstar Heavy Transport NV v Adkins [2013] EWCA Civ 886.

PROPORTIONALITY.

"166. It is in my view a mistake to approach proportionality as a test under the Human Rights Act which is insensitive to considerations of institutional competence and legitimacy. The qualifying objectives reflected in article 8.2 of the Convention can engage responsibilities normally attaching in the first instance to other branches of the state, whether the executive or the legislature. When considering whether a particular measure is necessary and all the more when considering whether it is justified on a balancing of competing and often incommensurate interests, courts should recognise that there can still be wisdom and relevance in the factors mentioned in the preceding two paragraphs. This is all the more so when the court is considering the scope of the Convention rights, as enacted domestically, in a situation, like the present, which the European Court of Human Rights has held to fall within the United Kingdom's international margin of appreciation. That Parliament has regularly addressed the general area and is still actively engaged in considering associated issues in the context of Lord Falconer's Assisted Dying Bill 2013 underlines the significance of the point. This does not mean that there is a legal rule that courts will not intervene (as to which see Lord Steyn, extra-judicially in *Deference: A Tangled Story*, [2005] PL 345, commenting on *R. (ProLife Alliance) v British Broadcasting Corp* [2003] UKHL 23, [2004] 1 AC 185, paras 74–77 per Lord Hoffmann) or that the courts have no role. It means merely that some judgments on issues such as the comparative acceptability of differing disadvantages, risks and benefits have to be and are made by those other branches of the state in the performance of their everyday roles, and that courts cannot and should not act, and do not have the competence to act, as a primary decision-maker in every situation. Proportionality should in this respect be seen as a flexible doctrine."
Nicklinson R. (on the application of) (Rev 1) [2014] UKSC 38.

PROPORTIONATE.

"Proportionality requires that the measure is both 'appropriate' ('suitable') to secure the objective and 'necessary' as a means of doing so. A measure is suitable only if it genuinely reflects a concern to attain the objective in a consistent and systematic manner (*Commission v Austria*, no. C–28/09, 21 December 2011, paras 125–126). The court accepts that a measure cannot be necessary if there is an alternative which has a less restrictive effect on intra-European Union trade. In both respects, the court does not agree that the test for a successful challenge to a measure which infringes article 34 is that it requires to be 'manifestly inappropriate' to attain the objective. The court does not therefore accept that the level of judicial scrutiny can be described as 'low'. The ECJ is clear in its requirement that the member state demonstrate that the measure is proportionate; that is to say appropriate and necessary in the manner already described. The court accepts the petitioners' submission that 'manifestly inappropriate' is language used by the ECJ in relation to testing European Union institution measures (or national measures implementing EU law) (see e.g. *R v Secretary of State for Health ex parte British American Tobacco (Investments)* [2002] ECR I–11453, para.123). There the balance is between private and public interests. It is not applicable when testing the legitimacy of state measures against fundamental principles contained in the EU Treaties where the balance is between EU and state interests (see generally Tridimas, *General Principles of EU Law*, (2nd edn), pp. 137–138)."

Collis v The Lord Advocate [2012] ScotCS CSIH 80.

PROPOSAL.

"The word 'proposal' is defined in the *Oxford English Dictionary* as 'a putting forward of something for acceptance'; the verb 'propose' is defined as 'to put forward for acceptance'.

[49] Thus in our opinion, the language chosen by Parliament is significant. If not called in, a 'proposal' is converted to a workable decision (i.e. a decision that can be proceeded with) by the passage of six weeks and the specific statutory provision: section 15(6) and (7). But if the proposal is called in, all action on the part of the Council must be suspended (despite their earlier decision to implement the proposal in terms of section 15(1) and (3)). The proposal can only become a workable decision (i.e. a decision that can be proceeded with) as and when the Ministers choose to make it so: section 16(2)–(4). Thus in our opinion the Ministers are not, in terms of the statute, mere checkers of procedural aspects leading to a decision; rather they are part of the decision-making process itself."

Comhairle Nan Eilean Siar (Constituted As The Western Islands Council) v The Scottish Ministers [2013] ScotCS CSIH 6.

PROPRIETARY TRADING.   Stat. Def., Financial Services (Banking Reform) Act 2013 s.11.

PROSECUTOR.

"I would answer these questions by saying that the phrase 'the prosecutor' in section 31 of the [Animal Welfare Act 2006] is not limited to prosecutors

who prosecute pursuant to a power conferred by some statutory provision but applies to anyone who initiates a prosecution under the Act."
Lamont-Perkins v Royal Society for the Prevention of Cruelty to Animals (RSPCA) [2012] EWHC 1002 (Admin).

PUB. See TIED PUB.

PUBLIC AREA. Stat. Def., "a place in the open air to which the public has access, without payment, as of right, and which is not in a market area," Licensing of Pavement Cafés (Northern Ireland) Act 2014 s.1.

PUBLIC AUTHORITY. Stat. Def., Public Service Pensions Act 2013 s.37.

"219. The Defendants contend that section 6(3)(b) applies to the Claimant, on the bases that (a) it provides housing in the public sector (and in this case granted the Defendants a tenancy after a referral from the local housing authority and further to an arrangement between the Claimant and that authority) and (b) its functions are of a public nature.

220. The Defendants rely especially on *R. (Weaver) v London and Quadrant Housing Trust* [2010] 1 WLR 363. There, the Court of Appeal explained that in determining whether a body is a public authority there is 'no single test of universal application' (per Lord Nicholls in *Aston Cantlow and Wilmcote with Billesley Parochial Church Council v Wallbank* [2003] UKHL 37; [2004] 1 AC 546) and the courts should adopt what Lord Mance in *YL v Birmingham City Council (Secretary of State for Constitutional Affairs intervening)* [2007] UKHL 27; [2008] AC 95 described as a 'factor-based approach'. . . .

222. It is of course correct that the Claimant provides social housing. But that is not, in isolation, sufficient (and see per Elias LJ in *Weaver* at [72]).

223. In contrast to the position in the *Weaver* case (see paragraphs [220]–[221] above) which did not concern a fully mutual housing co-operative, and where the claimant was and is a large social landlord managing some 70,000 homes (compared to the Claimant's 36 homes), the unquestioned evidence shows that:

(1) The Claimant does not rely on any public subsidy to operate. The Claimant was set up with the benefit of a Housing Corporation grant and finance from private mortgages. The grant is repayable to the Housing Corporation on a disposal of the Claimant's properties, so is in effect a loan. The Claimant has received no further public funds. It derives its income from rent charged to its tenants/members and interests on reserves.

(2) The Claimant does not take the place of local government in providing social housing; its allocations are not controlled by a local authority, nor has it obtained its housing stock from local government. The Claimant has an informal nominations arrangement with Wandsworth Council,

but the Claimant retains ultimate autonomy over the approval of new tenants. There has been no voluntary transfer of housing stock from a public authority to the Claimant.

(3) The Claimant does not charge market rents. However, it does not provide 'subsidised' housing; it receives no subsidy. It has low rents because it exists for the benefit of its members (rather than to make profit). As a very small landlord, it does not contribute significantly to the achievement of the Government's housing objectives.

(4) Whilst there is an incidental, albeit small, public benefit in the provision of housing by the Claimant, its raison d'être is the provision of a benefit for its members. Indeed, it is a requirement of its registration as an industrial and provident society for it to operate for the benefit of its members, rather than for society at large.

(5) Fully mutual housing associations are not subject to statutory regulation in the same way as other housing associations. The very complaint made by the Defendants in these proceedings is that their tenancy is not afforded assured or secure status by the statutory regime. This is because the government has decided that such protections are not necessary or appropriate. Any tenant becoming a member of a fully mutual housing association will sign up to the association's principles and thus must be taken to be aware of its regulatory status. As a result, it cannot be said that fully mutual housing associations form part of a public interest scheme to protect the vulnerable or less well off.

(6) The Claimant is regulated by the Financial Conduct Authority as a co-operative, and by the Homes and Community Agency ('HCA') as a housing association. Unlike London and Quadrant, the Claimant is regulated as a small provider. Regulation does not extend far beyond annual scrutiny of its accounts and regulatory return.

224. Moreover, and as stressed by the Claimant, its mutual nature, and the fact that its members own and control it, is a further inconsistency with the notion that the Claimant stands as a public authority in respect of the Defendants or that it exercises functions which can properly be described as public for the Defendants' benefit.

225. In all the circumstances disclosed by the evidence filed on behalf of the Claimant and not disputed by the Defendants, I accept the submission of the Claimant and the SoS that the Claimant should not be considered to be exercising functions of a public nature for the purposes of section 6(3)(b)."

Southward Housing Co-Operative Ltd v Walker [2015] EWHC 1615 (Ch).

PUBLIC EXPENDITURE.

"The question that lies at the heart of this appeal is how the words 'public expenditure' should be interpreted. In relation to local authorities, do they mean expenditure incurred by local authorities in discharging their functions under the Education Acts as defined in section 573 of the 1996 Act ('education functions') (the narrow meaning); or do they mean expenditure incurred by any public authority as a result of the discharge by the local authority of the education functions (the wider meaning)? There is also a possible intermediate meaning, namely that 'public expenditure' means expenditure incurred by a local authority in the discharge of any of its functions (including, but not limited to, education functions). Neither party contends for this intermediate meaning. In my view, they are right not to do so. . . . In my view, the correct meaning of the words 'public expenditure' in section 9 is expenditure incurred by a public body, as opposed to 'private expenditure' (ie expenditure incurred by a private body). There are three linguistic points to be made. First, this interpretation accords with the natural and ordinary meaning of the words. If it had been intended to limit the expenditure referred to in section 9 to expenditure incurred by the Secretary of State or local authorities in the exercise of education functions, the section could and would have said so. Instead, Parliament chose the general words 'public expenditure'. Secondly, if the public expenditure were limited to expenditure incurred by the Secretary of State or local authorities in the discharge of their education functions, the word 'public' would have been unnecessary. The Secretary of State and the local authorities are public bodies and expenditure incurred by them in discharging these functions is bound to be 'public' rather than 'private' expenditure. The word serves the important purpose of distinguishing the expenditure from private expenditure. Thirdly, the language of para 3(3) of Schedule 27 should be contrasted with that of section 9. Para 3(3) requires the local authority to specify the name of the school preferred by the parent unless the attendance of the child at the school would be incompatible inter alia with 'the efficient use of resources'. As we have seen, this phrase has been interpreted as referring to the resources of the LEA (now the local authority) and no other authority. In section 9 Parliament could have used the words 'so far as that is compatible with the . . . avoidance of the inefficient use of resources'. If it had done so, it would have been clear (in the light of the authorities on para 3(3)) that the relevant expenditure was that incurred in the discharge of education functions and no other. I accept, of course, that Schedule 27 post-dated the predecessor to section 9. But the contrast in language in nevertheless striking. In enacting para 3(3), Parliament did not seek to reproduce the language of section 9. It follows that a natural reading of section 9 clearly supports the wider interpretation."

Haining v Warrington Borough Council [2014] EWCA Civ 398.

PUBLIC HEALTH SERVICES. Stat. Def., Health and Social Care Act 2012 s.234.

PUBLIC PLACE. Stat. Def., any place to which the public or any section of the public has access, on payment or otherwise, as of right or by virtue of express or implied permission, Anti-social Behaviour, Crime and Policing Act 2014 s.74.

PUBLIC SERVICE PENSIONS LEGISLATION. Stat. Def., Pension Schemes Act 2015 s.7.

PUBLICATION. Stat. Def., Crime and Courts Act 2013 s.42.

"67. Turning to the definition of 'publication' in the Contempt of Court Act 1981, I admit to having some real difficulties, particularly in the context of section 11. One possible answer may be that section 2(1) does not in terms define 'publication', but rather merely confirms that it includes any communication addressed to at least 'any section of the public', thus arguably merely emphasising the breadth of the term as used in the Act rather than imposing a restriction. However, as Elias LJ indicates, as a matter of construction, there is difficulty with the notion of a private disclosure to one individual in this statutory context being a 'publication'—I should add that I find his suggestion as to why the difficulty arises compelling —and, as the point I make with regard to the ambit of section 2(1) was not fully argued before us, I would hesitate to say more without some such debate. But, in any event, I am sure that section 11 of the 1981 Act does not exhibit an intention on the part of Parliament to restrict the powers of the court designed to ensure that justice is done. In my view, far clearer words would have been necessary to have had that effect."
Yam, R. (on the application of) v Central Criminal Court [2014] EWHC 3558 (Admin).

PUBLISH. Stat. Def. (but only by reference to the common law), Defamation Act 2013 s.15.

"44. . . . I base that conclusion on a straightforward interpretation of the statutory formula in section 118(1)(b) of the 2008 Act—'the day on which the order is published' or, if later, 'the day on which the statement of reasons for making the order is published'. The words mean what they say. What they mean, in their ordinary sense, is the day on which the order, or the statement of the Secretary of State's reasons for making it, is put into the public domain. The concept of publication in this context, I think, reflects the normal meaning of the verb to 'publish'—to '[make] generally known, declare or report openly; announce . . . ' (*Shorter Oxford English Dictionary*, 6th edn). The same may be said of the concept of the Secretary of State's reasons for a refusal of development consent being 'published', as the parallel provision for that eventuality is framed in section 118(2)(b). Here again the focus is on the reasons for the Secretary of State's decision being made known to the general public, as well as to those members of the public particularly affected by it. The critical step, which starts the period for challenge, is the publication of the Secretary of State's reasons for his decision.

45. The way in which an order and the Secretary of State's statement of reasons for making it are to be 'published' is not prescribed by section 118. But in my view the placing of the order on the Planning Inspectorate's infrastructure planning website on 12 September 2014, together with the Secretary of State's decision letter and the Examining Authority's report, and, on the same day, the notification of interested parties, both by e-mail and by post, that this had been done, was enough to constitute publication of the order, and the reasons why it was made, within the meaning of section 118. . . .

46. I do not accept that the provisions of section 117 point to some other understanding of section 118. There is clearly a difference between the concept of publishing a development consent order by making it known to the public that the order has been made, and the concept of the formalities involved in the making of a statutory instrument. Section 117(3) allows the Secretary of State to publish an order granting development consent 'in such manner as [he] thinks appropriate' unless the order falls within the ambit of section 117(4), in which case it 'must be contained in a statutory instrument'. The status of a development consent order as a statutory instrument, if it has to be in that form, requires a particular statutory process to be followed. That process has to be followed, no matter how the Secretary of State has initially published the order and his reasons for making it. The relevant provisions of the 1946 Act and 1947 regulations lay down the procedure by which statutory instruments are to be promulgated, and provide differently for local instruments and general instruments in the formal steps required. In this case it was necessary for the development consent order to be contained in a statutory instrument. As a local instrument it was exempt from the requirements of section 2(1) of the 1946 Act. Mr Hunter does not suggest that any of the necessary formalities under the 1946 Act and 1947 regulations were neglected. But in any event the order and the Secretary of State's reasons for making it were in the public domain on 12 September 2014, and interested parties had been told on the same day that this was so. That is the crucial point.

47. If Parliament had intended to include in section 118 different concepts of a development consent order being 'published' depending on whether or not it was required to be contained in a statutory instrument, I think it would have done so. Had the intention been to provide that the period for challenge would start only when a particular requirement of the 1946 Act or the 1947 regulations had been discharged, this could have been done. But it was not. I doubt that such provisions would have been conducive to clarity, certainty and consistency in the statutory regime for challenging decisions on applications for development consent orders. The fact is, however, that section 118 was not drafted in that way. And I do not think the court should imply into it provisions that Parliament did not see fit to insert. . . .

49. So one is left with the simple concept of a development consent order being published on the day when the order itself and the Secretary of

State's reasons for making it are made known to the public. That is how section 118(1)(b) of the 2008 Act should be understood."
Williams, R. (on the application of) v Secretary of State for Energy and Climate Change [2015] EWHC 1202 (Admin).

PUBLISHES. See PERSON WHO PUBLISHES.

PUBS CODE. Stat. Def., Small Business, Enterprise and Employment Act 2015 s.42.

PURPOSE.

"21. On the other hand, the meaning of the word 'purpose' in any particular provision must depend on the context. 'Purpose' is a 'protean concept', and how it has to be established 'will depend on the construction of the statute in the light of the mischief to which it is directed' (to quote from Lord Sumption in *Hayes v Willoughby* [2013] UKSC 17, [2013] 1 WLR 935, at paragraph 9). While, therefore, 'purpose' is frequently determined by reference to subjective intentions, that it is not always the case. The point can be illustrated by reference to *Pi Consulting (Trustee Services) Ltd v Pensions Regulator* [2013] EWHC 3181 (Ch), [2013] PLR 433. That case was concerned with whether certain schemes or arrangements were 'occupational pension schemes' within the meaning of section 1 of the Pension Schemes Act 1993. Under that provision, an 'occupational pension scheme' has to be established 'for the purpose of providing benefits to, or in respect of, people with service in employments of a description' or 'for that purpose and also for the purpose of providing benefits to, or in respect of, other people' (emphasis added in each case). It was submitted to Morgan J, and he accepted, that the relevant 'purpose' was 'the purpose of the scheme and not the purpose of one, or even all, of the parties to the documents which established the scheme' and that 'the relevant purpose was an objective matter, which turned upon the meaning and effect of the scheme so that it did not turn upon subjective matters such as the motives or the intentions or the beliefs of one or even all of the parties to the documents which established the scheme' (see paragraphs 36–39 of the judgment). . . .

24. On balance, accordingly, it seems to me that, in the context of regulation 2(1)(d), the 'purposes' for which a guarantee is given, or other arrangements are made, must be determined objectively rather than on the basis of the relevant public authority's subjective intentions."
FSS Pension Trustees Ltd v The Board of the Pension Protection Fund [2014] EWHC 1397 (Ch).

PURPOSE CONNECTED WITH.

"19. A central issue is thus whether, under section 22(2)(b), that part of the Heysham/M6 development which does not fall within schedule 5 to the

Order is a highway to be 'constructed for a purpose connected with a high-way for which the Secretary of State is (or will be) the highway authority.'

20. Much time and energy was devoted in argument to the issue of what the words 'a purpose connected with' mean. . . .

22. Ultimately, however, I conclude that: i) 'A purpose connected with' are ordinary English words which can and should be given an ordinary English meaning. ii) The meanings of common words and phrases, particularly (as in this case) those which are conceptually abstract, may well vary in accordance with the statutory context in which those words are to be found. Divorcing interpretation from context may tend to mislead rather than to inform. iii) There is no ambiguity, obscurity or absurdity about the language of the section which entitles me to have regard to *Hansard* (in any event, I did not find the passages which were brought to my attention to be of particular help). iv) If Parliament had intended to elaborate further upon the meaning of these words then it could easily have done so. I see no benefit, in the circumstances of this case, in attempting to put a gloss on the words themselves. In *Re Sevenoaks Stationers (Retail) Ltd* [1991] Ch 164, Dillon LJ, referred to judicial statements on section 6 of the Company Directors Disqualification Act 1986 which he described as 'ordinary words of the English language', at page 176F: 'Such statements may be helpful in identifying particular circumstances in which a person would clearly be unfit. But there seems to have been a tendency, which I deplore, on the part of the Bar, and possibly also on the part of the official receiver's department, to treat the statements as judicial paraphrases of the words of the statute, which fall to be construed as a matter of law in lieu of the words of the statute. The result is to obscure that the true question to be tried is a question of fact—what used to be pejoratively described in the Chancery Division as "a jury question".' In my view, these observations apply with equal force to the wording of section 22(2)(b) of the 2008 Act.

23. In the circumstances of this case I am entirely satisfied that the dual carriageway which is intended to fall within the auspices of Lancashire as highway authority ('the Lancashire highway') was indeed constructed for a purpose connected with the highway in respect of which the defendant is intended to be the highway authority (the defendant's highway")."

R. (on the application of Gate) v Secretary of State for Transport [2013] EWHC 2937 (Admin).

PUTCHER RANK.

"1. The claimant, Mr Nigel Mott, is the leasehold owner, jointly with the interested party Mr Merrett, of a right to fish for salmon at Lydney in the estuary of the River Severn using a putcher rank, that is, an array of 650 basket-like traps into which adult salmon swim as they make their way from the sea to spawn. The putcher is a very old fishing method and traditionally was made of woven wood, but the claimant's are now made of steel. The claimant's putcher fishery is a commercial operation; in the years prior to the decisions challenged the claimant's evidence is that he caught an average of 600 salmon per year with an approximate value of £60,000 and that the fishery represents his full time occupation and livelihood, supporting his family and that of Mr Merrett."

Mott, R. (on the application of) v Environment Agency [2015] EWHC 314 (Admin).

Q

THE QUEEN'S PEACE.

"Finally, in an article entitled 'Murder Under the Queen's Peace' [2008] Crim LR 541, Professor Michael Hirst traces the ambit of the meaning of the term 'the Queen's peace' in the offence of murder. He concludes that the phrase essentially goes to jurisdiction and the ambit of the offence of murder under English law, but may be of relevance to the killing of a victim in a time of war.

33. The law is now clear. An offender can generally be tried for murder wherever committed if he is a British subject, or, if not a British subject, the murder was committed within England and Wales. The reference to 'the Queen's peace', as originally dealt with in the cases to which we have referred, went essentially to jurisdiction. Although the Queen's Peace may play some part still in the elements that have to be proved for murder as regards the status of the victim (and it is not necessary to examine or define the ambit of that), it can only go to the status of the victim; it has nothing whatsoever to do with the status of the killer. The argument was completely hopeless. We have set out at some length why it was hopeless; it should never have been advanced. We dismiss this ground of appeal as entirely misconceived."

R. v Adebolajo [2014] EWCA Crim 2779.

REALISATION.

"42. This issue turns on the meaning of the words 'realisation of the security' in section 106(d). Neither the Act nor any associated legislation contains a statutory definition of the term 'realisation' applicable to section 106(d). Mr Say relied on *Wilson v Howard* [2005] EWCA Civ 147. In that case the claimant entered into 67 successive agreements with the defendant pawnbroker, under which she successively pawned 13 groups of objects. Under the arrangements, she was treated as periodically paying off the capital and interest purportedly due under each agreement and at the same time re-pledging the goods under a fresh agreement. A feature of the defendant's system was that the claimant was charged a full month's interest for a period short of a month—sometimes a single day—often calculated from a foreshortened redemption date. The use of the fresh agreement would then enable the defendant to set off against the principal notionally advanced under the new agreement the debt (including interest) owed under the previous agreement. The trial judge held that each successive agreement was a fresh agreement and not merely a variation of the prior agreement. He held that eight of the agreements were unenforceable because they contravened the principles of fair dealing and for other reasons. He ordered the return of the goods purportedly pledged under the agreements and awarded the claimant a sum equal to all the amounts notionally paid to the pawnbroker by each 'rolling up' even though in actual fact the claimant had only made a single payment. . . .

48. Neither that notional realisation nor the notional payment off of the outstanding capital and interest when each new agreement was made had anything to do with redemption. Despite Mr Say's submission, I cannot see any analogy between the 'realisation' of a security within section 106(d) and the redemption of a mortgage. In conventional legal terms the realisation of a security is something carried out by or on behalf of a creditor to release the value of the security so that the value can be applied in discharge of the debt. Redemption is something done by a debtor (viz. payment of what is outstanding) in order to obtain the return of the secured property. I can see no good reason why 'realisation' of the security for the purposes of section 106(d) should bear any meaning other than its conventional meaning. Sections 120 and 121 of the Act support that conclusion. Section 120 sets out the circumstances in which 'the pawn becomes realisable by the pawnee' where the pawn has not been redeemed at the end of the redemption period. Section 121, which is headed 'Realisation of pawn', provides for the pawn to be 'realisable' by the pawnee selling it.

49. That conventional interpretation of section 106(d) is consistent with a coherent legislative policy to preclude a creditor from circumventing the need to obtain an enforcement order by simply 'realising' the security. That policy is apparent from sections 142(1) and 113(3)(d) which are the gateways to section 106(d). Furthermore, that conventional interpretation achieves the policy—expressly stated in section 113(1)—that the security provided in relation to a regulated agreement cannot be enforced so as to benefit the creditor to any greater extent than would be the case if the security were not provided. The respondents' interpretation, on the other hand, would put a debtor who has provided security in a far better position than a debtor who has not provided security. Expressed differently, contrary to the policy objective stated in section 113(1), it would put the creditor in a worse position than if no security had been provided. On the respondents' argument, the debtor who has provided security is entitled under section 106(d) to repayment of all money paid by the debtor to discharge the debt and interest whether or not the money has come from the proceeds of sale of the security. A debtor who has not provided security, on the other hand, cannot recover any money paid in discharge of the debt unless he or she falls within the unfair relationship provisions of section 140A."
London Scottish Finance Ltd (in administration), Re [2013] EWHC 4047 (Ch).

REALISTIC.

"A 'realistic' claim is one that carries some degree of conviction. This means a claim that is more than merely arguable: *ED & F Man Liquid Products v Patel* [2003] EWCA Civ 472 at [8]."
Stemcor UK Ltd v Global Steel Holdings Ltd [2015] EWHC 363 (Comm).

REASONABLE.

"28. The question is then whether, as Dr Krebs alleges, the defendant has acted unreasonably or otherwise than as a responsible public body in seeking to terminate his contract (Dr Krebs does not allege bad faith). That, in turn, raises the question whether breach of the obligation under clause 10 of the contract to 'act reasonably and as a responsible public body' can only be held to have occurred if, in the *AP Picture Houses v Wednesbury Corporation* [1948] 1 KB 223 sense, the defendant has acted in a way no other responsible or reasonable public body would do or whether the word 'reasonably' can have a wider meaning.

29. If contracts between the private parties require either party to act reasonably in any particular respect as when, for example, a contract gives a discretionary power to one of the parties to take some decision for the purposes of the contract, the courts have traditionally been reluctant to import principles of public law as a guide to construction. Thus in *The Product Star* where a charterparty entitled the owners of a vessel to decline to proceed to a port which they considered to be dangerous as a result of

war, this court declined to import the Wednesbury test into an assessment whether the owners had made a reasonable decision that a port was dangerous as a result of the Iran-Iraq war. Leggatt LJ (with whom Balcombe and Mann LJJ agreed) said:

' . . . the exercise of judicial control of administrative action is an analogy which must be applied with caution to the assessment of whether a contractual discretion has been properly exercised ... In my judgment the authorities show that not only must the discretion be exercised honestly and in good faith, but, having regard to the provisions of the contract by which it is conferred, it must not be exercised arbitrarily, capriciously or unreasonably.' See *Abu Dhabi National Tanker Co v Product Star Shipping Ltd* [1993] 1 Lloyds Rep 397, 404.

30. Similarly in *Braganza v BP Shipping Ltd* [2013] EWCA Civ 230 and [2013] 2 Lloyd's Rep 351 where a death in service payment to an employee was not payable if 'in the opinion of BP or its insurers' the death resulted from the employee's wilful act or default, this court assessed the reasonableness of BP's opinion without regard to any Wednesbury considerations.

31. In the light of those authorities, I do not think the word 'reasonable' in clause 10 of the contract should be read in a restricted Wednesbury sense even though Dr Kreb's contract was made with a public body and even though clause 10 itself refers to the concept of a responsible public body. The fact that courts are now prepared to dilute the Wednesbury test in appropriate cases where the context so dictates, see *Kennedy v Information Commissioner* [2014] 2 WLR 808 per Lord Mance at paras 51–54, supports this conclusion.

32. In this respect, therefore, I differ from the judge who seems to have thought that as a matter of private law 'reasonableness' (even in the Wednesbury sense) did not come into the equation as a result of clause 11 of the contract. That way of looking at the matter would effectively negate clause 10 which cannot, in my view, be right. Clause 11 can mitigate the consequences of clause 10 (as I have already said) but cannot entitle a court to treat clause 10 as a dead letter."
Krebs v NHS Commissioning Board [2014] EWCA Civ 1540.

See ALL REASONABLE ENDEAVOURS.

REASONABLY PRACTICABLE.

"19. The effect, therefore, is that local authorities have a statutory duty to accommodate within their area so far as this is reasonably practicable. 'Reasonable practicability' imports a stronger duty than simply being reasonable. But if it is not reasonably practicable to accommodate 'in borough', they must generally, and where possible, try to place the household as close as possible to where they were previously living. There will be some cases where this does not apply, for example where there are clear benefits in placing the applicant outside the district, because of domestic violence or to break links with negative influences within the district, and others where the applicant does not mind where she goes or actively wants to move out of the area. The combined effect of the 2012 Order and the Supplementary Guidance changes, and was meant to change, the legal landscape as it was when previous cases dealing with an 'out of borough' placement policy, such as *R. (Yumsak) v Enfield London Borough Council* [2002] EWHC 280 (Admin), [2003] HLR 1, and *R. (Calgin) v Enfield London Borough Council* [2005] EWHC 1716 (Admin), [2006] HLR 4, were decided."

Nzolameso v City of Westminster [2015] UKSC 22.

RECALL PETITION. Stat. Def., Recall of MPs Act 2015 s.22.
ITV Plc v Pensions Regulator [2015] EWCA Civ 228.

RECOURSE.
"18. As it seems to me, Burton J was there espousing the view expressed by VDB that there was an important distinction between 'ordinary recourse' and 'extraordinary recourse'; and recognising that although the possibility of the latter does not prevent an award being binding under the Convention (and also s103(2)(f) of the 1996 Act) that is not so (or at least not necessarily so) with regard to the former. Of particular importance, in my view, is the conclusion reached by Burton J in [26] when he states: 'As I conclude, the binding effect of an award depends upon whether it is or remains subject to ordinary recourse. Once it is binding, it does not cease to be so as a result of some event in the home jurisdiction; and the absence of such impediment does not make it so.' As I read the Judgment in *Dowans*, the proceedings before the Tanzanian Court to set aside or to remit the ICC award were, in effect, treated by Burton J as "extraordinary recourse" and it was for that reason that he concluded that such proceedings were irrelevant for the purposes of enforcement as a matter of English law under s103 of the 1996 Act. In my view, the result is that if an award is subject to 'ordinary recourse', it will not be binding.

19. I fully recognise that there may be a problem of definition i.e. what constitutes 'ordinary recourse' as opposed to 'extraordinary recourse'; that there may well be a fine line between the two categories; that the recognition of such a distinction carries with it the potential danger of reintroducing the abandoned 'double exequatur' (or at least a modified form of it) by the back door which should be avoided; and that it remains necessary to consider the proper approach as to how the English court should determine whether or not the award is subject to 'ordinary recourse'. But it seems to me that these problems are inherent in the wording of Article V of the Convention and s103(2)(f) of the 1996 Act. . . .

21. Whilst recognising the distinction between 'ordinary recourse' and 'extraordinary recourse', I am extremely reluctant to provide any definition of either category; and in my view it would be inappropriate to do so particularly because (i) as appears above, those responsible for drafting

the Convention appear to have shied away from such exercise; (ii) the parliamentary draughtsman did not provide any definition of 'binding' in the 1996 Act; (iii) it seems unnecessary to do so in the circumstances of the present case; and (iv) even if Mr Cox is right that the term 'ordinary course' would embrace a 'genuine appeal on the merits', I am not persuaded that the concept of such term should necessarily be defined in such way."
Diag Human Se v Czech Republic [2014] EWHC 1639 (Comm).

REFERENCE.
"73. Finally, there was discussion during the hearing why Parliament used the expression 'reference' as opposed to 'appeal'. There is a precedent for using this term in FSMA. In my judgment, the term 'reference' is a recognition that the hearing before the Upper Tribunal is the first judicial hearing that there is in the PA04 scheme to consider the liability of the targets to the regulatory action which TPR proposes. It is noteworthy that TPR cannot refer a matter to the Upper Tribunal. Section 103(3) PA04 makes it clear that this is to be a full hearing and that there is no restriction on the evidence which may be adduced to (say) that which was before TPR when the Determinations Panel made its decision, as might be the case on a judicial review application. I therefore do not accept a submission that Lord Pannick made that this must be a lesser form of review because Parliament had to introduce section 103(3) PA04."

REFERRED. For a discussion of the meaning of referral in the medical context see *Hussein v The General Medical Council* [2013] EWHC 3535 (Admin).

REGISTER OF PARLIAMENTARY ELECTIONS. Stat. Def., Recall of MPs Act 2015 s.22.

REGULATORY FUNCTION. Stat. Def., Deregulation Act 2015 s.111.

REGULATORY FUNCTIONS. Stat. Def., Regulatory Reform (Scotland) Act 2014 s.1.

REGULATORY REQUIREMENT. Stat. Def., Regulatory Reform (Scotland) Act 2014 s.1.

RELATING TO.
"24. As a matter of ordinary English, I would read 'relating to' in the phrase 'sells any food after the date shown in a "use by" date relating to it' as synonymous with 'referring to'; or, in other words, as meaning simply that the food sold is the subject of a mark or label with a 'use by' date. It denotes a factual connection rather than a legal requirement. The word 'relating' is similarly used, for example, in regulation 35. Dealing with the

ways in which marking may be done, that regulation permits certain particulars to appear on the 'commercial documents relating to the food'. (In fairness to the Divisional Court, Mr Kirk acknowledged that its attention was not drawn to this point or to other examples in the regulations where 'relating to' is used in the sense of 'referring to'.)"
Torfaen County Borough Council v Douglas Willis Ltd [2013] UKSC 59.

RELIEF. See ANY APPROPRIATE RELIEF.

RELIGION.
"34. There has never been a universal legal definition of religion in English law, and experience across the common law world over many years has shown the pitfalls of attempting to attach a narrowly circumscribed meaning to the word. There are several reasons for this—the different contexts in which the issue may arise, the variety of world religions, developments of new religions and religious practices, and developments in the common understanding of the concept of religion due to cultural changes in society. While the historical origins of the legislation are relevant to understanding its purpose, the expression 'place of meeting for religious worship' in section 2 of PWRA has to be interpreted in accordance with contemporary understanding of religion and not by reference to the culture of 1855. It is no good considering whether the members of the legislature over 150 years ago would have considered Scientology to be a religion because it did not exist. . . .

51. Unless there is some compelling contextual reason for holding otherwise, religion should not be confined to religions which recognise a supreme deity. First and foremost, to do so would be a form of religious discrimination unacceptable in today's society. It would exclude Buddhism, along with other faiths such as Jainism, Taoism, Theosophy and part of Hinduism. The evidence in the present case shows that, among others, Jains, Theosophists and Buddhists have registered places of worship in England. Lord Denning in *Segerdal* [1970] 2 QB 697, 707 acknowledged that Buddhist temples were 'properly described as places of meeting for religious worship' but he referred to them as 'exceptional cases' without offering any further explanation. The need to make an exception for Buddhism (which has also been applied to Jainism and Theosophy), and the absence of a satisfactory explanation for it, are powerful indications that there is something unsound in the supposed general rule. . . .

56. It might be argued that the expression 'religious worship' in section 2 of the 1855 Act shows that Parliament intended the word 'religious' to be given a narrow interpretation. I would reject that argument. The language of the section showed an intentionally broad sweep. It included 'Protestant Dissenters or other Protestants', 'persons professing the Roman Catholic religion', 'persons professing the Jewish religion' and 'any other body or denomination of persons'. It may be that the members of the legislature in 1855 would not have had in mind adherence to other faiths such

as Buddhism, but that is no ground for holding that they were intended to be excluded from legislation passed to remove religious discrimination. . . .

57. Of the various attempts made to describe the characteristics of religion, I find most helpful that of Wilson and Deane JJ. For the purposes of PWRA, I would describe religion in summary as a spiritual or non-secular belief system, held by a group of adherents, which claims to explain mankind's place in the universe and relationship with the infinite, and to teach its adherents how they are to live their lives in conformity with the spiritual understanding associated with the belief system. By spiritual or non-secular I mean a belief system which goes beyond that which can be perceived by the senses or ascertained by the application of science. I prefer not to use the word 'supernatural' to express this element, because it is a loaded word which can carry a variety of connotations. Such a belief system may or may not involve belief in a supreme being, but it does involve a belief that there is more to be understood about mankind's nature and relationship to the universe than can be gained from the senses or from science. I emphasise that this is intended to be a description and not a definitive formula."

Hodkin, R. (on the application of) v Registrar-General of Births, Deaths and Marriages [2013] UKSC 77.

REMUNERATION. Stat. Def., including disbursements, Legal Aid, Sentencing and Punishment of Offenders Act 2012 s.42.

REPAIR.
"26. Repair is the converse of disrepair. A state of disrepair connotes a deterioration from some previous physical condition. Accordingly, that which requires repair is in a condition worse than it was at some earlier time: *Quick v Taff Ely Borough Council* [1986] QB 809; *Post Office v Aquarius Properties Ltd* (1987) 54 P & CR 61. If it is shown that property is worse than it was at some earlier time, it does not matter whether the deterioration resulted from error in design, or in workmanship, or from deliberate parsimony or any other cause: *Post Office v Aquarius Properties Ltd.* In our case the hereditament was, in this sense, worse than it was at some earlier time because of the decision to strip out the interior. Why that decision was taken does not matter. The intentions of the particular property owner or ratepayer are irrelevant since value must be objectively assessed; and in any event we are in a world of hypothetical parties. Mr Reade objected that this violated the principle stated by Lush J because it was looking back into the past at what the hereditament had once been. But as I have said, the principle of reality must yield to any counter-factual assumption which the valuation framework requires. In order to decide whether works are works of repair fairly so-called it is necessary to compare the hereditament in its actual state with its previous state. This comparison is a necessary preliminary to the making of the assumption that

the statute requires. I thus agree with the Valuation Tribunal that on the material date the hereditament was 'an office suite in disrepair'."

Newbigin (Valuation Officer) v S J & J Monk (a firm) [2015] EWCA Civ 78.

REPAY.

"75. . . . 'Repay' can properly describe the means of refunding the amount of the tax to whoever has a legal claim for its recovery. . . .

76. Although the word 'repay' taken in isolation is obviously capable of describing the satisfaction of any claim for the recovery of overpaid or undue tax, we consider that the natural meaning of the phrase 'credit or repay any amount accounted for or paid to them by way of VAT' read in context is the refunding of the tax to the taxpayer. The use of 'repay' merely reflects the provisions of s.80(2A) which were intended to extend to taxpayers who were repayment traders. Since the terminology of s.80(7) is explicable by and reflective of the earlier provisions of s.80, we are not persuaded that it should be given some wider and much less natural meaning. But if resort is to be made to a purposive approach to construction then that exercise has, we think, to involve a consideration of the legislative history. The judge undertook this exercise but thought it was unhelpful. We take a different view."

Investment Trust Companies v Revenue and Customs Commissioners [2015] EWCA Civ 82.

REPRESENTATION. Stat. Def., Legal Aid, Sentencing and Punishment of Offenders Act 2012 s.42.

REQUIRED.

"20. The debate in this court has centred on two parts of the definition: 'required by . . . administrative provisions' and 'set the framework for future development consent . . .'."

R. (on the application of Buckinghamshire CC) v Secretary of State for Transport [2014] UKSC 3.

REQUIRED BY ADMINISTRATIVE PROVISIONS.

"21. As explained by the CJEU, the word 'required' in this context means no more than 'regulated': I-E Bruxelles para 31. But it is less clear how that concept applies to administrative, as opposed to legislative or regulatory, provisions. In *Walton v The Scottish Ministers* [2012] UKSC 44; [2013] PTSR 51, at para 99, I said:

'There may be some uncertainty as to what in the definition is meant by "administrative", as opposed to "legislative or regulatory", provisions. However, it seems that some level of formality is needed: the administrative provisions must be such as to identify both the competent authorities and the procedure for preparation and adoption.'"

HS2 Action Alliance Ltd, R. (on the application of) v The Secretary of State for Transport [2014] UKSC 3.

RESIDENCE. See DWELLING.

See ORDINARY RESIDENCE.

RESIDENT.

"In the JM case the Court of Appeal refused to declare that 'resident' in section 117(3) [of the Mental Health Act 1983] means the same as 'ordinarily resident' in section 24 of the National Assistance Act 1948. That is not surprising because Parliament used a different formula in each Act and included in the 1948 Act both a deeming provision and a special provision for the Secretary of State to resolve disputes, neither of which is present in MHA. It might be a great deal more convenient and sensible if there were a match between the two provisions, rather than this mismatch, and at least one party in the JM case hoped to achieve such a match, but it did not succeed. In *R (Stennett) v Manchester City Council* [2002] UKHL 34 the House of Lords held that section 117 is a free-standing provision, not to be construed so as to align it with the 1948 Act. It might very well be better for the Secretary of State to be able to resolve issues of the present kind, as under the 1948 Act, rather than for it to be necessary to have recourse to the courts, with the time and expense that is inevitably involved in litigation, but that would require primary legislation."

Sunderland City Council, R. (on the application of) v SF [2012] EWCA Civ 1232.

RESIGNATION.

"1. The issue in this appeal concerns the meaning of the word 'resignation' as that term is used in the rules (the 'rules') of the Principal Civil Service Pension Scheme ('PCSPS'). . . .

25. Leaving the wording of the introduction to rule 3.11 to one side, it seems to me that there are clear indications that rules 3.11 and 3.12 are concerned with both voluntary and involuntary departure from the Civil Service. I say that for the following 5 reasons:

i) First and foremost, the term 'resignation' is defined in rule 1.13 as meaning 'termination of service or voluntary retirement from the Civil Service before pension age'. Had the words 'termination of service' been intended to be limited to voluntary termination, it would have been easy to move the word 'voluntary' to qualify both 'termination of service' and 'retirement from the Civil Service before pension age'. Moreover, there is, as the judge herself acknowledged, nothing to prevent a draftsman defining a narrow term as having a broad meaning. As Mr Cheetham said, 'black' can, if desired, be defined to mean or include 'white'.

ii) Rule 3.12 is the rule that makes the pension age 60 for those covered by rule 3.11, yet it expressly excludes those who have retired early under the Compensation Scheme, which is the method by which prison staff would have been made redundant. If the draftsman did not think that 'resignation' prima facie included both voluntary and involuntary methods of termination, this exclusion would have been unnecessary.

iii) Rule 3.14 allows a preserved pension to be brought into immediate payment if the person suffers an illness that would have led to retirement on medical grounds had they remained in the Civil Service. One of the pre-conditions in rule 3.14 is that the person has 'left the service'. The formulation is apt to describe either a voluntary or an involuntary departure, providing some indication that the rules under the heading were concerned with both.

iv) Rule 3.10a allows a person, who is eligible for a preserved pension under rule 3.11, to opt for a pension at any time after age 50 (for pre-Fresh Start employees) subject to an actuarial reduction. The words used to describe the termination of the relevant service are, however, instructive. They say that the rule applies '[w]here a civil servant . . . ceases to be a civil servant'. The concept of ceasing to be a civil servant is apt to include those who have left either voluntarily or involuntarily.

v) Under the 'dismissal' heading, rule 3.18a provides that a civil servant who is dismissed will be awarded the same benefits 'as if he had resigned voluntarily'. This formulation provides a pointer to the fact that the draftsman must have thought it possible to 'resign' involuntarily; otherwise, the word 'voluntarily' would have been superfluous.

26. Standing back from this construction, it seems to me that, even if the definition of 'resignation' in rule 1.13 were ambiguous, which I do not think it is, it makes business sense to think that the draftsman would have wanted to make provision somewhere for involuntary departures from Civil Service employment. I accept that transfers of undertakings out of the public sector may have been infrequent in 1972, but that does not mean that the draftsman did not contemplate involuntary departures. He clearly did. There is no reason in the rules to think that he was making provision for what should happen on dismissal or redundancy but not for any other kind of involuntary departure. Whilst section 71 of the Pension Schemes Act 1993 protecting short service benefit had not yet been enacted in 1972, it would be strange if the draftsman had not considered the need to do so in all reasonably conceivable circumstances."

Ellis v Cabinet Office [2015] EWCA Civ 252.

RESPECTABLE AND RESPONSIBLE.

"The expression 'respectable and responsible' in relation to a proposed sub-tenant or assignee is frequently used in commercial leases and has a long history. . . .

It seems to me that there is merit in adopting the defender's two-stage approach: in other words, to address first the question whether a proposed sub-tenant is respectable and responsible. . . .

The question is one of the proper construction of that expression, having regard to the relevant surrounding circumstances, being the circumstances which were reasonably within the knowledge of the parties to the lease at the time when it was granted. In my opinion, the parties to the lease must be taken to have been aware when they included this commonly-used expression in sub-paragraph 16.3 that it had been the subject of interpretation by the courts. They would be aware that 'respectability' had been held to refer to the manner in which the company in question conducted its business and to its reputation (*Wilmott*, per Cozens-Hardy MR at 531) and that 'responsibility' had been held to refer to financial capacity (ibid, per Farwell LJ at 537). In my opinion, the defender is well founded in its submission that these characteristics must be borne by the particular entity proposed as a sub-tenant. I consider this to be more obviously the case with regard to responsibility. By using the word 'responsible' in sub-paragraph 16(3), the parties agreed, in my opinion, that the landlord would be entitled to be satisfied as to the financial solidity of any proposed sub-tenant. It is not unheard of for one of the members of a group of companies to become insolvent while others survive; nor is it improbable that a company owned and directed by an individual would suffer insolvency yet that the owner and other corporate entities owned and controlled by him would continue to trade successfully. In my opinion a landlord who stipulates that a proposed sub-tenant must be responsible is reserving to himself the right to be satisfied as to the financial soundness of the sub-tenant itself and not as to the soundness of individuals or entities who might or might not provide assistance in the event of financial difficulty. So far as respectability is concerned, it may be that little should be required to satisfy the landlord, but once again I consider that evidence of respectability should relate to the proposed sub-tenant itself. A company does not acquire respectability automatically along with its certificate of incorporation, although it may not be long before its mode of carrying on business affords sufficient indication that it could not reasonably be regarded as anything other than respectable. That is not, in my view, the same as an assessment of the respectability of the company's owners or of other companies in common ownership."
Burgerking Ltd v Castlebrook Holdings Ltd [2014] ScotCS CSOH 36.

RESPONSE ACTION. Stat. Def., Antarctic Act 2013 s.13.

RETIREMENT INCOME. Stat. Def., Pension Schemes Act 2015 s.7.

RETIREMENT LUMP SUM. Stat. Def., Pension Schemes Act 2015 s.7.

RETURN.
"1. The issue in this case is whether the High Court of England and Wales has jurisdiction to order the "return" to this country of a small child who

has never lived or even been here, on the basis either that he is habitually resident here or that he has British nationality. . . .

63. In my view, there is no doubt that the jurisdiction exists, insofar as it has not been taken away by the provisions of the 1986 Act. The question is whether it is appropriate to exercise it in the particular circumstances of the case."

A (Children), Re (Rev 1) [2013] UKSC 60.

For the meaning of "return" in the context of the Taxes Management Act 1970 see *Cotter v Revenue & Customs* [2013] UKSC 69.

RIGHT.

"As a matter of substance, I do not consider that the holder of an EUA [European Union Allowance] has a 'right' which he or she can enforce by way of civil action. It is not a 'right' (in the Hohfeldian sense) to which there is a correlative obligation vested in another person. It does not give the holder a 'right' to emit CO_2 in this sense. Rather it represents at most a permission (or liberty in the Hohfeldian sense) or an exemption from a prohibition or fine. But for the entitlement to the EUA, the holder would either be prohibited from emitting CO_2 beyond a certain level or at least would be required to pay a fine if he did so. In this way, the holding of the EUA exempts the holder from the payment of that fine. An EUA is a creature of the ETS. As a matter of form an EUA exists only in electronic form. It is transferable automatically by electronic means within the registry system. Under the ETS legislation it is transferable under the terms of the ETS Directive. It has economic value, first because it can be used to avoid a fine, and secondly, because there is an active market for trade in EUAs. The evidence before me establishes that substantial amounts of money change hands between a transferor and a transferee. Each EUA has its own unique number and can be located by reference to that number."

Armstrong DLW GmbH v Winnington Networks Ltd [2012] EWHC 10 (Ch).

" . . . that Beresford is authority for the following propositions: (a) That there is a distinction between a use of land 'by right' and a use of land 'as of right'. (b) That if a statute properly construed confers a right on the public to use land for recreational purposes their use of that land will be by right and not as of right."

Barkas v North Yorkshire County Council [2012] EWCA Civ 1373.

RIGHTS (OF CHILDREN). Stat. Def., Children and Young People (Scotland) Act 2014 s.4.

RISK. See SIGNIFICANT RISK.

ROUTE.

"28. The better interpretation of 'route' in the body of s12, therefore, is that the police can give a direction based on what they understand of the organisers' intentions and based on what they believe is reasonably possible.

That may not be an objectively provable fact; it may be no more than a reasonable belief based on what has been gleaned from a variety of sources. But once it is recognised that the power to give a direction as to route precedes certain knowledge of the future route, it follows that a direction can be given in respect of what the police reasonably believe to be possible future routes at a time when the actual future route is not known. The fact that the route is uncertain, for whatever reason, necessarily implies the existence of a variety of reasonably possible routes to which the direction can apply. The crucial requirement before a preventive direction is given is therefore not the identification of the precise route to be followed, but the reasonable belief that one or more of the reasonably possible routes may lead to serious disruption."

Powlesland v Director of Public Prosecutions [2013] EWHC 3846 (Admin).

RULE.

"8. In *R (Alvi) v Secretary of State for the Home Department* [2012] 1 WLR 2208, which was heard with *Munir* and decided on the same day, this court considered in detail what constituted a rule dealing with the practice to be followed for regulating entry into and stay in the United Kingdom. The principal judgments were delivered by Lord Hope and Lord Dyson. They were agreed upon the basic requirement of section 3(2) and on the test for distinguishing a 'rule' from something that was merely advisory or explanatory, although not on every aspect of its application to the facts of that case. Lord Walker of Gestinghorpe, Lord Clarke of Stone-cum-Ebony and Lord Wilson delivered concurring judgments agreeing with both of them on the points on which they were agreed. Lord Hope put the point in this way at para 41:

'The content of the rules is prescribed by sections 1(4) and 3(2) of the 1971 Act in a way that leaves matters other than those to which they refer to her discretion. The scope of the duty that then follows depends on the meaning that is to be given to the provisions of the statute. What section 3(2) requires is that there must be laid before Parliament statements of the rules, and of any changes to the rules, as to the practice to be followed in the administration of the Act for regulating the control of entry into and stay in the United Kingdom of persons who require leave to enter. The Secretary of State's duty is expressed in the broadest terms. A contrast may be drawn between the rules and the instructions (not inconsistent with the rules) which the Secretary may give to immigration officers under paragraph 1(3) of Schedule 2 to the 1971 Act. As Sedley LJ said in *ZH (Bangladesh) v Secretary of State for the Home Department* [2009] Imm AR 450, para 32, the instructions do not have, and cannot be treated as if they possessed, the force of law. The Act does not require those instructions or documents which give guidance of various kinds to caseworkers, of which there are very many, to be laid before Parliament. But the rules must be. So everything which is in the nature of a rule as to the practice to be followed in the administration of the Act is subject to this requirement.'

At para 94, Lord Dyson, in a conclusion expressly endorsed by Lord Hope, at para 57, said:

'a rule is any requirement which a migrant must satisfy as a condition of being given leave to enter or leave to remain, as well as any provision "as to the period for which leave is to be given and the conditions to be attached in different circumstances" (there can be no doubt about the latter since it is expressly provided for in section 3(2)). I would exclude from the definition any procedural requirements which do not have to be satisfied as a condition of the grant of leave to enter or remain. But it seems to me that any requirement which, if not satisfied by the migrant, will lead to an application for leave to enter or remain being refused is a rule within the meaning of section 3(2). That is what Parliament was interested in when it enacted section 3(2). It wanted to have a say in the rules which set out the basis on which these applications were to be determined."'

New London College Ltd, R. (on the application of) v Secretary of State for the Home Department [2013] UKSC 51.

S

SALAMI SLICING.
"4. On behalf of the Secretary of State Mr Forsdick submitted that 'salami slicing' is the term applied to the splitting up of projects into small sub-projects with the effect of each part coming below the thresholds for Environmental Impact Assessment ('EIA') and therefore avoiding (whether deliberately or not) the need for EIA. In the two leading Spanish cases a single long distance rail construction project was split into small 'local' projects with the result that the section in question . . . and the project as a whole) was not subject to EIA (*Commission v Spain* [2005] Env LR 20 [52]-[54] and a single project for the upgrade of the Madrid Ring road was split into 15 sub-projects with the result that the section in question (or the project as a whole) was not subject to EIA (*Ecologistas nen Accion v Ayuntamiento de Madid* [2009] PTSR 458 [25], [44]-[45]. In both cases it was held that that approach was impermissible under the Environmental Impact Assessment Directive 2011/92/EU ('the Directive'). It impermissibly constituted what is commonly called 'salami slicing'. The true project was in each case in fact the wider whole—the complete ring road or the long distance train line."
R. (Save Britain's Heritage) v Secretary of State for Communities and Local Government [2013] EWHC 2268 (Admin).

SALARY (FINAL SALARY).   Stat. Def., Public Service Pensions Act (Northern Ireland) 2014 s.34.

SALES PITCH.
"110. I agree with TNL that the term 'sales pitch' is in the nature of opinion or value judgment. But in itself it is a neutral term; it depends on what is being sold. The term is only defamatory here because of the context in which it is used. It is part of the wording that contributes to the second defamatory meaning I have identified. It is artificial to regard it as a separate and distinct defamatory imputation which the ordinary reader would take from the articles."
Yeo MP v Times Newspapers Ltd [2014] EWHC 2853 (QB).

SATISFIED.
"30. The Secretary of State places great weight on the word 'satisfied' within the terms of the prohibition in section 40(4) of the Act against making an order for deprivation 'if [she] is satisfied that the order would make a person stateless'. In providing for her satisfaction in this regard, the subsection replicates the requirement in subsections (2) and (3) that she be

'satisfied' of the existence of one or other of the two grounds for making the order. The word 'satisfied' in the subsections should, if possible, be given some value. I confess, however, that I do not find it easy to identify what that value should be. Parliament has provided a right of appeal against her conclusion that one or other of the grounds exist and/or against her refusal to conclude that the order would make the person stateless; and it has been held and is common ground that such is an appeal in which it is for the appellate body to determine for itself whether the ground exists and/or whether the order would make the person stateless (albeit that in those respects it may choose to give some weight to the views of the Secretary of State) and not simply to determine whether she had reason to be satisfied of those matters (*B2 v Secretary of State for the Home Department* [2013] EWCA Civ 616, Jackson LJ, para 96). Mr Hermer suggests that the word 'satisfied' means only that the Secretary of State must bring her judgement to bear on the matters raised by the subsections. His suggestion may afford some slight significance to the word in subsections (2) and (3). But does it work in relation to subsection (4)? If an order would make a person stateless but the Secretary of State has failed even to bring her judgement to bear on the possibility of that consequence, the order can hardly escape invalidity on the basis that the Secretary of State was never satisfied that the order would have that effect. Irrespective, however, of whether the word 'satisfied' in subsection (4) can sensibly be afforded any significance at all, I am clear that it cannot bear the weight which Mr Swift seeks to ascribe to it. He contends that it confers latitude upon the Secretary of State—and, in the event of an appeal, upon the Tribunal or the Commission—to look beyond the ostensible effect of the order to the active cause of any statelessness and, in particular, to the facility of the person to secure restoration of his previous nationality. But a requirement that I should be satisfied of a fact does not enlarge or otherwise alter the nature of the fact of which I should be satisfied. Whether the requirement is that the fact should exist or that I should be satisfied of it, the nature of the fact remains the same; it is only the treatment of the fact in my mind which, subject to the context, is governed by the word 'satisfied'."
Secretary of State for the Home Department v Al-Jedda [2013] UKSC 62.

SCHOOL (MAINSTREAM). Stat. Def., a maintained school that is not a special school, or an Academy school that is not a special school, Children and Families Act 2014 s.83.

SCHOOL (MAINTAINED). Stat. Def., a community, foundation or voluntary school, or a community or foundation special school not established in a hospital, Children and Families Act 2014 s.83.

SCOTS LAW.
"The question that arises in the present proceedings for judicial review is the meaning of the expression 'Scots law' in the legislation governing legal aid, and in particular section 6(1) of the Legal Aid (Scotland) Act 1986. Under section 6(1), advice and assistance is available to a client of a solicitor 'on the application of Scots law to any particular circumstances which have arisen in relation to the person seeking advice'. . . . Scots law includes rules of private international law that refer to the law of other jurisdictions. For example, if a Scot is injured in a road accident in England, he may go to a Scottish solicitor for advice, and would obtain legal assistance for a diagnostic interview. In such a case, however, the solicitor's function would be to indicate that the accident was governed by English law, not Scots law, and would direct his client to an English lawyer. That is a fairly straightforward piece of advice, and it is easy to see why it would be covered by a diagnostic interview. Likewise, Scots law has a rule, discussed in paragraph [12] above, that international treaties have no direct effect in domestic law. Thus if a solicitor's client seeks to found on an international treaty such as the Convention, the advice required would be very straightforward, namely that as a matter of Scots Law he cannot do so. In both of these cases the merits of the claim in England or in the Strasbourg Court are not part of Scots law; the application of Scots law is confined to identifying this rule and advising that in consequence the client must look for advice elsewhere. . . . In all the circumstances, therefore, I am of opinion that the expression 'Scots law' as used in section 6(1) of the 1996 Act does not extend to the giving of advice as to the making of an application to the European Court of Human Rights. Consequently the respondents' refusal to treat the advice given to the petitioner as a distinct matter for the purposes of the Legal Aid (Scotland) Act 1986 and the Advice and Assistance (Scotland) Regulations 1996 was correct."
Donaldson, Re Judicial Review [2012] ScotCS CSOH 176.

SCOTTISH FISHING BOAT. Stat. Def., "means a fishing vessel which is registered in the register maintained under section 8 of the Merchant Shipping Act 1995 and whose entry in the register specifies a port in Scotland as the port to which the boat is to be treated as belonging" (Aquaculture and Fisheries (Scotland) Act 2013 s.53).

SCRAP (SUPPLY FOR). Stat. Def., "that is to say, for the value of materials included in the products rather than for the value of the products themselves" (Construction Products Regulations 2013 reg.8(7)(a)(ii)).

SCRAP METAL. Stat. Def., Scrap Metal Dealers Act 2013 s.21.

SCRAP METAL DEALER. Stat. Def., Scrap Metal Dealers Act 2013 s.21.

SEA FISHERIES LEGISLATION. Stat. Def., Aquaculture and Fisheries (Scotland) Act 2013 s.53.

SECONDARY LEGISLATION. Stat. Def., Welfare Reform Act 2012 s.39.

SECURITIES SETTLEMENT SYSTEM. Stat. Def., Financial Services (Banking Reform) Act 2013 s.113.

SELLER.
"I am conscious that the FTT held in the alternative that the term 'seller' in article 29(3)(a) [of Council Regulation (EEC) No 2913/92] should be construed as applying separately to the hanger suppliers (in relation to the hangers) and to the clothing suppliers (in relation to the clothing). It did so in order to avoid what it thought would be an 'arbitrary or fictitious customs value'. In my judgment, this approach was not open to the FTT. The word 'seller' in article 29(3)(a) of the Code is a clear unambiguous term understood by commercial men in the UK and across the world. It cannot be salami sliced in the way the FTT suggested. The seller of a consignment of goods is the person selling those goods to the buyer. In this situation, there were three separate transactions which ought not to be elided or confused: (a) the sale of the clothing and the hangers by the clothing supplier to Asda, (b) the sale of the hangers by the hanger suppliers to the clothing supplier, and (c) the agreement between Asda and the hanger suppliers whereby they rebate to Asda a part of the purchase price of the hangers paid to them by the clothing supplier. The transactions may be inter-related, but transaction (b) is clearly a free-standing purchase by the clothing supplier before the goods are either sold to Asda or imported into the customs territory of the EU."
Asda Stores Ltd v The Commissioners for Her Majesty's Revenue And Customs [2014] EWCA Civ 317.

SERIOUS.
"60. In this context, I consider that on proper interpretation of paragraph 55.10 it is important to give full value to the word 'serious', in the phrase 'serious mental illness' (and indeed in the other cases qualified by that word, in the fourth and seventh bullet points), since that formula defines a class of case to which the 'very exceptional circumstances' test will be applied. Although application of the 'very exceptional circumstances' test does not prevent detention in all cases, it does—obviously—make it significantly more difficult to justify detention (and hence increases the risk that a person, not being detained as a result of application of that test, might abscond to avoid his removal and the effective implementation of immigration controls in his case). On a proper interpretation, the circumstances in which that more restrictive test falls to be applied should be relatively narrowly construed, since otherwise the effective, firm and fair operation of immigration controls may be excessively undermined.

61. In my view, 'serious mental illness' connotes a serious inability to cope with ordinary life, to the level (or thereabouts) of requiring in-patient medical attention or being liable to being sectioned under the Mental

Health Act 1983, or a mental condition of a character such that there is a real risk that detention could reduce the sufferer to that state—for instance, if there were a real risk that they could have a break-down in prison."
Das, R. (on the application of) v Secretary of State for the Home Department [2013] EWHC 682 (Admin).

"The use of the word 'serious' obviously distinguishes the statutory test from the common law as stated in *Thornton*. The threshold identified in *Thornton* was that the statement should 'substantially' affect attitudes in an adverse way, or have a tendency to do so. The *Jameel* test also requires a tort to be 'substantial'. As Bean J noted in *Cooke v MGN Ltd* [2014] EWHC 2831 (QB), [2014] EMLR 31 [37], examination of the Parliamentary history of the section shows that the word 'serious' was chosen deliberately in place of the word 'substantial'. It follows that the seriousness provision raises the bar over which a claimant must jump, as compared with the position established in the two cases mentioned."
Ames v Spamhaus Project Ltd [2015] EWHC 127 (QB).

SERIOUS CRIME. For discussion of the concept of serious crime in the context of refugees see *AH (Algeria) v Secretary of State for the Home Department* [2012] EWCA Civ 395.

SERIOUS HARM. Stat. Def., Defamation Act 2013 s.1.

SERVICE.
"Although in normal social parlance, 'delivering' a document 'personally' would often be understood to mean service by the sender personally, I do not consider that that is the natural meaning in a provision such as clause 13.2. After all, in the case of a notice on behalf of Mr Hormell, this would mean that Mr Hormell would have to deliver the Notice: that cannot be right, and is not suggested by Mr Bompas. So the normal social meaning cannot be invoked. Secondly, the concept of 'personal service' is well understood to mean service on the recipient personally, not service by the server (or anyone else) personally—see e.g. per Lord Bridge and Lord Goff in *Allison Limited v Limehouse & Co* [1992] AC 105, 113 and 124 respectively. Although it is true that the well known expression 'personal service' has not been used, it seems to me that the legally familiar concept of personal service is redolent in the relevant words of clause 13.2. The reason why the word 'delivering' rather than 'serving' is used in clause 13.2 is that having used the word 'served' as a generic term, it was then thought appropriate to distinguish between two types of service, namely, handing over ('delivering') and posting ('sending')."
Ener-G Holdings Plc v Hormell [2012] EWCA Civ 1059.

"Specifically, the issue focuses upon the meaning of the word 'serving' of legal proceedings in respect of a claim for breach of warranty. Although this judgment addresses particular words used in a particular agreement it appears from previous case law that the clause and the phrase in dispute is not untypical of other share purchase agreements. . . .

53. First, the perspective from which the provision must be interpreted is that of the parties, not the reasonable lawyer. Neither party submitted to me that simply because the critical word in dispute—'serving'—concerned an aspect of legal process that the relevant perspective was to be altered to that of a lawyer or even a business man with a lawyer permanently hovering at his shoulder whispering advice. Lord Clarke in the passage cited at [35] above in *Rainy Sky v Kookmin Bank* referred to the process of construction as involving determining 'what the parties meant that the language used' and the 'parties' are the parties to the agreement, not third party advisers. This has some significance in the present case because whilst the word 'serving' used in Schedule 4(3) and the surrounding phrases ('legal proceedings' etc) refer broadly to legal concepts the draftsmen has neither defined those terms in the SPA nor linked them to any specific procedural rule save to say that English law governs.

54. This is especially the case with a phrase such as 'serving'. The expression is one which can bear a number of different and conflicting meanings covering points in time before, on, and after receipt. For instance it can mean dispatch in the sense that a document is 'served' from the point in time of its dispatch or sending and therefore prior to its receipt. In such cases the modes of dispatch are frequently spelled out (fax, DX, first class recorded post, etc). The parties by this method in effect agree a risk transfer away from the sender and on to the other party: see the discussion of such clauses in *Ener-G Holdings Plc* (ibid) at paragraphs [23], [29], [30], [35] per Lord Neuberger MR. Alternatively, the phrase 'service' (and its cognates) might be read simply to mean delivery in a form which brings the contents of the document being served to the actual attention of the intended recipient. In such circumstances a document or other instrument will be served only when it is proven that the intended recipient was in actual possession of the document or instrument in issue. This is in my view the normal meaning of the concept of 'service'. And yet further it is possible that 'service' (and cognates) may be treated as having occurred at a point of time after actual receipt by the inclusion in the contract of provisions which define service as having occurred, for example, 'x' days or hours following proof of actual receipt. This analysis shows that the phrase 'serving' is not a term which necessarily imports a fixed or technical meaning. Its ordinary meaning is delivery upon and receipt by the intended recipient, but that can be modified by contractual provisions. This is not, in my view, one of those cases where the parties have carefully and deliberately chosen a very precise legal term of art which, accordingly to consistent case law, should be accorded its technical meaning and which the parties would accordingly understand as having a precise legal meaning: see the discussion of legal terms of art in Lewison, *The Interpretation of Contracts* (5th edition, 2011) section 5.08 et seq."

Ageas (UK) Ltd v Kwik-Fit (GB) Ltd [2013] EWHC 3261 (QB).

Stat. Def., "includes facility" (Health and Social Care Act 2012 s.150).

SERVICE (ADVOCACY). Stat. Def., "Advocacy services" are services which provide assistance (by way of representation or otherwise) to persons for purposes relating to their care and support, Social Services and Well-being (Wales) Act 2014 s.181.

SERVICE COMPLAINTS OMBUDSMAN. Stat. Def., Armed Forces Act 2006 s.365B inserted by the Armed Forces (Service Complaints and Financial Assistance) Act 2015 s.1.

SERVICE TO THE PUBLIC.
"If the Directive meant to confine its application to transport undertakings to those which are subject to a public service obligation, it would have said so. On the contrary, I consider that the wording 'service to the public' is used by way of distinction from the situation where an operator provides a service to only a limited class of persons, e.g. a railway carrying only freight, or the post office underground railway that operated in London until 2002."
Alstom Transport v Eurostar International Ltd [2012] EWHC 28 (Ch).

SERVING OFFICER. Stat. Def., Police Reform Act 2002 Sch.3 as inserted by Police (Complaints and Conduct) Act 2012.

SEXUAL COMMUNICATION WITH A CHILD. Stat. Def., Sexual Offences Act 2003 s.15A as inserted by the Serious Crime Act 2015 s.67.

SHALL.
"41. Here 'shall be' is used in the sense of 'must be'. It is not looking to the future. It is looking to the present. Temporality is conveyed by 'prior to and after'."
Napier Park European Credit Opportunities Fund Ltd v Harbourmaster Pro-Rata Clo 2 B.V. [2014] EWCA Civ 984.

"The word 'shall' has frequently been construed as permissive rather than mandatory; for example, *Stroud's Judicial Dictionary of Words and Phrases* (7th edn), Vol.3, pages 2522–2525, gives 17 examples of cases where the word has been so construed, usually with reference to the underlying policy of the Act in question. In the present case, we are of opinion that the policy underlying the existence of the roll of solicitors demands that the second respondent should have an element of discretion as to whether a request to remove a solicitor's name from the roll should be granted, at least immediately. Provided that good cause exists for doing so, we consider that the second respondent should be entitled to refuse a request for removal. The likelihood of significant disciplinary proceedings would clearly provide a sufficient reason. Under the new wording of section 9, this result seems to be quite clear."

Opinion of the court delivered by Lord Drummond Young in the appeal by Michael Louis Karus against Scottish Legal Complaints Commission and Law Society of Scotland [2014] ScotCS CSIH 59.

SHARED OWNERSHIP LEASE. Stat. Def., Prevention of Social Housing Fraud Act 2013 s.11.

SHARES.
"2. 'Shares' in clause 3.1.1 is defined as meaning:
'all shares (if any) specified in Schedule 1 (Shares), and also all other stocks, shares, debentures, bonds, warrants, coupons or other securities now or in the future owned by the Chargor in Corporal from time to time or any in which it has an interest.'
3. The particular issue which divides the parties is whether this definition encompasses the rights of Fons under two shareholder loan agreements dated 17th October 2007 and 15th February 2008 ('the SLAs') under which Fons made unsecured loans to a company, Corporal Limited ('Corporal'), in which it held both ordinary and preference shares. The loan under the first SLA was £563,500 and Fons was the sole lender. Under the second SLA, BG Holding EHF ('Baugur') and Fons acted as joint lenders and advanced £1.5m in proportion to their respective shareholdings in Corporal. Fons provided 35 per cent of the loan. As in the case of the first SLA, the loan was unsecured. . . .
19. In terms of shedding any further light on the scope and meaning of 'Shares', clause 3.1.3 is therefore of no assistance. But the definition of 'Distribution Rights' does at least confirm that 'Shares' was intended to include assets which are capable of generating 'income paid or payable' and 'rights, benefits and advantages' other than dividends or further derivative share issues. Although this does not go as far as to provide a clear identification of whether the SLAs are within the type of assets which are included within the definition of 'Shares', it does at least confirm that they are not certainly excluded. The definition extends to 'debentures, bonds, warrants, coupons or other securities' which are income producing. If the SLAs can as a matter of ordinary language properly be treated as falling within one or more of those descriptions, there is no contra-indication in clause 3.1 to suggest that they should be given a narrower meaning. . . . The words 'or other securities' appear at the end of a list of items all of which can loosely be described as investments. Clause 1.2.6 of the Charge confirms that the plural is to include the singular and it is not therefore possible to exclude the SLAs from being 'debentures' on the basis that they were not part of a series or that they did not include security in the form of a charge. What they did represent was relatively long-term loan capital for Corporal not repayable before the company's

principal loan facility with RBS. From Fons's point of view this could reasonably be regarded and described as an investment in Corporal secured
by the terms of the SLAs.

44. Armed with this knowledge, I can see no reason why the reasonable
observer should regard the reference to 'other securities' as limiting
'debentures' to a meaning which would exclude the SLAs in this case.
Once it was clear from a reading of the Charge that they did not have to
include a charge over Corporal's assets he would, I think, have read
'debentures' as having its ordinary meaning of an acknowledgement of
debt recorded in a written document. The judge has not suggested any
alternative meaning which would have been obvious from the admissible
background."

Fons Hf v Corporal Ltd [2014] EWCA Civ 304.

SHELLFISH FARMING. Stat. Def., "the cultivation or propagation of
shellfish with a view to their sale or their transfer to other waters or land; but
only where such activity is required to be authorised as an aquaculture production business under regulation 6 of the Aquatic Animal Health (Scotland) Regulations 2009 (S.S.I. 2009/85)" (Aquaculture and Fisheries
(Scotland) Act 2013 s.63).

SHOW.
"True it is that the word 'show' or 'shows' is used in Section 31(1) and (2),
but in our judgment it is being used in a neutral way without defining the
standard of proof. As Makuwa indicates, in Section 31(1) the word 'show'
covers both the situation where there is an evidential burden on the applicant and also where he has to prove matters on the balance of probabili-
ties."

Sadighpour v R. [2012] EWCA Crim 2669.

SIBLING. Stat. Def., "means a sibling of the full blood or the half blood"
(Presumption of Death Act 2013 s.20).

SIGN.
"55. In brief, the description of the mark as including not just the colour
purple as a sign, but other signs, in which the colour purple predominates
over other colours and other matter, means that the mark described is not
'a sign.' There is wrapped up in the verbal description of the mark an
unknown number of signs. That does not satisfy the requirement of 'a sign'
within the meaning of Article 2, as interpreted in the rulings of the CJEU,
nor does it satisfy the requirement of the graphic representation of 'a sign',
because the unknown number of signs means that the representation is not
of 'a sign.' The mark applied for thus lacks the required clarity, precision,
self-containment, durability and objectivity to qualify for registration."

Société Des Produits Nestlé SA v Cadbury UK Ltd [2013] EWCA Civ 1174.

SIGNIFICANT.

"25. The first matter is the meaning of the word 'significant'. In this regard Parliament chose to help the court to a limited extent by providing in section 31(10) [of the Children Act 1989] as follows: 'Where the question of whether harm suffered by a child is significant turns on the child's health or development, his health or development shall be compared with that which could reasonably be expected of a similar child.' When we read this subsection together with the definition of 'harm' in the preceding subsection, we conclude that, whereas the concept of 'ill-treatment' is absolute, the concept of 'impairment of health or development' is relative to the health or development which could reasonably be expected of a similar child. This is helpful but little more than common sense.

26. In my view this court should avoid attempting to explain the word 'significant'. It would be a gloss; attention might then turn to the meaning of the gloss and, albeit with the best of intentions, the courts might find in due course that they had travelled far from the word itself. Nevertheless it might be worthwhile to note that in the White Paper which preceded the 1989 Act, namely The Law on Child Care and Family Services, Cm 62, January 1987, the government stated, at para 60: 'It is intended that "likely harm" should cover all cases of unacceptable risk in which it may be necessary to balance the chance of the harm occurring against the magnitude of that harm if it does occur.' It follows that when, in *Re C and B (Care Order: Future Harm)* [2001] 1 FLR 611, Hale LJ (as my Lady then was) said, at para 28, that 'a comparatively small risk of really serious harm can justify action, while even the virtual certainty of slight harm might not', she was faithfully expressing the intention behind the subsection. But the other interesting feature of the sentence in the White Paper is the word 'unacceptable'. I suggest that it was later realised that whether the risk was 'unacceptable' was a judgement which fell to be made at the welfare stage of the inquiry; and so a different adjective was chosen."

B (a Child), Re [2013] UKSC 33.

SIGNIFICANT RISK.

"'Significant risk' is more than the mere possibility of occurrence and means 'noteworthy, of considerable amount or importance'—see *R v Lang* [2005] 1 Cr App R(S) 34."

Nouri, R. v [2012] EWCA Crim 1379.

SINGLE INVESTEE COMPANY.

"The board's submission was simple. The phrase 'single investee company' should be given its primary meaning in ordinary speech. It meant a distinct corporate entity in which an investment was made. SEI's case involved treating the aggregate of the companies in the MR group as a 'single investee company'. That case is irrelevant. Mr McGregor referred me to well-known cases which vouch that the separate personality of a company is a real thing (*Salomon v Salomon & Co Ltd* [1897] AC 22, *Woolfson v Strathclyde Regional Council* 1978 SC (HL) 90, *Adams v Cape Industries plc* [1990] 1 Ch 433 and *Watt's Trustee v SPS (Holdings) Ltd* 2000 SC 371). . . . [17] I do not think that the word 'company' in the phrase 'single investee company' should be given an extended meaning. I have reached this view for the following four reasons. First, the deed of trust and the constitution were drafted by skilled solicitors who had extensive commercial experience. They must be taken to have been very familiar with the principle of separate corporate personality. There is no ambiguity in the phrase 'single investee company'. If they had wished to express a limit on the power of the board to invest in companies within a group of companies, they could have chosen words which clearly achieved that result. Secondly, the document is a formal constitution which delimits the powers and duties of the board and the trustees. It is important that there is clarity in such a document. Mr Simpson sought to persuade me that the limit was on investing in a single undertaking or business. But the concept of a business or an undertaking in which a group of companies is involved is much less clear than that of a single company. There would be difficult questions as to the degree of financial inter-dependence required for a group of companies to be a 'single investee company' for the purposes of the constitution. It would be necessary to decide whether there had to be cross-guarantees or a particular degree of integration of the businesses carried on by separate companies within a group. [18] Thirdly, consistency of construction of phrases used in the deed of trust and the constitution points towards the ordinary meaning of the phrase. The phrase 'investee company' is used in clause 1.1 of the deed of trust in the definitions of 'loan' and 'security' where the recipient of a loan or the granter of a security would have to be a single corporate entity. Fourthly, I consider that if I were to uphold Mr Simpson's submission I would be doing violence to the language that the parties had used. This is not a case where the contract is unclear or where one can infer that the parties have made a mistake in the words they have chosen to express their agreement. In *Pink Floyd Music Ltd v EMI Records Ltd* [2010] EWCA Civ 1429, Lord Neuberger MR stated (at para 22) ' . . . before the court can be satisfied that something has gone wrong, the court has to be satisfied both that there has been "a clear mistake" and that it is clear "what correction ought to be made" (per Lord Hoffmann in *Chartbrook* [2009] 1 AC 1101, paras 22–24, approving the analysis of Brightman LJ in *East v Pantiles (Plant Hire) ltd* (1981) 263 EG 61, as refined by Carnwath LJ in *KPMG LLP v Network Rail Infrastructure Ltd* [2007] Bus L R 1336).' I am not confident that there was a mistake or that the parties would have agreed a restriction which referred to a single investee business or a single investee undertaking because of the uncertainty inherent in such phrases. It is not open to the court in these circumstances to substitute for the parties' contract an arrangement which it considers to be more sensible."

Symphony Equity Investments Ltd v Shakeshaft [2013] ScotCS CSOH 102.

SITE.

"48. I accept Mr Martin's submission that in the context of this dispute the word 'site' must be construed in a manner that accords with how it would be understood in the industry.

49. I can find no error of law in the conclusion set out at paragraph 18 of the ET's judgment (set out in paragraph 44 above). I do not consider that the ET was adopting a strict 'perimeter fence' approach, although it may well have taken that as its starting point. I agree with Ouseley J. that there is no 'bright line' solution to the question of where a particular site begins or ends: it is really a matter of impression. The authorities show that an impressionistic approach to problems of this sort is entirely appropriate. That was the approach adopted by the ET on a site by site basis.

50. I can discern no ambiguity in the meaning of 'site' as construed by the ET. It may be that there will be borderline cases when the answer to the question of whether a person is or is not a site employee, but that does not mean that there is an ambiguity."

On Line Design & Engineering Ltd v Engineering Construction Industry Training Board [2013] EWHC 287 (Admin).

SLAVERY. Stat. Def. (by implication), Modern Slavery Act 2015 s.1.

SLUSH FUND.

"The natural meaning of 'slush fund' is that money is either being used for improper purposes or, at the very least, for purposes which the provider of the funds is not prepared publicly to acknowledge because he fears that legitimate criticism of use of such funds can be made. In the context of local authority expenditure, the ordinary reader would regard the use of the term 'slush fund' as an imputation that the provider of the funds is acting corruptly. The purpose of using the word 'slush' as part of the term 'slush fund' is to imply that the money is dirty money."

Thompson v James [2014] EWCA Civ 600.

SMALL DONATION. Stat. Def., Small Charitable Donations Act 2012 s.3.

SOCIAL CARE. Stat. Def., Health and Social Care Act 2012 s.233.

SOCIAL ENTERPRISE. Stat. Def., Social Services and Well-being (Wales) Act 2014 s.16.

SOME OTHER COMPELLING REASON.

"The phrase 'some other compelling reason' is a robust and stringent test. Various judges have used different words in an attempt to elucidate the phrase. These have included 'very high prospects of success', 'strongly arguable', 'legally compelling', 'a sufficiently serious legal basis' and 'perverse and plainly wrong'. All of these phrases should be read within the

context of the decisions in Cart and Eba. The clear intention of the Supreme Court was to provide that the courts would only intervene in very exceptional cases where there was a clear need for them to do so."
Y.H. for Judicial Review of a Decision of the Upper Tribunal (Immigration and Asylum Chamber) [2013] ScotCS CSOH 94.

SPAM.
"1. This is a case about spam, which for present purposes is adequately defined as unwanted email sent in bulk. It can also be described as the internet version of junk mail."
Ames v Spamhaus Project Ltd [2015] EWHC 127 (QB).

SPECIAL EDUCATIONAL NEEDS. Stat. Def., Children and Families Act 2014 s.20.

SPECIAL EDUCATIONAL PROVISION. Stat. Def., Children and Families Act 2014 s.21.

SPECIAL POLICE FORCE. Stat. Def., Crime and Courts Act 2013 s.16.

SPECIALIST PRINTING EQUIPMENT. Stat. Def., Specialist Printing Equipment and Materials (Offences) Act 2015 s.2.

SPECULATION. See HEDGING.

SPECULATIVE INVOICING.
"Consumer Focus contends, however, that the present claim is a manifestation of a more unsavoury practice called 'speculative invoicing', which has attracted considerable media attention in the last couple of years. Consumer Focus describes this as follows. In essence, it involves the sending of letters before action to thousands of internet subscribers whose internet connection is alleged to have been used for small-scale copyright infringement and whose names and addresses have been obtained by means of Norwich Pharmacal orders against their IPSs. Without seeking to confirm whether the internet subscriber was the person responsible for the uploading/downloading of the copyright work that has been detected, the internet subscriber is requested to pay a substantial sum which has no relation to the actual damage caused by the alleged copyright infringement or the costs incurred. Typical sums demanded are in the range £500 to £1000. Invariably, there is a profit-sharing arrangement between the party conducting the litigation and the client, with the former getting the lion's share. The tactic is to scare people into paying the sums by threatening to issue court proceedings. If this does not work, proceedings are not normally issued. This is because the economic model for speculative invoicing means that it is more profitable to collect monies from those who pay rather than incur substantial costs in pursuing those who do not pay

in court. Where proceedings are issued, they are not pursued if a default judgment cannot be obtained."
Golden Eye (International) Ltd v Telefonica UK Ltd [2012] EWHC 723 (Ch).

SPEEDILY. For discussion of the meaning of "speedily" in Article 5(4) of the European Convention on Human Rights see *Faulkner, R. (on the application of) v Secretary of State for Justice* [2013] UKSC 23.

SPOUSE. Stat. Def., Marriage (Scotland) Act 1977 s.2 inserted by Marriage and Civil Partnership (Scotland) Act 2014 s.1.

SPREAD.
"The verb 'spread' may, no doubt, in some contexts indicate the occupation of or penetration into a greater geographic area. But in the context of disease it connotes, or may readily connote, an intensification or increase of the incidence of the disease, whether or not over a greater area, and in particular may connote, as it does naturally here, the spread of disease from one species to another: from badgers to cattle."
Badger Trust, R. (on the application of) v SSEFRA [2012] EWCA Civ 1286.

SPREAD BETTING. For a judicial definition of spread betting see *Spreadex Ltd v Battu* [2005] EWCA Civ 855 at [2]–[3].

STAFF. Stat. Def., Public Service Pensions Act 2013 s.37.

STATELESS.
"95. The word stateless in section 40 (4) means de jure stateless, not de facto stateless in the sense discussed above: see *Fransman's British Nationality Law,* third edition, paragraph 25.4 and *Abu Hamza v The Secretary of State for the Home Department* (SIAC, 5th November 2010).
96. The words 'if he is satisfied that' in section 40 (4) of the 1981 Act do not mean that the Secretary of State's opinion is the yardstick. These words must be construed in a manner which is consistent with article 8.1 of the 1961 Convention. In the result therefore the Secretary of State cannot make an order depriving a person of British citizenship if the consequence will be to render that person de jure stateless."
B2 v Secretary of State for the Home Department [2013] EWCA Civ 616.

STATEMENT. Stat. Def. "words, pictures, visual images, gestures or any other method of signifying meaning" (Defamation Act 2013 s.15).

STATUTORY FUNCTION. Stat. Def., Public Service Pensions Act 2013 s.37.

STRATEGY.
"The *Oxford English Dictionary* defines a 'strategy' as a 'plan of action designed to achieve a long term or overall aim'. In adopting only the 'architecture and principles', the Executive adopted something that was inchoate. There is no evidence before me that this inchoate strategy was ever finalised. There is no evidence that it was ever crafted into a road map designed to tackle the issues referred to in the section [46]. A strategy is intended to guide, to set a course. It must therefore be implicit in the idea of a strategy that that strategy must be identifiable, it must be complete, it must have a start, a middle and an end, it must aim to be effective, its effectiveness must be capable of measurement and the actions which are taken in attempting to implement that strategy must be referable back to that overarching strategy. In order for a strategy to fulfil these implicit requirements and to inform all the many stakeholders that an anti-poverty strategy must necessarily inform, it must be a written document (or a collection of strategy level documents intended to be read together as such). It must be capable of being referred back to and of providing policy level guidance to the stakeholders charged with achieving its goals."
Committee on the Administration of Justice (CAJ) and Brian Gormally's Application [2015] NIQB 59.

SUBJECTIVE DEVALUATION. See *Benedetti v Sawiris* [2013] UKSC 50.

SUBJECTIVE OVER-VALUATION. See *Benedetti v Sawiris* [2013] UKSC 50.

SUBSTANTIAL WEIGHT.
"127. I turn to consider the irrationality argument. I would make the preliminary observation that expressions such as 'substantial weight', or for that matter 'limited weight', do not have some uniform meaning, or even carry some numerical evaluation. Their significance depends upon the particular context in which they have been used. They often represent no more than a summary expressing how the decision-maker has pulled together a number of judgmental factors. It is difficult to see how in the present type of case a rationality challenge could succeed merely on the basis that a decision-maker has decided to give 'substantial weight' to a policy. Instead, the challenge ought to be directed to the process of reasoning which has been adopted."
Luton Borough Council, R. (on the application of) v Central Bedfordshire Council [2014] EWHC 4325 (Admin).

SUCCESS.
"'Success' for the purposes of the CPR is 'not a technical term, but a result in real life' and 'is a matter for the exercise of common sense': see Lightman J. in *BCCI v Ali* (No 4) 149 NLJ 1734 at paragraph 7."

Jones v Secretary of State for Energy And Climate Change [2012] EWHC 3647 (QB).

SUCH.

"In common usage, the phrase 'such person' is often employed to refer back to a class of person identified by reference to particular distinguishing features, without having to repeat those distinguishing features. The point may be too obvious to require illustration, but an example is to be found in the opinion of the court in *Donaldson*. Following the passage which I have quoted in paragraph [17] above, in which the First Division concluded that the regulations afford no protection to persons present in a workplace as visitors but not as workers, the court continued: 'That does not mean that such persons are left unprotected. They continue to have the protection afforded to visitors to premises by the antecedent, and subsisting, law relating to occupiers' liability.' The distinguishing feature of 'such persons' as are referred to there is that they are present in a workplace as visitors but not as workers. The only distinguishing feature of 'such person' as is referred to in the inclusion provision that can be read out of the general provision is that such person is one to whom premises or part of premises have been made available as a place of work. There is nothing in the wording of regulation 2(1), in my opinion, to suggest an intention that someone, A, who is present in premises which have been made available to another person, B, as a place of work and are, therefore, B's workplace, should enjoy the protection of the regulations for no reason other than that A happens to be at work there."

Brown v East Lothian Council [2013] ScotCS CSOH 62.

SUPPLEMENTARY.

"49. Section 41 is, as the heading to that congeries of sections heralds, supplementary. Supplementary means what it says: it is added to the power in s.9 to fill in details or machinery for that which the Act, and in particular s.9(2), does not itself provide. It enables that which the Act empowers to be effective."

Public Law Project, R. (on the application of) v Secretary of State for Justice [2014] EWHC 2365 (Admin).

SUPPLIER. Stat. Def., Groceries Code Adjudicator Act 2013 s.22.

SUPPLY AGREEMENT. Stat. Def., Groceries Code Adjudicator Act 2013 s.22.

SURVIVING SPOUSE.

"The issue in this appeal is simply whether the Appellant, Miss Latisah Ouaha, was properly to be regarded as 'the surviving spouse' of Mr Khawan Al-Faisal ('Mr Al-Faisal') when he died on 19 November 2010. . . . It seems to me that the question of whether a spouse under a valid foreign

marriage might or might not constitute the surviving spouse for the purposes of paragraph 2(1) could raise some difficult points of law that would
require full argument and maybe evidence before they could be determined. . . . In my judgment, these authorities, taken together with *Dukali
v Lamrani* to which I have already referred, demonstrate, as is obvious
from the context of paragraphs 2(1) and 2(2) that the term 'the surviving
spouse' has rather more formality about it than the term 'a person who
was living with the original tenant as his or her wife or wife or husband' in
paragraph 2(2)(a). It is not, therefore, to be given the flexible meaning that
was adopted by the Court of Appeal for the word "family" in then equivalent provisions. (See *Brock v Wollams* [1949] 2 KB 388 at page 394 per
Bucknill LJ and page 395 per Cohen LJ). The flexibility in the schedule to
the Rent Act 1977, as it seems to me and as was pointed out by Lord Slynn
in the passage that I have cited, is provided by paragraph 2(2) which refers
to persons 'living with the original tenant as his or her wife or husband'.
That provision did not, of course, apply here because Mr Al-Faisal had, as
the judge found, left the Appellant in 2002 or 2003. . . . In my judgment,
the judge was right because there was no formal marriage ceremony valid
under English law upon which the Appellant was able to rely. I would prefer to leave open whether the judge was right to hold that the only way in
which a person can qualify as 'the surviving spouse' for the purposes of
paragraph 2(1) is by showing that they underwent a ceremony of marriage
valid under the Marriage Acts. It may be that some or all foreign cere-
monies of marriage would allow a person to qualify, but we do not need to
decide that point today. What I can say is that the Appellant, on the evidence before the judge, never went through any valid ceremony of marriage recognised in the country in which the ceremony took place.
Accordingly, she did not, I think, reach the starting blocks. The words 'the
surviving spouse' as used in paragraph 2(1) seem to me obviously to contemplate in relation to a person relying upon a marriage ceremony a person who, by that ceremony, became legally the wife or husband in the
country in which the ceremony took place."
Northumberland & Durham Property Trust Ltd v Ouaha [2014] EWCA Civ
571.

SUSTAINABLE DEVELOPMENT.

"6. The relevant national policies are set out in the NPPF, in which 'sustainable development' is the key concept. There is no specific definition of
'sustainable development', but it is to be defined in terms of development
which meets the needs of the present without compromising the ability of
future generations to meet their own needs. That is reflected in the first
words of the Ministerial Foreword to the NPPF, which state:

'The purpose of planning is sustainable growth. Sustainable means
ensuring that better lives for ourselves don't mean worse lives for future
generations. Development means growth. We must accommodate the new

ways in which we will earn our living in a competitive world. We must
house a rising population . . . ."
*Milwood Land (Stafford) Ltd v Secretary of State for Communities and
Local Government* [2015] EWHC 1836 (Admin).

SUSTAINED OR CONTRACTED.   See Employers' Liability Insurance
"Trigger" Litigation: *BAI (Run Off) Ltd v Durham* [2012] UKSC 14.

SYSTEMIC.
"The adjective 'systemic' may mean 'systematic'; that is to say something
which is 'arranged or conducted according to a system, plan, or organised
method' (Shorter Oxford English Dictionary sub nom 'systemic' and 'systematic'). The court notes the reference in its remit being to determine
"how systemic or widespread" the problem is, but it is not immediately
clear whether these two adjectives are to be regarded as synonymous. It
will proceed on the basis that if corruption is 'widespread' in a judicial
system, it can properly be regarded as systematic and 'systemic'."
Fatjon Kapri v Her Majesty's Advocate (for the Republic of Albania) [2014]
ScotHC HCJAC 33.

T

TAG-ALONG RIGHTS. Stat. Def., "tag-along rights", in relation to shares in a company, means the right of the holders of a minority of the shares to sell their shares, where the holders of the majority are selling theirs, on the same terms as those on which the holders of the majority are doing so, Employment Rights Act 1996 s.205A as inserted by the Growth and Infrastructure Act 2013 s.35.

TAX ADVANTAGE. Stat. Def., Finance Act 2013 s.208.

TAX ARRANGEMENTS. Stat. Def., Finance Act 2013 s.207.

TAX AVOIDANCE.
"I should interpolate that 'tax avoidance schemes' in the present context means special arrangements made by a taxpayer so as to minimise his or her tax liability. There is no question or suggestion of dishonesty—that is called tax evasion. What HMRC contends is that some film schemes are ineffective and in particular that the schemes or most of them involving partnerships to finance film-making promoted by Mr McKenna via Ingenious are so. That is hotly disputed and is currently the subject of substantial proceedings in the relevant tax tribunal."
Ingenious Media Holdings Plc, R. (on the application of) v HM Revenue & Customs [2015] EWCA Civ 173.

TELECOMMUNICATIONS.
"61. I also agree with Mr Malynicz that the term 'telecommunications services' has a broad meaning, which includes services such as digital audio visual streaming via broadband connections or mobile or fixed line telephone networks of audio visual TV content to mobile telephones and other devices, including to set top boxes."
Total Ltd v YouView TV Ltd [2014] EWHC 1963 (Ch).

TELEVISED. Stat. Def., "shown (on a screen or by projection onto any surface) whether by means of the broadcast transmission of pictures or otherwise" (Offensive Behaviour at Football and Threatening Communications (Scotland) Act 2012 s.4).

TEMPORARY.
"The judge noted that the words of the relevant covenant were far from clear, but that the parties agreed that some animal usage was permissible,

but only if it was 'temporary'. . . . The meaning to be given to the word
'temporary' is the meaning that the word has in the context of the Conveyance. It plainly does not have a single legal meaning in all legal contexts:
each party on the appeal recognised that the other's reading of the word
was one which the word could bear. I consider that the judge correctly
recognised that the word was an ordinary English word containing within
it a variety of nuances (some of which would be more prominent than others when the word came to be applied to different sets of facts). I consider
that he correctly held that whether a particular use (or combination of
uses) was 'temporary' was a question of fact and degree: and I would not
disturb the application by an experienced County Court Judge of the
working document he construed to the facts he found."
Giles v Tarry [2012] EWCA Civ 837.

TENANT. Stat. Def., "in relation to a lease, means the person who has right
as tenant under the lease, whether or not such person has completed title
(and where more than one person comes within that description, the person
who most recently acquired that right)" (Long Leases (Scotland) Act 2012
s.80).

TERMS.
"112. A worker is a person who cannot establish that he is an employee. It
is common ground that section 43K(1) was enacted primarily to protect
agency workers.
    113. The conclusion which I have reached above that there was no con-
tract means that there is also no contract for the purposes of section
43K(1)(b). The only question is whether there also needs to be a contract
for the purpose of section 43K(1)(a). The EAT held that on the true interpretation of this provision there was no requirement for a contract.
    114. Mr Bowers essentially submits that where Parliament refers to con-
tract, it uses the word 'contract' and so when it refers to 'terms' there need
be no contract. Mr Linden submits that this is wrong. The word 'terms' is
used because there have to be terms imposed. The sub-section is not
intended to apply to non-contractual situations: it has likewise been held
that measures to combat discrimination to persons in their occupations do
not apply to volunteers: *X v Mid-Sussex Citizens Advice Bureau* [2013] 1
All ER 1038.
    115. In my judgment this is a short point. It must inevitably follow from
the statutory reference to 'term on which he is or was engaged to do work'
that there must be a contract."
Sharpe v Bishop of Worcester [2015] EWCA Civ 399.

TERRORISM.
"The essence of terrorism is the commission, organisation, incitement or
threat of serious acts of violence against persons or property for the pur-

pose of intimidating a population or compelling a government or international organisation to act or not to act in a particular way (see, for
example, the definition in article 2 of the draft comprehensive Convention), as Sedley L.J. put it in the Court of Appeal, 'the use for political ends
of fear induced by violence' (para.31). It is, it seems to us, very likely that
inducing terror in the civilian population or putting such extreme pres-
sures upon a government will also have the international repercussions
referred to by the UNHCR."
Al-Sirri v Secretary of State for the Home Department [2012] UKSC 54.

"The appeal raises the issue of the meaning of 'terrorism' in section 1 of
the Terrorism Act 2000 ('the 2000 Act'). . . .

23. The case for the prosecution is that the definition of terrorism in
section 1 of the 2000 Act, and, in particular, in subsections (1) and (2), is
very wide indeed, and that it would be wrong for any court to cut it down
by implying some sort of restriction into the wide words used by the legislature. On that basis, the appellant was rightly convicted and the answer to
the certified question must be 'yes'.

24. The case for the appellant, as it developed in oral argument, had
three strands. The first is that the 2000 Act, like the 2006 Act, was
intended, at least in part, to give effect to the UK's international treaty
obligations, and the concept of terrorism in international law does not
extend to military attacks by a non-state armed group against state, or
inter-governmental organisation, armed forces in the context of a non-
international armed conflict, and that this limitation should be implied
into the definition in section 1 of the 2000 Act. The second, and closely
connected, argument is that it would be wrong to read the 2000 or 2006
Acts as criminalising in this country an act abroad, unless that act would
be regarded as criminal by international law norms. The third argument
raised by the appellant is that, as a matter of domestic law and quite apart
from international law considerations, some qualifications must be read
into the very wide words of section 1 of the 2000 Act.

25. Although it was advanced as an alternative argument to the contentions based on international law, we propose to start by addressing the
appellant's case based on the relevant statutory provisions by reference to
the familiar domestic principles, and then to consider whether that meaning conflicts with international law. . . .

27. The effect of section 1(1) of the 2000 Act is to identify terrorism as
consisting of three components. The first is the 'use or threat of action',
inside or outside the UK, where that action consists of, inter alia, 'serious
violence', 'serious damage to property', or creating a serious risk to public
safety or health—section 1(1)(a), (2) and (4). The second component is
that the use or threat must be 'designed to influence the government [of the
UK or any other country] or an [IGO] or to intimidate the public'—
section 1(1)(b) and (4). The third component is that the use or threat is

'made for the purpose of advancing a political, religious, racial or ideo-logical cause'–section 1(1)(c).

28. As a matter of ordinary language, the definition would seem to cover any violence or damage to property if it is carried out with a view to influencing a government or IGO in order to advance a very wide range of causes. Thus, it would appear to extend to military or quasi-military activity aimed at bringing down a foreign government, even where that activity is approved (officially or unofficially) by the UK government.

29. It is neither necessary nor appropriate to express any concluded view whether the definition of 'terrorism' goes that far, although it is not entirely easy to see why, at least in the absence of international law considerations, it does not. For present purposes it is enough to proceed on the basis that, subject to these considerations, the definition of terrorism in section 1 in the 2000 Act is, at least if read in its natural sense, very far reaching indeed. Thus, on occasions, activities which might command a measure of public understanding, if not support, may fall within it: for example, activities by the victims of oppression abroad, which might command a measure of public understanding, and even support in this country, may well fall within it.

30. The Crown argues that, particularly given the purpose of the 2000 Act, 'terrorism' cannot be narrowly defined, if one is to allow for the many disparate forms which terrorism may take, and the inevitable changes which will occur in international relations, in political regimes in other countries, and in the UK's foreign policy. Accordingly, runs the argument, a very wide definition was deliberately adopted, but, recognising the risks of criminalising activities which should not be prosecuted, the 2000 Act has, through section 117, precluded any prosecution without the consent of the Director of Public Prosecutions ('DPP') or, if the activities under consideration occurred abroad, the Attorney General.

31. It is clear that it is very hard to define 'terrorism'. Thus, Lord Lloyd of Berwick, who wrote an Inquiry into the Legislation against Terrorism (Cm 3420) which contained recommendations which were reflected in the 2000 Act, observed in a speech on the second reading of the Bill which later became that Act that 'there are great difficulties in finding a satisfactory definition of "terrorism", and suspected that "none of us will succeed". That view has been cited with agreement in reports produced by the two successive Independent Reviewers of the legislation appointed under section 36 of the 2006 Act, Lord Carlile of Berriew QC and Mr David Anderson QC.

32. In reports produced in 2006 and 2007 Lord Carlile concluded that the statutory definition of terrorism was 'practical and effective' and advised that, save for small amendments, the definition should remain as originally drafted. More specifically, he observed that 'the current definition in the Terrorism Act 2000 is consistent with international comparators and treaties, and is useful and broadly fit for purpose . . . '. Lord

Carlile also stated that 'the discretion vested in the authorities to use or not to use the special laws is a real and significant element of protection against abuse of rights'. . . . Despite the undesirable consequences of the combination of the very wide definition of 'terrorism' and the provisions of section 117, it is difficult to see how the natural, very wide, meaning of the definition can properly be cut down by this Court. For the reasons given by Lord Lloyd, Lord Carlile and Mr Anderson, the definition of 'terrorism' was indeed intended to be very wide. Unless it is established that the natural meaning of the legislation conflicts with the European Convention on Human Rights (which is not suggested) or any other international obligation of the United Kingdom (which we consider in the next section of this judgment), our function is to interpret the meaning of the definition in its statutory, legal and practical context. We agree with the wide interpretation favoured by the prosecution: it accords with the natural meaning of the words used in section 1(1)(b) of the 2000 Act, and, while it gives the words a concerningly wide meaning, there are good reasons for it. . . .

39. We are reinforced in this view by the further consideration that the wide definition of terrorism was not ignored by Parliament when the 2000 Act was being debated. It was discussed by the Home Secretary who also, in answer to a question, mentioned the filter of section 117 (see *Hansard* (HC Deb) 14 December 1999, cols 159, 163). This is not a case in which it is appropriate to refer to what was said in Parliament as an aid to statutory interpretation, but it provides some comfort for the Crown's argument. Of rather more legitimate relevance is the fact that Parliament was content to leave the definition of 'terrorism' effectively unchanged, when considering amendments or extensions to the 2000 Act, well after the 2007 report of Lord Carlile, which so clearly (and approvingly) drew attention to the width of the definition of terrorism—see eg the Crime and Security Act 2010, the Terrorist Asset-Freezing etc Act 2010 and the Terrorism Prevention and Investigation Measures Act 2011. . . .

62. While acknowledging that the issue is ultimately one for Parliament, we should record our view that the concerns and suggestions about the width of the statutory definition of terrorism which Mr Anderson has identified in his two reports merit serious consideration. Any legislative narrowing of the definition of 'terrorism', with its concomitant reduction in the need for the exercise of discretion under section 117 of the 2000 Act, is to be welcomed, provided that it is consistent with the public protection to which the legislation is directed."

Gul, R. v [2013] UKSC 64.

See ACT OF TERRORISM.

TIED PUB. Stat. Def., Small Business, Enterprise and Employment Act 2015 s.68.

TIES.
"38. In my judgment, however, Aikens LJ, by referring to 'support', was not there intending to lay down a defining qualification of ties. As Christopher Clarke LJ pointed out in the course of argument, a person may have very close ties with another state but in the particular circumstances little or no prospect of support. . . . Consideration of whether a person has 'no ties' to such country must involve a rounded consideration of all the relevant circumstances."
CG (Jamaica) v Secretary of State for the Home Department [2015] EWCA Civ 194.

TOWN GREEN.
"40. I acknowledge that there may be a legal distinction to be drawn between town or village greens, which were newly defined by section 22 CRA 1965, and rights of common which, though described in section 22, were not exhaustively defined."
Littlejohns, R. (on the application of) v Devon County Council [2015] EWHC 730 (Admin).

TRADE.
"As an ordinary word in the English language 'trade' has or has had a variety of meanings or shades of meaning. Its meaning in tax legislation is a matter of law. Whether or not a particular activity is a trade, within the meaning of the tax legislation, depends on the evaluation of the activity by the tribunal of fact. These propositions can be broken down into the following components. It is a matter of law whether some particular factual characteristic is capable of being an indication of trading activity. It is a matter of law whether a particular activity is capable of constituting a trade. Whether or not the particular activity in question constitutes a trade depends upon an evaluation of all the facts relating to it against the background of the applicable legal principles. To that extent the conclusion is one of fact, or, more accurately, it is an inference of fact from the primary facts found by the fact-finding tribunal."
Eclipse Film Partners No.35 LLP v Revenue and Customs Commissioners [2015] EWCA Civ 95.

TRADER. Stat. Def., "a person acting for purposes relating to that person's trade, business, craft or profession, whether acting personally or through another person acting in the trader's name or on the trader's behalf" (Consumer Rights Act 2015 s.2).

TRAFFIC DATA (COMMUNICATIONS). Stat. Def., Prisons (Interference with Wireless Telegraphy) Act 2012 s.4.

TRAFFICKING. Stat. Def., Modern Slavery Act 2015 s.2.

TRANSACTION.
"32. As I have explained, the term 'transaction' is widely defined in s.436 as including a gift or arrangement. If it were necessary for the purposes of this decision, I would therefore be disposed to find it is broad enough to encompass a payment made by a company or by an agent of the company acting within the scope of his authority. But to focus unduly on the term 'transaction' risks obscuring the need for the second and vital element, namely the requirement that the transaction be something that the company has 'entered into'. This expression connotes the taking of some step or act of participation by the company. Thus the composite requirement requires the company to make the gift or make the arrangement or in some other way be party to or involved in the transaction in issue so that it can properly be said to have entered into it, and of course it must have done so within the period prescribed by s.240."
Hunt (Liquidator of Ovenden Colbert Printers Ltd) v Hosking [2013] EWCA Civ 1408.

TRANSGENDER IDENTITY. Stat. Def., "any of the following—
  (i) transvestism,
  (ii) transsexualism,
  (iii) intersexuality,
  (iv) having, by virtue of the Gender Recognition Act 2004 (c.7), changed gender,
  (v) any other gender identity that is not standard male or female gender identity" (Offensive Behaviour at Football and Threatening Communications (Scotland) Act 2012 s.4).

TRAVEL DOCUMENT. Stat. Def., Specialist Printing Equipment and Materials (Offences) Act 2015 s.2.

TREATMENT. For the meaning of the concept of medical treatment in the context of abortion see *Doogan, Re Judicial Review* [2012] ScotCS CSOH 32.

TREE.
"6. I note that part of the evidence submitted in the appeal on behalf of the Claimant by Julian Forbes-Laird, an expert aboriculturalist, criticised the TPO's description of W2, 'all trees of whatever species' for using 'excruciatingly vague language' (see rebuttal proof paragraphs 3.4.2–3.4.3). Ignoring the hyperbole, the short answer is that the description was not legally uncertain. The order meant exactly what it said. Any specimen qualifying as a 'tree' fell within the scope of the restrictions contained in the TPO. In any event, as emerged during oral argument in this appeal, there was no real issue before the Inspector as to what should be understood in the legislation by the word 'tree'. There should not have been any

doubt therefore as to the obligations imposed by the TPO before the Claimant gave instructions for works to be carried out. . . .

12. The Act does not contain a definition of 'tree'. The issue raised by the Claimant concerning the extent to which the definition applies to young specimens (to use a neutral word) applies just as much to section 197 as to sections 198 and 206 to 208. A restrictive approach as to what may be considered to be a 'tree' would not only affect the scope of the protection afforded by TPOs, but also the ambit of the local planning authority's power to require the preservation or planting of trees when determining planning applications. . . .

39. The Claimant accepts that the word 'tree' includes saplings, but argues that it does not include seeds or seedlings. It is submitted that in so far as Cranston J suggested otherwise in *Palm Developments Limited v Secretary of State for Communities and Local Government* [2009] 2 P. & C.R. 16 his judgment was incorrect and should not be followed. It is submitted that the same error was made in the Council's evidence and in the Inspector's decision. . . .

45. Mr Boyle Q.C. criticised the evidence of Ms Leonard on behalf of the Council for treating seedlings as falling within the definition of 'tree' (see paragraphs 4.4 and 4.7). He also criticised references to the seed bearing trees in the vicinity. But on a fair reading the Council's evidence did not rely upon mere seeds as such, but on the likelihood of seedlings and saplings having developed in the W2 area (see e.g. Willow and Ash can seed prolifically preceded by the phrase 'there may have been plenty of seedlings/saplings on site prior to the clearance works'.

46. In his main proof Mr Forbes-Laird did not deal with the 'young tree' issue. Even more telling, in point 3 of paragraph 3.3 of his rebuttal, Mr Forbes-Laird quoted Ms Leonard's reference to 'seedling/saplings on site prior to the clearance works' and did not make any criticism at all of her inclusion of seedlings. Similarly, he did not raise the point that seedlings should be excluded from 'trees' because of the inability to differentiate them from the scrub in sense of 'stunted forest growth'. His response at paragraphs 3.6.1 to 3.6.4 simply asserted that there were no young trees in the cleared area relying upon the declaration of Mr Logsdon which was defective in this respect.

47. Mr Boyle Q.C. accepted that paragraph 8 of the Inspector's decision letter, summarising the relevant part of the decision on *Palm*, was impeccable. It refers to 'saplings' as 'trees'. Mr Boyle accepted that ground 2 depends upon the four words in the first sentence of paragraph 9 of the decision letter which follow the reference to 'saplings', namely 'or other potential trees'. He submitted that the Inspector had been influenced by the Council's reference to 'seedlings' and that the word 'potential' indicated that he was taking into account specimens which had not become trees.

48. Ground 2 is untenable. The Inspector was entitled to produce a decision letter with reasons briefly stated and addressed to an audience famil-

iar with the arguments and points. The position facing the Inspector was that the Claimant did not disagree with the Council's use of the term 'seedlings/saplings'. The Inspector was entitled to rely upon that uncontroversial position. The words 'and other potential trees' should not be read as referring to specimens which are not trees at all, but simply to the unchallenged 'seedlings/saplings' term used by the Council. For these reasons I reject ground 2."
Distinctive Properties (Ascot) Ltd v Secretary of State for Communities and Local Government [2015] EWHC 729 (Admin).

TRUST.
"The first thing is that, while Scots law has no difficulty in using the word 'trust' in this context, the concept is more accurately and precisely analysed by referring to the fiduciary duty that the agent owes to his client with regard to money that he holds on his client's behalf. So the fact that a statutory trust is rejected by section 139(3) of the 2000 Act in favour of agency in the application of section 139(1) to Scotland, while at first sight surprising, does appear to have some basis in the language that was used to explain the relationship in *Jopp v Johnston's Trustee.*"
Lehman Brothers International (Europe), Re [2012] UKSC 6.

TRUSTEE. Stat. Def., "includes an executor, administrator or personal representative" (Presumption of Death Act 2013 s.20).

TURNOVER. Stat. Def. (in context of a society), Co-operative and Community Benefit Societies Act 2014 s.102.

TURPITUDE. For examination of the meaning of turpitude in the context of the impact on a claim or defence see *RTA (Business Consultants) Ltd v Bracewell* [2015] EWHC 630 (QB).

UK FINANCIAL SYSTEM. Stat. Def., Financial Services and Markets Act 2000 s.1I as inserted by Financial Services Act 2012 s.6.

UNABLE TO PAY ITS DEBTS.
"It is in my judgment clear from Eurosail and its approval of Cheyne Finance that the balance sheet test in section 123 (2) [of the Insolvency Act 1986] is not excluded merely because a company is for the time being in fact paying its debts as they fall due."
Bucci v Carman (Liquidator of Casa Estates (UK) Limited) [2014] EWCA Civ 383.

UNDER.
"29. However it arises, it is plain that liability for mis-selling would not arise 'under' the contract of insurance. The insurer's primary liability under an insurance policy is its liability to pay claims in the event of an insured loss: see, e.g. *Sprung v Royal Insurance (UK) Ltd* [1997] CLC 70 at [80]."
PA (GI) Ltd v GICL 2013 Ltd [2015] EWHC 1556 (Ch).

UNDERGROUND WORKS.
"40. In my judgment s.3(2) has no application to the work that has been carried out. The purpose of the 1931 Act is, as the long title states, 'to provide for the preservation and for restricting the user of certain squares gardens and enclosures in the administrative county of London and for other purposes'. I agree with Mr Straker that s.3(2) is to be construed as allowing unrestricted use of the subsoil of a protected square so long as the square is unaffected or, provided there is consent, use of the subsoil of the square which brings with it such use of the surface as is reasonably necessary and proper for such subsoil use. Such use of the surface as can occur must be for an underground purpose, namely for the construction and maintenance of underground works and underground buildings or for the erection of temporary buildings and for entrances exits and ventilations shafts in relation to such works and buildings.

41. In my view 'underground' in s.3 means below the surface of the ground. That accords with its ordinary English meaning as defined by the *Oxford English Dictionary*; and the definitions of it given in the *Collins English Dictionary* are not inconsistent with this interpretation. Indeed Collins gives 'below the surface' as a synonym for 'below ground'. I reject Mr Maurici's submission that works which are situated below the ground

level of a protected square are underground works for the purposes of the
1931 Act, irrespective of whether they are, or are not, exposed to the sky.

42. There is, in my view, force in Mr Straker's submission that underground works and buildings carry the same meaning in both parts of
s.3(2). However if the Claimant's contention that an underground work
can be open and on the surface is correct, then underground works are
given a different meaning in the second part of s.3(2) from the first part.
Section 3(2) refers in its first part to owners not being prevented from
using the subsoil for the construction and maintenance of underground
works and buildings. It therefore contemplates the subsoil as the place for
such work. The surface is separately referred to by the Act. As a matter of
ordinary English the subsoil is always under something, namely the top-
soil.

43. The Royal Commission recommended that any proposals in connection with the use of the subsoil, if they affected the surface, should
require consent (para.103(4)(c); and see para.69 on the construction of
underground garages). I agree with Mr Straker that this is only consistent
with the second part of s.3(2) dealing with something underneath the
ground.

44. In my judgment the surface use of the protected square by the
Claimant was not for or in relation to the construction and maintenance
of underground works or buildings. None of the works (the courtyard, the
lightwell, the bridge or the stairs) are underground works or buildings for
the purposes of s.3(2) of the 1931 Act."

*Eliterank Ltd, R. (on the application of) v Royal Borough of Kensington &
Chelsea* [2015] EWHC 220 (Admin).

UNLAWFUL. See WITHOUT LAWFUL AUTHORITY.

UNNECESSARY MATERIAL.
"66. 'Unnecessary material' was defined in clause 728(2) of the Company
Law Reform Bill in the same terms as in section 1074(2) of the 2006 Act.
The Explanatory Notes stated in relation to clause 728: '1311. This clause
provides for cases where a delivered document contains unnecessary material (i.e. material for which there was no legal requirement) . . . ' It is
unclear whether this explanation was intended to reflect clause 728(2)(a)
('not necessary in order to comply with an obligation under any enactment') alone, or clause 728(2)(b) ('not specifically authorised to be delivered to the registrar') as well. On the one hand, the phrase 'legal
requirement' is more apt to refer to clause 728(2)(a) alone. On the other,
the explanation appears to have been intended to refer to the entire clause.
On either view, I consider that this explanation supports what I would in
any event hold to be the meaning of section 1074(2)(a), namely that it
relates to legal requirements alone. . . .

67. Accordingly, I consider that the issue of whether the requirement in

section 1074(2)(a) is made out falls to be determined on an entirely objective basis, by reference to legislation, and that the Applicant's perception of whether or not material 'is necessary in order to comply with an obligation under any enactment' has nothing to do with that issue. . . .

72. Mr Margolin submitted that to interpret section 1074 as meaning that anything that is not required or authorised by legislation to be included in a document is 'unnecessary material' would produce a surprising result. I disagree. I consider that it would be more surprising if the content of "unnecessary material" depended on the extent to which a person had been "specifically authorised" to include that material in documents.

73. Mr Margolin also submitted that to interpret section 1074(b) as referring to what is not specifically authorised by legislation means that it adds nothing to section 1074(a). I do not agree with this either. Section 1074(a) refers to the requirements of legislation, whereas section 1074(b) refers to what is authorised by legislation, which is different."

The Registrar of Companies v Swarbrick (Administrators of Gardenprime Ltd) [2014] EWHC 1466 (Ch).

UPSTREAM.

"26. Nothing turns on the CJEU's use of the words 'upstream' and 'downstream'. *Bonik* may have been among the first cases in which the CJEU used these actual terms but, in *Kittel* at [43], [44], [45] and [49], the CJEU referred to transactions occurring prior and subsequent to the purchase giving rise to the input tax on which the trader relied, which comes to the same thing. Those words simply go to timing."

Fonecomp Ltd v HM Revenue and Customs [2015] EWCA Civ 39.

USE.

"The word 'use' is employed as a noun in section 298(2)(b) and in other sections where that word appears in this part of POCA. The noun 'use' has various connotations, but in this case I think that its sense, when used in conjunction with some other noun (such as 'cash' as in this instance) is that of 'the application' of the other thing (in this case the cash) for some purpose which, in this case, is that of intended unlawful conduct. However, to my mind, the appellant did not intend to apply this cash in any positive sense to deceive the benefit authorities. The unlawful conduct of concealing the fact that the appellant had more than the limit of savings of £6,000 would have occurred whether or not the appellant had the money in cash. She could, after all, have had the additional £1,150 in a bank account or, indeed, all £7,150 in a bank account. The intent was to conceal the fact of having that sum of money in savings. In my view, the unlawful conduct that was intended by this appellant was to conceal the fact that she had savings greater than the limit of £6,000 in order that her benefits would not be reduced. That does not amount to the 'use' of the cash in the unlawful conduct intended in this case. In fact, it was the very opposite of

a 'use'. The appellant intended to conceal the fact that she had the money, but did not intend its use in any other way in order to further her intended unlawful conduct."
Begum v West Midlands Police [2012] EWHC 2304 (Admin).

See IN USE.

VALUE.

"In favour of the tenants' construction it can be said that, if it had been intended that the schedule of dilapidations should include binding estimates of the costs of repair, it would have been more natural to use the expression 'costs of repair' rather than 'value'; that would have made it clear that the schedule was intended to include estimates of cost and that those estimates were to be used to determine how the breach of the tenants' obligations in articles Fifth and Sixth was to be quantified, subject to a right to challenge individual items. 'Value', however, is a word of more general signification than 'cost'. Moreover, the purpose of the relevant part of article Twelfth is to deal with breaches of other clauses by the tenants. In that context, we are of opinion that the use of the word 'value' can be taken to indicate that the schedule of dilapidations is not an end in itself but a means to an end, namely the ascertainment of what is required to put the landlords in the position that they would have been in if the tenants had fulfilled their obligations under articles Fifth and Sixth."

Grove Investments Ltd v Cape Building Products Ltd [2014] ScotCS CSIH 43.

VICINITY.

"[28] The concept of vicinity is a chimera. Its definition may evolve under the impact of changing social and demographic conditions thus progressing the purpose and theme of the many authorities that deal with it."

Sainsbury's Supermarket Ltd v Winemark The Wine Merchants Ltd [2012] NIQB 45.

VICTIM.

"By way of elaboration on those observations we would remark that while we are conscious of a seemingly increasing, indiscriminate and often inappropriate use of the term 'victim' in the media and elsewhere, the word 'victim' nonetheless still unquestionably conveys that the person to whom it is applied has, as a matter of fact, suffered both the injury, insult or disadvantage relevant to the particular context and that such was caused by the actings of the person or persons responsible for the event in question. There will of course be many situations in which it is entirely appropriate and proper to refer to a person as being a victim. But in the context of criminal proceedings it will generally be the case that until guilt is admitted or proved it will not be appropriate to refer to a complainer as being a 'victim'. The very purpose of the criminal process is, of course, first to establish whether the alleged crime has been committed and secondly whether the accused was the perpetrator. In general it is only once the first

of these purposes has been achieved positively to the prosecutor that it may properly be said there is a victim of the crime charged. It is therefore important that in most aspects of the criminal process care is taken to avoid referring to a person making an allegation of criminal conduct towards him or her as a 'victim' other than in a context in which guilt is proved or is assumed for valid reasons. A particularly important part of the criminal process is, of course, the giving of instructions to the jury in cases prosecuted under solemn procedure, where correspondingly particular care should be taken. In that respect, users of the 'jury manual' should bear in mind the important note issued with the last amendment drawing attention to the observations in *Hogan v HM Advocate*."
Michael Wishart v Her Majesty's Advocate [2013] ScotHC HCJAC 168.

VICTIM OF SLAVERY. Stat. Def., Modern Slavery Act 2015 s.56.

VIDEO GAME. Stat. Def., Corporation Tax Act 2009 s.1217AA inserted by Finance Act 2013 Sch.17 para.1.

VILLAGE GREEN.
"40. I acknowledge that there may be a legal distinction to be drawn between town or village greens, which were newly defined by section 22 CRA 1965, and rights of common which, though described in section 22, were not exhaustively defined."
Littlejohns, R. (on the application of) v Devon County Council [2015] EWHC 730 (Admin).

VIOLENCE.
"11. I do not understand why the draftsman thought it necessary, in both section 177 and section 198, explicitly to include threats of violence as a sub-category within the definition of violence. This seems to me to add an unnecessary level of complication. If such threats have been made, and—as the definition requires—are 'likely to be carried out', that would seem necessarily to establish that it was probable that actual violence would occur if the applicant continues to occupy the property, or returns to the district (as the case may be); and specific provision is redundant. But I make this point only in the interests of clear thinking: it does not seem to impinge on the issues which we have to decide. . . .
27. In the end, however, I have concluded that such an approach cannot be reconciled with the way that section 177(1A) is drafted. The structure which the draftsman has adopted is that there is a single concept of 'violence', of which 'domestic violence' is a sub-category. This is, I think, the same point as Lady Hale makes, 'on the other hand', in para.35 of her judgment in Yemshaw; and it appears also to be the basis of the views of Lord Rodger and Lord Brown that 'violence' must have a single meaning. Further, quite apart from this verbal point, on reflection I think that to distinguish between the meaning of 'violence' as it appears in the phrases

'domestic violence' and 'other violence' is unsatisfactory as a matter of substance. As Lady Hale observes, people who are at risk of intimidating or harmful behaviour from their near neighbours merit protection no less than those who run the same risk from partners or family members; and Lord Rodger's warning about 'playing down the serious nature of psychological harm' is not confined to the domestic context. . . . The burden which adopting a broader construction of 'other violence' may place on authorities is not of a nature, or inherently on a scale, that could justify the conclusion that Parliament cannot have intended it (still less so if, as I suspect, the additional impact caused by such a construction is likely to be less than that already caused by Yemshaw). . . .

31. In short, therefore, I believe that the phrase 'other violence' in section 177(1) covers not only physical violence (actual or threatened) but other threatening or intimidating behaviour or abuse, if of such seriousness that it may give rise to psychological harm. . . .

32. I should perhaps say a little more about 'psychological harm'. That term does not appear in the statute itself and it should not be treated as a formal requirement of section 177(1) that an applicant has suffered, or is likely to suffer, such harm as a result of the conduct in question. Rather, its significance is, as discussed above, that conduct cannot normally be described as 'violent', as opposed to merely anti-social, unless it is of such a nature and seriousness as to be liable to cause psychological harm. That being so, it is not necessary for officers making decisions under the homelessness provisions to search for some technical, still less medical, meaning. I think the broad sense in which the phrase is employed in *Yemshaw* is adequately well understood in ordinary usage. It connotes something more than transient upset or distress. Psychological harm will often shade into, or overlap with, a diagnosed psychiatric injury or illness, such as depression; but that need not always be so."

Hussain v London Borough of Waltham Forest [2015] EWCA Civ 14.

See CRIME OF VIOLENCE.

VOLUNTARY. See DETAINED.

WAREHOUSE CERTIFICATES/RECEIPTS.
"4. It should be noted that, when used in trade and financing, these documents are given various names, though probably the most common is
'warehouse receipts'. In this case, the documents are called 'warehouse
certificates'. The court was told that in Chinese it is the same word, and
can be translated either way.

54. Warehouse receipts are common instruments in trade and finance,
and may contain, or evidence, a contract between the warehouse and the
party on whose behalf the goods are stored. In the present case, the
receipts in dispute were made payable to the order of the bank which was
providing finance for trading in warehoused metal. The receipts thereby
constituted the bank's security, or more accurately an essential part of it.

55. A warehouse receipt represents goods in the possession of a warehouse. The document gives a description of the goods, and is a receipt for
the goods stored. At common law, warehouse receipts are not treated as
negotiable documents of title (unlike bills of lading). However, though not
in itself conferring possession of the goods on the holder, possession of a
warehouse receipt in effect gives the holder the right to possession of the
goods. The evidence in this case, for example, is that without receiving the
receipt back, the warehouse will not release the goods."

*Impala Warehousing and Logistics (Shanghai) Co Ltd v Wanxiang Resources
(Singapore) PTE Ltd* [2015] EWHC 811 (Comm).

WEEKLY.
Erratum: ignore the cross-reference to AVERAGE WEEKLY EARN-
INGS.

WEIGHT.
"127. I turn to consider the irrationality argument. I would make the preliminary observation that expressions such as 'substantial weight', or for
that matter 'limited weight', do not have some uniform meaning, or even
carry some numerical evaluation. Their significance depends upon the
particular context in which they have been used. They often represent no
more than a summary expressing how the decision-maker has pulled
together a number of judgmental factors. It is difficult to see how in the
present type of case a rationality challenge could succeed merely on the
basis that a decision-maker has decided to give 'substantial weight' to a
policy. Instead, the challenge ought to be directed to the process of reasoning which has been adopted."

*Luton Borough Council, R. (on the application of) v Central Bedfordshire
Council* [2014] EWHC 4325 (Admin).

WELL-BEING (OF A PERSON). Stat. Def., Social Services and Well-being (Wales) Act 2014 s.2.

WELLBOAT. Stat. Def., "a vessel that contains a tank or well for holding water (including sea water)—
    (a) into which live farmed fish may be taken, and
    (b) in which the fish may be subsequently kept,
for . . .
    (a) the transportation of farmed fish,
    (b) the storage of farmed fish,
    (c) the slaughter of farmed fish,
    (d) the treatment of farmed fish in connection with health, parasites, pathogens or diseases,
    (e) the grading of farmed fish." (Aquaculture and Fisheries (Scotland) Act 2013 s.4).

WELSH GOVERNMENT. Stat. Def., Wales Act 2014 s.4.

WIDOW. Stat. Def., includes a woman whose marriage to another woman ended with the other woman's death, Marriage (Same Sex Couples) Act 2013 Sch.3; Stat. Def., "includes a woman whose marriage to another woman ended with the other woman's death" (Marriage and Civil Partnership (Scotland) Act 2014 s.4).

WIDOWER. Stat. Def., includes a man whose marriage to another man ended with the other man's death, Marriage (Same Sex Couples) Act 2013 Sch.3; Stat. Def., "includes a man whose marriage to another man ended with the other man's death" (Marriage and Civil Partnership (Scotland) Act 2014 s.4).

WIFE. Stat. Def., includes a woman who is married to another woman, Marriage (Same Sex Couples) Act 2013 Sch.3.

WITHOUT LAWFUL AUTHORITY.
"The phrase 'unlawful mooring' as used in section 19 of the 1995 Act denotes a mooring in contravention of section 18 of the 1995 Act, such as to constitute a criminal offence under section 18 of the 1995 Act. It is a mooring in breach of the criminal law: and it is to be noted in that context the care taken in section 19(8) of the 1995 Act to ensure that a continued mooring after receipt of a notice served under section 19(1) is not, without more, to be unlawful in that sense. By contrast, the phrase 'without lawful authority' in section 8(1) of the 1983 Act focuses on the lack of lawful authority, not on breach of a regulation or provision regulating mooring (and constituting a criminal offence). The gist is not contravention, but lack of authority."
Moore v British Waterways Board [2012] EWHC 182 (Ch).

WITHOUT PREJUDICE TO THE GENERALITY.

"On the other hand, a statute can be passed with the deliberate Parliamentary intention that it is to be applied in a range of circumstances not necessarily foreseen or contemplated at the time it is passed. The words 'without prejudice to the generality' seem to me to convey that approach."
Shanks (t/a Blue Line Taxis), R. (on the application of) v The Council of the County of Northumberland [2012] EWHC 1539 (Admin).

WORK EQUIPMENT.

"Counsel for the appellant argued that once it was established that this was work equipment for cleaners/housekeepers employed by the defenders, then it became work equipment for the appellant. There are two flaws in this argument. First, the wardrobe (and the pole within) was not in the lodge for use at work, even by cleaners or housekeepers. It does not follow that because an item is cleaned by a cleaner that its practical purpose is for use at work by the cleaner. The walls and floors of a place of work may require to be cleaned, but that fact does not render them 'work equipment92 for the purpose of regulation 2(1)—*Smith v Northamptonshire County Council* at paragraph [21]; *Spencer-Franks* at paragraphs [52/53]. Second, an item may be "work equipment" when it is being used at work, but may not be 'work equipment' when it is being used away from work. A company car used for an entirely private journey (possibly not even by the employee) or the tools of an employed or self-employed builders trade which he uses at home to repair his own sink—these may be work equipment when used at work at one time, but not when used at another time when not at work—*Spencer-Franks* per Lord Mance at paragraph [84], and per Lord Rodger at paragraph [51]. Even if (contrary to the view expressed above) the wardrobe and the pole within were items of work equipment for cleaners/housekeepers when they were cleaning the lodge, on the evidence before the sheriff no cleaners or housekeepers came into the lodge when there were no paying guests using it, and when it was simply being occupied in return for payment by an employee. When the appellant was occupying the lodge (as he was at the time of the accident) there were no other employees of the defenders who had any occasion to come into contact with the wardrobe or the pole within. It follows (like the company car being driven for an entirely personal reason, perhaps by someone other than an employee) that, at least while the lodge was being occupied by the appellant, the wardrobe and the pole within were not work equipment."
Coia v Portavadie Estates Ltd [2015] ScotCS CSIH 3.

WORKER.

"It follows from the definition that all employees are workers, but not all workers are employees. The central feature of both concepts, however, is that the worker should be employed pursuant to a contract. If there is no

contract personally to perform work or services, then neither concept applies."
Ajar-Tec Ltd v Stack [2012] EWCA Civ 543.

For discussion of the principles to be applied in determining who is a "worker" in the healthcare context see *The Hospital Medical Group Ltd v Westwood* [2012] EWCA Civ 1005.

"Can a member of a limited liability partnership be a worker within the meaning of Section 230 of the Employment Rights Act 1996? That is the question of principle which arises in this case. . . . It may be that it was because of the uncertain effect which the creation of LLPs would have on the employment status of members that Parliament thought it appropriate to pass Section 4(4) so as to make the position clear. In my view it has achieved that objective—albeit in a curiously drafted provision—with the result that a member of an LLP cannot be regarded as employed by the LLP either as a worker or an employee by reason of his or her membership alone."
Clyde & Co LLP v Bates Van Winkelhof [2012] EWCA Civ 1207.

Stat. Def., Employment Rights Act 1996 s.43K as amended by Enterprise and Regulatory Reform Act 2013 s.20.

WORKING DAY. Stat. Def., Recall of MPs Act 2015 s.22.

WORKS.
"22. The expression 'works' is defined in section 2 as: 'Works of any nature whatever in, under or over the Thames or which involve cutting its banks other than those referred to in section 73 (Licensing of dredging, etc.) of this Act.'
23. It is common ground that the placing of mooring roots where Mr Lacey has his roots would fall within the expression 'works'. There is a dispute as to whether two of his actual fixings and associated chains fall within the definition of 'works' (because Mr Lacey says they are fixed to a wall and not placed in the Thames), and that is a question which I will have to deal with hereafter. . . .
243. So there is nothing in the ancient moorings exemption which would save these chains if they are 'works' within the 1968 Act. I consider that they are 'works'. The definition of 'works' appears above. I do not consider that the mere affixing of plates on wall with rings for mooring would necessarily be 'works' for these purposes (they are not in, under or over the Thames; nor do they amount to 'cutting of [its] banks' as suggested by Mr Harpum). But running chains to it must involve something 'over' (or 'under', if they are below the water or the silt) the river, and in my view they would be works. Mooring chains as such can be 'works' (that is implicit in section 63), and laying an unfixed chain for mooring to (if sensible) would amount to "works" for these purposes. So running one to a

fixing on the wall amounts to 'works'. Such a chain would plainly be capable of having as much effect on navigation and the operation of the Thames as a chain fixed to the river bed, so it is within the mischief of the Act. Accordingly, I hold that the running and fixing of those chains and their attachment to the wall are 'works' requiring a licence under the Act."

The Port of London Authority v Tower Bridge Yacht & Boat Co Ltd [2013] EWHC 3084 (Ch).

WORSHIP. Scientology does not conduct "worship"—see *Hodkin, R. (on the application of) v Registrar General of Births, Deaths and Marriages* [2012] EWHC 3635 (Admin).

Y

YOGHURT.

"5. At its simplest, yoghurt is a form of fermented milk, usually (now) from cows. It may be sold on its own, usually called 'plain', mixed or layered with fruit, honey, nuts or other products, or in twin-pots where the yoghurt and the flavouring are kept separate. Thick and creamy yoghurt is derived from ordinary yoghurt by two main processes. The first, generally called straining, involves the separation and removal of the watery whey. The second involves the use of thickening agents, such as concentrated or dried milk products. Traditionally, straining was achieved by the use of cloth bags through which the fluid but not the solid elements in the fermented milk were able to pass. More modern industrial processes include ultra-filtration and separation by centrifuge. They are perhaps less appropriately described as straining than is the cloth bag method. Nonetheless, like Chobani's expert Mr Michael Hickey, I shall refer to all yoghurt made thick and creamy by the extraction of fluid as strained."

Fage UK Ltd v Chobani UK Ltd [2013] EWHC 630 (Ch).